Canned coffee and Kimonos
**A Memoir of
Four Years Living and Teaching in Japan
Tom Fitzmaurice**
ISBN: 978-1-8384686-5-1

Published By: -

i2i

PUBLISHING

i2i Publishing. Manchester.
www.i2ipublishing.co.uk

For Ai

About the author

Tom Fitzmaurice is a teacher from Wiltshire. This is his first book.

One written word is worth a thousand pieces of gold.

Japanese Proverb

Author's Note

I have changed people's names out of respect for their privacy. I have not mentioned the name of the company for which I worked, and I have allocated different locations for the schools for anonymity's sake, but not for any other places mentioned in the book. A few of the memories I recount here are from subsequent holidays to Japan in the summers of 2015-2019, but the vast majority are from my four years living there between 2007 and 2011. This memoir is not written in chronological order, but instead organised by theme. This book was written nine years after I left Japan and so there are many events and tales I have simply forgotten with time. This book is what I *can* remember. The entirety of this book was written and edited solely by me, and all of the content within the book is my own and previously unpublished. This memoir is simply that, a recollection of time, places and events as I experienced them, internally and externally. It is the Japan I lived in and the Japan that lived in me.

Prologue

It was inevitable that before long I would break the rules, unwittingly but in spectacular fashion, and when I did, it happened in a swimming pool. After much befuddlement, a charming member of staff had helped me with the ticket vending machine at the entrance, for which I was very grateful. I didn't know what any of the buttons were for, there were at least twenty of them and all I wanted to do was swim. I had my brand-new swimming trunks and my goggles, I hadn't forgotten my 100-yen coin for the locker, and I knew what time the swimming pool closed. I had my locker key on its rubber band around my wrist and I'd showered before I got in. What more could you possibly need?

I dived in at the deep end and then it started. I heard the whistle while I was still underwater. It sounded as shrill and as loud as any noise I'd heard in my life. It was almost as if the very pitch of it conveyed the anger of the pool attendant. Muffled though it was to my submerged ears, I didn't want to come up. I wondered how long I could stay below the surface. How long could I hold my breath? Long enough that by the time I surfaced the stout little woman with the whistle would have forgotten about me? Alas, no. And as I slowly rose, my cheeks already flushed with embarrassment, I knew it was me. I knew *I* had been the idiot. I knew *I* had done something wrong. In those brief seconds I wondered what on Earth my transgression could be? I had concluded that there must be a 'no diving' rule. I'd apologise and vouch never to do it again.

As my head emerged from the water everyone had stopped and was looking my way. I had felt self-conscious enough walking to the edge of the pool with my hairy chest and hairy feet like some bizarre furry foreign hobbit, but my by-now bright red face was a glowing beacon to all. Look at the foreign prat. The eyes of the splashing families were laser beams but that was nothing. The squat little pool attendant removed the whistle from her mouth and pointed straight at me.

"Where is your swimming cap?"

My swimming cap? And then it dawned on me. As I looked around, with my stupid pasty hairy legs treading water frantically beneath me I noticed something that had at first completely passed me by. Everyone, absolutely everyone was wearing a swimming cap, including the cheerless pool attendant. She pointed with an angry finger back in the direction of the changing room.

Well, if people hadn't been staring at my strange semi-naked figure until this point, they certainly were now. I bowed and waved and grinned feebly as I apologised to the angry woman and headed back out to the changing room. I was so flustered I didn't even have the wherewithal to dry myself off and get changed. Instead, I traipsed dripping wet to the reception desk and the kind man who'd helped me obtain my ticket from the vending machine. The mouths of the children and their young father who were standing at the desk were agape. Who was this beast that had just crawled out of a swamp? Daddy, help!

I pointed at my head like a bad mime artist and shivered and said, "Swimming cap please." The man laughed with his female colleague and produced a tray from under the desk. It contained swimming caps, swimming caps for people who had been foolish enough to arrive without one. They were rented for 50 yen and looked like they had been sewn by a charitable grandmother. They were like a swimming-based dunce hat which not only highlights the misdemeanours of the person forced to wear it but makes them look like a clown at the same time.

"That'll be 50 yen please," said the man.

"Oh," I said as I dripped all over his pristine ledger.

He stared at me in disdain as he wiped off the drips. I flapped around in apology for my dripping locker key, my apologetically flailing limbs only serving to spray water further across the desk and the astonished children. I should have been glad by this point that I looked like Mr Bean, the Japanese loved him. But Mr Bean is perhaps only funny to watch from afar, to cringe at his buffoonish mistakes from the detached distance of your sofa. But when Rowan Atkinson's idiot character turned up at your workplace it was perhaps harder to see the funny side.

I plodded back into the locker room and discovered I hadn't a clue where my locker was. After five minutes of being viewed suspiciously by everyone in the changing room as I put my key into one locker after another, I found it. I trudged back out to the reception desk 50-yen in hand and waited still sopping wet behind a queue of newly arrived swimmers. After enduring the round of astonished looks and comments of the fresh arrivals I handed over my money and was given a swimming cap that looked like one of granny's tea cosies.

By this time, I almost didn't want to swim. I almost wanted to just give up and go home. I certainly didn't want to head back out to the pool and the queueing masses waiting for Bozo the clown to perform an encore, and I certainly didn't want to clap eyes on Mrs Trunchbull the pool attendant again. But I'd come this far so I bloody well would. I re-emerged and just in case it turned out that diving also was a transgression, I decided to use the metal steps. I tried to be light footed, I tried to be inconspicuous but the hairy chest and legs and hobbit feet and tea cosy on my head made this impossible. Worst of all, the only set of steps was next to Trunchbull. I smiled and bowed and to my enormous relief she grinned and nodded and laughed and she didn't seem so fierce after all. She almost seemed nice. And I've no doubt I'd provided her with an anecdote to tell at home and at parties for years to come. *First, he walks out looking like a pale gorilla, then he dives in without a swimming cap. Urgggh! So, we put a tea cosy on his head.*

The entire incident had left me so abashed that I didn't even have the energy to be giddy over the swimming trunks drying machine in the changing rooms which was like a cross between a hand dryer and a washing machine. And, in my new state of high alert, desperate to not make any more slip ups, I paid heed to the notice that warned you not to leave the swimming trunks in for more than ten seconds or they might catch fire. That would simply be too much. I had done enough for today. The dripping journeys to and from the reception desk, the hairy body, the strange feet, the tea cosy on my head and the vending machine incompetence were all enough without burning down the building.

Contents

1.   **How Do I Get to Kokubunji?**   17

Turning Japanese

2.   **Climbing Mt. Fuji and Looking for Love** 33

The first long summer

3.   **To-mu Sensei**   47

Becoming a teacher

4.   **The Biggest City on Earth**   67

Living in Tokyo

5.   **Sensory Overload**   81

Sights and sounds of the metropolis

6.   **White Gloves**   99

Craftmanship, service and the pursuit of perfection

7.   **Massive Wrapped Apples**   113

My students

8.   **Trains, Planes and Automobiles**   131

A country in transit

9.   **Gaijin**   149

The capsule hotel from Hell and bathing with the
yakuza

10.   **Lost in Translation**   169

Communication problems

11.   Love Hotels, the Robot Restaurant and a
Skewered Penis   189
Only in Japan: The bizarre and the ridiculous

12.   Banzai, Biscuits and Bearskins   217
East meets West

13.   'Get out of the Pool!'   243
Breaking rules and the sleep-deprived nation

14.   You Can't Sit There, That's Takako's Seat 261
Knowing your place: Sumo wrestlers and bossy old
ladies

15.   The Good, the Bald and the Ugly   277
My Colleagues

16.   Japan has Four Seasons   301
Japan as unique

17.   All is not as it Seems   319
A land of contradictions

18.   'Read the Sign, Damn it!'   333
Making a nuisance of myself in the provinces

19.   Bad Things Come in Threes   351
Earthquake, tsunami and nuclear disaster

20.   Twenty Asylum Seekers a Year   367
A changing Japan

21.   **Sayonara**   379
Saying Goodbye

Epilogue   385

Glossary   387

List of Proverbs & Sayings   399

Bibliography   403

Chapter 1

Turning Japanese

How do I get to Kokubunji?

Newly learned tactics are the origin of great blunders.
Japanese proverb

I arrived in Japan on 23rd April 2007, St. George's day, three months before my twenty-fourth birthday. My pre-flight nerves were eased when I met a small group of fellow teachers in the departure lounge at Heathrow. Great, I thought, I'm not alone. There was a girl from Brighton and a smattering of people from the home counties. On the plane I sat next to one of them, a short, fat rugby enthusiast. He told me that he'd lived and worked in Japan previously and was going back for the second time. Brilliant. I decided to pick his brains. After ten minutes he was fast asleep against the plane window and he didn't wake until the plane taxied on the runway in Japan.

When we emerged into the arrivals lounge a gaggle of smiling Japanese company representatives met us.

"You two," said one, as he read off two names, "are coming with me. We are catching a train to Saitama[1]."

They disappeared.

"You three," said a smiley lady, "are coming with me. We are going to Chiba[2]."

---

[1] A prefecture (county) immediately to the North of Tokyo.
[2] A prefecture immediately east of Tokyo across Tokyo bay.

They scuttled off. Only three of us remained, the final group. I smiled at the other two remaining new teachers, imagining the friendships we'd surely form.

"You two," said one of the two remaining women, "are coming with me. We are going to Kanagawa[3]."

And then I was left alone, like the last chicken on the shelf. A small, squat, cheerless middle-aged woman with short curly hair and milk-bottle glasses stood staring at me.

"You are coming with me," she said. "We are going to Tokyo."

She set off at a brisk pace, while I tried to keep up as I trailed my heavy and cumbersome luggage behind me. We hopped on an escalator, then a bus, then a train and then two more. Jetlagged and bewildered, I desperately tried to keep sight of her through the busy crowds, while simultaneously attempting not to mow down Japanese commuters with my leviathan of a suitcase. Somehow, I managed to keep the woman in sight. It was a disorientating introduction to the city. We passed through impossibly crowded train stations and onto and then off immaculate trains. I didn't really take it all in, I couldn't process it. To do so would have been to distract me from my sole task of not getting left behind. I didn't have a clue where I was or where I was going. I memorised the exact hue of her jacket and her distinctively officious gait, the only things that distinguished her rapidly moving mop of black hair amongst a sea of other rapidly moving mops of black hair. I had one sole mission. Don't lose her. It was enough of a shock to have watched as my fellow

---

[3] A prefecture immediately south of Tokyo.

teachers were gradually plucked from my company to head off to their respective regions. Now I was alone, the one thing I mustn't do was lose track of the one human being who knew to where I was bound.

We stepped off the final train onto the busiest train platform I had ever seen. This is where things would get really tricky. As I broke into a half run, praying that a wheel on my suitcase would not break at such an inopportune moment, my gargantuan luggage was dodged, tripped over, and tutted at. I didn't know it at the time but, jetlagged, bewildered and nervous, I was standing in the centre of the busiest train station on Earth at rush hour. Everywhere I looked there were people, people, people. I felt more out of place than I had ever done. More than the uniform mops of black hair and the tired end-of-work-day screensaver facial expressions of the obligatorily black-suited workers, it was their sense of purpose that set them apart from me. Speedily and efficiently, without undue fuss or noise, they were heading to platforms and trains and homes. They were not even paying attention to their surroundings. Like a hive of well-drilled worker ants rushing about the colony, they moved in well-rehearsed patterns, and then there was me, a bewildered and incongruous slug, dishevelled and ungainly in the midst of their organised chaos.

Finally, out of the enormous and brightly lit subterranean concourse, we were out in the open air, my first sight of real Tokyo, but once again I hadn't any time to take in any of it. We got in a taxi and sped off into the Tokyo night. The vast neon expanse of the metropolis whizzed by in a blur as I stared wearily out of the window from the back seat. Building upon building seemed to fill every conceivable space. The woman sat wordlessly in the front seat for the entire journey, and I was left alone with my thoughts.

Thirty minutes later we arrived in a non-descript, poorly lit little street.

"This is your apartment," said the brusque lady.

As I exited the taxi before me stood a white, tiled two-storey building that looked like a cross between a public swimming pool and a strip club. In large gold 3D letters on the side of the building were the words 'Whity Spot'. This was to be where I would live for the next year. Well, the contract said a year, and even then, I wasn't sure I'd see out more than five or six months in such an utterly alien and bewildering land. Of course, I didn't live there for the next five or six months, or the next year. I lived there for the next four years.

My flat, number 101, was on the ground floor on the outside edge of a block which consisted of two floors of five apartments each. When the lady opened the door and took me inside, I waited for her to show me the rest of it. There was no rest of it. I hear people talk about living in a small flat and then they take me there or show me pictures and I scoff at them. They have no idea. The entire property consisted of a bedroom-cum-living room-cum-dining room, a tiny bathroom and a miniscule kitchen and was twelve square metres in total. The kitchen was so small in fact that when two people stood in it, they were pressed up tightly against each other. It housed a tiny steel sink and a single ring hob above a double shoebox-sized fridge that didn't work.

The bathroom was an all-in-one plastic coated wet-room and consisted of a toilet, sink and bath. I only attempted to sit in the bath once and felt like I needed a chiropractor afterwards. I'm not exactly lofty at just shy of five foot eight, but still my knees were pulled up against my chest just to fit in. The toilet was by the door and angled inwards to fit in the tiny room. The tiny sink hung over the toilet on one side and the bath on the other and when I sat on the toilet my elbows rested on the sink. I could touch the walls long ways with flat palms, and I could span the width of the room with my elbows pressed against my sides, touching the walls with my palms. The 'bathroom', and I use that term very loosely, had a sliding plastic door which was quite see-through. The sliding door wasn't a design choice on the part of the architect. There was no room for either an inward opening door (it would have bashed the toilet) or an outward opening one (it would have taken up the entirety of the kitchen). It quite literally couldn't have been smaller. I've seen wardrobes with more space.

The main room had a bed, a clothes rail, a fridge (this one actually worked), a small coffee table, a television, a tiny bookshelf and pretty much nothing else. I couldn't even do a press up, so little floor space was there. My flat did not have a single proper window but luckily had a sliding glass patio door, which would have let in some sunlight, were it not for a building a mere eight feet away. The patio door opened onto a two-foot-wide strip of concrete and a two-foot-wide area beyond that of moss-covered soil. I had a washing machine on the concrete strip outside and the unit for the air conditioner beside that.

Having come from the rural south west of England with its open expanses of fields, woodlands and plains, this was quite a shock. I came to see that this would just have to do. A little voice nagged inside my head that surely, I must have known that this is what I was letting myself in for, but as I surveyed my new prison-like surroundings, I thought, 'Well, I don't think we're in Wiltshire any more Toto.'

Without ceremony, the lady placed the key and two A4 sheets of paper on the coffee table and picking up one of them, an indecipherable map, she pointed and said, "You need to be here at 10am tomorrow. Don't be late." With that she bade me goodbye, walked out, shut the door behind her and left me entirely alone. I never saw her again. I sat on my tiny excuse for a bed, raised on its flimsy wooden structure barely one foot off the ground and surveyed my bleak, windowless surroundings. The realisation began to sink in that in the space of twenty hours I had gone from my comfortable and familiar family home to this place. The phrase 'culture shock' didn't quite cut it. The fact was that I knew not a soul in Tokyo, in Japan, indeed for over five thousand miles. I suddenly felt quite alone.

Worst of all I spoke not a single word of Japanese. Well, that's not strictly true, I knew one, 'sayonara' which means goodbye. I didn't even know the word for 'hello' or 'yes' or 'please' or 'thank you'. I couldn't even count to five, but rest assured I could wave people off with polite and accurate sentiments. In fact, even that wasn't strictly true. I'd picked up my one and only Japanese word from that great font of linguistic scholarship known as 'Teenage Mutant

Hero Turtles' when I was a seven-year-old boy. And, as it turns out, 'sayonara' is rarely used in daily conversations. It really means 'farewell' rather than a casual goodbye and is far too formal to use commonly. The Japanese had a far more complex term for saying goodbye, 'Bye bye'.

I left my flat and tentatively headed up the road in search of dinner. As I walked, I gazed at the impossibly thick tangle of electric wires overhead. Everything was unfamiliar. The jumble of streets, the road signs, the sounds and the smells. I stopped at the first shop I came to and immediately noticed that it differed from the shops back home in that a good portion of its stock was outside the front door on the side of the road. There were stacks of large plastic bottles of green tea, barley tea, beer and juice. This is a common feature of grocers and drug stores in Japan, although I did not know it at the time, and it speaks to the safety of the country. The proprietors of these businesses didn't seem to worry that their goods might get stolen, and of course it was a wise use of space.

I walked mesmerised along the aisles of this, the first shop I'd ever been into in Japan. I didn't recognise a lot of the food and of course all the packaging was covered in Japanese writing which I could not decipher. In desperation I grabbed hold of the first recognisable item. It was a small tin of corned beef, at least I took it to be such judging by the small picture of a cow on its side and the opening key. I returned to my house, sat down on my small wooden bed and began to open my one and only source of nutrition. And then the key snapped. I sat, utterly despondent, staring at the now unopenable can. I walked into the kitchen and opened the meagre cutlery drawer. There was no tin opener. I picked up a fork and returned to my corned beef. I vainly tried to prize out hunks of meat from the jagged hole left by the snapped key with the fork, but I was getting nowhere, only succeeding in digging out half-rice grain sized lumps with each attempt. I lay back on my bed utterly despondent and felt like crying.

I don't know how long I lay there but I must have at some point realised that I was being pathetic. I found within myself a steely resolve, realising that lying on my bed mourning the corned beef just wouldn't do. I ventured out once more into the night. This time I took with me the second A4 sheet the woman had left on my coffee table, upon which was written my address. I wandered back up the road past the convenience store from which I had purchased the corned beef and headed towards a busy area near the station. As I walked, I gazed at the unfamiliar signage, not daring to go into any establishment with my non-existent Japanese language skills. And then I saw it, the heavenly golden arches brightly beckoning me. It was a wonderful feeling to sit and gorge my way through an ungodly amount of fast food.

With a spring in my step, I began the return journey to my new flat. After I had walked down the road for five minutes I suddenly realised, as the brightly lit area around the station quickly receded behind me, that I hadn't the faintest idea where I was. I looked down one side street after another, but they all looked the same and I had no idea what my address was or even the name of the street so it wasn't as if I could exactly ask for directions. And even if I did, in whatever language you ask, "Where do I live?" It's as sure a sign of a madman as are the questions "What's my name?" and "What day is it?" And then it struck me, I had brought the piece of paper with me with my address written on it in Japanese. I could now ask a local without them thinking I had amnesia.

I stopped the first passer-by, a tall, fat man in his late thirties with glasses. I thrust the piece of paper at him. Like an idiot, I pointed at it and said in English, "Excuse me, Where's my house?" He smiled and nodded and, to my enormous delight, led me home. I saw that man once more in my time in Japan. It was about four months later. He was standing in the street eating something and as I passed by, he looked at me and said in broken English whilst pointing to a first-floor flat that had police and the fire department swarming all around it, "In there. Suicide. Gas. Man. Dead."

***

My second day in Japan got off to an equally inauspicious start. I studied the piece of paper that I'd been given the day before. I was to be at my company's head office by 10am in a place called 'Kokubunji'. The instructions told me that I ought to buy a PASMO[4] train card so, in my smartest shirt and tie, my shoes polished to a brilliant shine, I headed off to the train station. The wrong one as it turned out.

I asked the man behind the counter for a PASMO card. He didn't understand me, so I repeated it again

---

[4] A rechargeable, contactless smart card used on public transport and as a payment card for vending machines and stores.

more loudly and more slowly like a British tourist ordering lunch on the Costa del Sol. He looked at me as if I'd just announced that I was sleeping with his daughter before turning around and beckoning to a colleague. I got the impression that this was the guy they called for when weirdos and foreigners turned up. I gathered from his hand gestures and broken English that I couldn't buy one there. How stupid of me to think I could purchase a rail card at a train station. I fumbled in my pocket for change and managed to somehow buy a ticket to I didn't know where on a train that was possibly going in the right direction but more probably wasn't.

It wasn't. The train arrived at a station called 'Takadanobaba', a name that I scarcely believed wasn't a form of elaborate joke that some clown had plastered over the real station name to mess up my day. I asked the train guard there for a PASMO. He made a similarly dismissive gesture to the man at the station from which I'd come. The expression that crossed his face can best be described as a mixture of how you'd speak to a senile great-grandfather and how you'd approach a raving axe murderer.

"How do I get to Kokubunji?" I asked forlornly. "Can I buy a PASMO here?"

He puffed out his cheeks as if I'd just asked him to give me the formula for pi. He put out a hand and smiled apologetically before turning to speak to a colleague. I received more puffed out cheeks, scratched temples, groans, sighs, mumbles and even a full-on taking off of the glasses and rubbing of the face, before the original train guard returned saying, "You cannot buy PASMO here." Eventually, I discovered through a hastily hand-drawn map that Kokubunji was back in the direction from which I'd come and on a different train line. I'd have to get on another train line just to get to that train line. Therefore, I needed a new ticket for both. I hurried on to the first of my next trains and missed the station I needed to change at.

I did eventually make it to Kokubunji, late. I walked into the office at about 10:30 and was met with fury and bluster by my new boss, a tall, blonde Australian lady. Nothing like a good first impression, eh?

"You're late!" she barked before I seated myself next to the other three new employees in the intake.

I apologised profusely before explaining that I'd only arrived in country the evening before and had got lost on the train network. It didn't wash. A bad start to say the least.

I would love to say that my train blunders ended after day one, but they didn't. On the Thursday of the first week, I was required to attend a meeting in 'Hibarigaoka'. I scanned the train maps. Aha, I'd found it. There it was writ large on the 'Toei Oedo' underground line, coloured pink on the map. With a great sense of pride in my independent city-slicker navigation skills I arrived at the station. It said in the training manual that the school was visible from the station. I looked and looked but couldn't for the life of me see it. I promptly phoned up one of my trainers.

"I'm here at the station. It says in the training manual that you can see the school building from the station, but I can't."

"Are you sure you're in the right place?" came the reply.

"Yes," I said, turning around and re-reading the train station sign, pronouncing each syllable of the name slowly over the phone.

"Oh, for crying out loud! You're in 'Hikarigaoka'. You're supposed to be in Hibarigaoka. Why didn't you check carefully?"

Hibarigaoka, it turned out was in an entirely different part of the city. Once again, I turned up late, tail between my legs.

On my second night in Japan, I discovered a small games arcade called 'Game Beat'. It had an eighties feel to it with its little neon sign outside. In those early days on most evenings, I was its only customer. I'd stroll down late in the evening and have fun playing Time Crisis 2, enjoying the childlike thrill of shooting baddies alone in the arcade and getting through an ungodly number of 100-yen coins in the process. Amongst the old-fashioned fighting and football games and shoot-em' ups, was a curious game tucked away in one corner. I slotted a 100-yen coin into the machine and watched in fascination as a man on the screen ordered a woman to strip. A piece of her clothing disappeared before a flashing sign on the screen instructed me to insert another coin for another garment to come off. I got fed up pretty quickly. I was shortly five hundred yen down and she still had her skirt and blouse on, so I traipsed off through the night back to Whity Spot.

My first week in the country was spent in training. The other trainees were mostly male and mostly in their twenties or thirties. Among a few I befriended early on was Nigel, a 23-year-old media graduate from Ipswich with a dry sense of humour who'd been to Japan before and could speak a little of the language. Then there was Stew, half-Japanese, from Hastings who annoyingly spoke quite a lot of Japanese. After sitting through a raft of training activities and demo lessons Nigel, Stew and I decided one evening to go out for dinner. I was excited to eat some decent food since I was still subsisting mainly on McDonalds and snacks. A steak would have been nice, a pizza, some noodles. I could even have tolerated sushi. What did we have? Chicken heart, testicles and raw liver.

Nigel and Stew were drinking sake[5] and I decided to join in. Drinking alcohol may sound completely innocuous but I shouldn't have had any at all. Three years prior to coming to Japan I'd developed an intolerance to alcohol. Through sheer stubbornness, and not wanting to be left out, I decided to ignore this fact and gulped the Japanese alcohol like it was going out of fashion.

Saying farewell to my colleagues at the station I headed for home. Up to this point I'd felt fine, but a dull ache began in my abdomen. On the train journey home, it grew in both intensity and area and by the time I got off at my station the painful swelling sensation was spreading down my left thigh and it felt as if something within me was about to burst. I was sweating, my heart was beating fast, and I began to panic. I thought I was going to die. I fumbled in my pocket for the mobile phone I'd been issued by the company on arrival. I didn't know the number for the

---

[5] A traditional Japanese alcoholic beverage made by fermenting rice.

emergency services and besides, I didn't have the language ability to talk to the phone operator in order to call an ambulance. I phoned the angry Australian boss and explained my predicament to her.

"Do you really need a hospital?!"

"Well, I am in a lot of pain and I think something has burst inside."

"Oh well, look in the manual you've been given. It gives a list of nearby facilities such as hospitals. Are you sure this is an emergency?"

I put down the phone and decided instead to return to my miniscule flat and die quietly rather than make any further fuss. Of course, being the hypochondriac that I am, nothing had burst inside, but I spent the remainder of that training week trying desperately to get through the lectures without visibly squirming in my chair too much. It was all I could do to sit still, whilst I surreptitiously wriggled into a more comfortable position. It was my own fault because I was, and am, a complete idiot. Needless to say, I didn't drink again.

On our first day off after training Nigel and I met in Nakano and strode through the streets looking for something to do. As we stood outside a shop a lanky teenager with a centre parting approached and challenged me to an arm wrestle. I accepted and was trounced and left with a sore arm making lame excuses. Japan 1, England 0.

We then headed to Yoyogi park in Harajuku, central Tokyo. Yoyogi park is a popular hangout spot and in recent years has gained quite a reputation as a tourist trap. The rockabilly dancers were out in force dressed in leather and tight denim. It was an incongruous sight, this snapshot of 1950's American popular culture in the middle of East Asia's largest city in the 21st century. Middle-aged Japanese men with huge, exaggerated teddy boy quiffs and greased-back hair and shades and dolled up Japanese ladies with bright red lipstick and polka-dot dresses twisted and jived to all the 1950s rock hits blasting from their large sound systems on the asphalt. These rockabilly gangs are a famous and quirky Tokyo subculture, and the retro-style personalised leather jackets of the various gangs sport such slogans as 'Black Shadow' 'Strangers-Greaser on the Road', 'Tokyo Rockabilly Club' and my personal favourite 'Lebels' (presumably a misspelling of 'Rebels'). Was I still in Tokyo or had I stepped onto the set of 'Happy Days'?

Nigel and I continued walking through the park until we heard a commotion from among the trees at the park's edge. I don't know what surprised us more, that strung between the trees were the ramshackle dwellings of the homeless (something which I would see replicated in many city parks in Japan in the coming years) or that after we followed the noise we emerged into a clearing where a rave was taking place, all tents and tie dye and massive booming sound systems and people off their head on something.

I'd imagined that the curiosity and the intrigue of those first weeks would dimmish with time, that everything would become familiar and mundane but, as I was to find out, Japan still had plenty of surprises in store for me.

Chapter 2

Climbing Fuji and Looking for Love

The first long summer

A man who never climbs Mt. Fuji is a fool. A man who climbs Mt. Fuji more than once is a fool.
Japanese proverb

Japan was interesting and exciting in its ridiculous, otherworldly, kitsch, bizarre kind of way, but there was something lacking. I had found my lack of Japanese language ability was proving an impenetrable barrier to approaching ladies and so, as summer got into full swing, I was still very much on the lookout for a charming companion with whom I could spend my free time.

One of the girls who worked in the local 'Family Mart' convenience store was very smiley, so I decided to try my luck. I had been into the shop numerous times and always received the same shy glances and eyelash-fluttering grins, so I thoroughly believed I was on to a winner. I made a plan. I scrawled my name and mobile number on a small scrap of paper and decided that the next time I went in I'd go to her checkout and hand it over. When I did, she looked bemused and laughed a little and never ever called me. I'm sure this incident only served to confirm in her mind just how odd and creepy foreign men truly are.

In early July Nigel managed to secure us a double date. A wealthy middle-aged student of his had matched us up with her 18-year-old niece Ayumi and her 19-year-old friend Tomoka. I shouldn't have looked a gift horse in the mouth because it was kind of her, but I was slightly perturbed that the aunt decided to chaperone the four of us on our date. Maybe this was just the way things normally happened in Japan. The benefit of having the over-protective aunt with us was that she paid in full for our meal at a luxury restaurant in one of Tokyo's most exclusive districts. It was a really interesting set up. Dotted around the restaurant's large dining room were square cooking stations closed on three sides and surrounded by stools. Inside the cooking station, behind a wooden counter, a chef prepared a wide variety of vegetables, meats and fish on little wooden skewers and then deep fried them one at a time before handing them to us over the wooden counter. Worryingly, the aunt seemed fonder of us than the girls. She spent the evening fluttering her eyelashes at both of us and giggling like a schoolgirl. Ayumi and Tomoka on the other hand were sadly far more subdued.

We'd obviously wooed the aunt successfully enough, if not the girls, because a fortnight later a follow-up date was arranged, this time minus the aunt, in a restaurant in Shinjuku. Nigel and I tried our best to impress and seemed at last to be making a little headway. Tomoka and Ayumi were laughing at our jokes, no doubt out of politeness, as the chances of them understanding what we said, let alone finding it funny, was highly unlikely. Luckily for me, Tomoka lived on my train line, about half an hour further out of the city. I sensed an opportunity and accompanied her on the journey home. With nothing to lose, as the train pulled into my station, I leant over and gave her a peck on the cheek. She froze like I'd burped in her face and stared at me in silence, open-mouthed, with a look of utter shock on her face. As I got off the train, with the other passengers glaring at me in disapproval, I waved through the window as the train pulled away. She turned in her seat and stared at me through the window. I'd got her! Or so I thought.

A few days later I decided to have all my hair shaved off. I don't know why. Perhaps subconsciously it was part of the rebranding. Living in a foreign country you have the opportunity to start all over again, anonymous, and besides, maybe Tomoka would go for the rough and ready look. When I arrived at work the next day my students thought I had gone completely mad.

"Your head is blue!" shrieked one of my students. "Urghhh."

"You look like Bruce Willis," said another.

Strangely, she still insisted I looked like Bruce Willis even when my hair had grown back.

Nigel and I decided that we needed another double date to seal the deal. The plan was Tokyo Disneyland. Perfect. On a sweltering day in late July Ayumi drove us there by car. Apart from nearly crashing at several points on the journey and getting pulled over by the police, the ride was eventless. By the way, a word for any Japanese policemen reading this: If you ever happen to pull over a car with two beautiful young ladies in the front and you then look in the back at two Western men sweating profusely, one of them with a shaven head and lounging in the back seat in jogging bottoms, I do forgive you for thinking that the vehicle has been hijacked. Luckily for us, if that's what the fat middle-aged policeman who pulled us over had thought, he had clearly decided that it was a nice day for hostage-taking and waved the us on with warnings to be more careful in future. I tried every trick in the book that day. I used the cover of the more hair-raising rides to clutch Tomoka's hand every time she screamed. Later, thinking that a show of manly strength might impress her, I hoisted her up onto my shoulder and then spent the next week with a strained back regretting what I'd done.

One warm summer's evening a week or so after the Disneyland double-date Nigel and I accompanied the girls to the biggest annual fireworks display in Tokyo. In their summer kimonos, with traditional wooden sandals on their feet and flowers in their hair they looked resplendent. The display, though magnificent and beautiful with the pyrotechnics in the night's sky reflecting on the glistening Sumida river, sadly did not prove to be a metaphor. There didn't seem to be any fireworks between us and our respective dates.

We had one more date, just the two of us this time. We went to a bowling alley on the basement floor of the Nakano Sun Plaza, a large wedge-shaped building near my home. Perhaps sticking my fingers inside large spherical objects and launching them powerfully along narrow lanes of maple and pine would convince this girl that I was the man for her. It didn't. I'd like to blame my paltry double-digit score as the cause of my failure to woo her but, just like at the sides of the lane each time she went to bowl, she had her bumpers firmly up that day. Alas, that was the last time I saw her. I was sad that things didn't work out between Tomoka and me. The only consolation was that they didn't work out between Ayumi and Nigel either. I believe Nigel kept in contact with Ayumi, but the great romance it could have been never materialised and, as the summer grew ever hotter and July turned to August, I sympathised whole-heartedly with the increasingly feverish whine of the cicadas in the trees whose anguished screams built into a fever pitch in the relentless summer heat.

***

By August, the rainy season had finished, leaving behind a simple, searing, humid heat, which was inescapable in the densely populated city. August in Japan is a time of festivals and dances and lantern parades. It is also the time of Obon[6], a week-long holiday where family members return from the big cities to their hometowns and villages in the country. Tokyo is a strange place to be during Obon in mid-August as I discovered that first summer. For the best part of a week, I wandered up and down Tokyo's usually bustling streets wondering where on Earth everyone had gone. It wasn't completely deserted of course. For some people Tokyo itself was home, or they just hadn't the means or inclination to go. However, for those several days the metropolis I now called home was noticeably and eerily a lot quieter.

---

[6] A family reunion holiday derived from a Buddhist custom to honour the spirits of one's ancestors.

August is also significant because it is the season for climbing Mt. Fuji. Mt. Fuji is the most famous and important of Japan's three 'holy mountains', with perhaps the most well-known depiction of the mountain being Hokusai's[7] Edo-era[8] woodblock print 'The Great Wave off Kanagawa'. It seemed a bit of a rite of passage, one of the things to do when in Japan, a tick off the must-do-list.

Japan's tallest and most sacred mountain is only open to climbers for a brief three-week window in July and August, so Nigel and I booked a coach and took the two-hour journey one evening in early August to the fifth station of the great mountain. I say the fifth station because those who start climbing Fuji rarely start from its true base which splays out over miles across its forested lower reaches. Coaches and other vehicles park up at the fifth station where there is a large car park, a restaurant, gift shops and toilets that are pretty rank. We bought the obligatory walking staff with attached bell on the end of a piece of colourful silk ribbon, stocked up on drinks and snacks and began our ascent.

We were told it was a good idea to reach Fuji's summit by sunrise, so we set out at 10pm on our climb. The gradient was steady to start with but, with increasing altitude, the route upwards became steeper, and the path and my breath became ever thinner. I knew we were doing badly when a white-haired man and his little scotty dog raced on ahead of

---

[7] A famous Japanese woodblock print artist whose most famous piece, 'The Great Wave off Kanagawa' was published around 1830.

[8] The Edo era, also known as the Tokugawa period, lasted from 1603-1868.

us. I'd wanted to macho it out in front of Nigel, but my asthma was getting the better of me. Huffing on my inhaler, we stopped at various stations along the way, each of which was marked out by a little wooden torii[9] gate. These are usually found at the entrance to Shinto[10] shrines and serve as a reminder of the mountain's holy stature. Each 'station' consists of a small wooden shack selling snacks and drinks and the higher ones even have little wooden bothies in which you can sleep. There is usually a bench or two on which you can sit to admire the view but, as the entirety of our climb took place after dark, there wasn't much to look at other than the swirls of clouds illuminated by the moon which started above us and through which we gradually passed. At the sixth station the toilets were dirtier than at the fifth, at the seventh dirtier still and by the eighth I simply couldn't face using them.

Despite it being mid-August I wore two woolly hats and two pairs of jogging bottoms. When we got to the ninth station, we purchased the obligatory drinks and a cup of corn soup and, having manfully refused to purchase them from the large shop at the beginning of our ascent, I also bought a couple of cans of oxygen to relieve my wheezing breath. We peered into a little bothie to see a huddle of people asleep on

[9] A traditional Japanese gate which is usually found at the entrance to a Shinto shrine. They are usually painted vermilion. Each torii marks the transition from the mundane to the sacred.

[10] A religion originating in Japan, often regarded as Japan's indigenous religion, it is a religion of nature and pre-dates Buddhism's arrival in Japan from China and Korea.

the floor, wisely having decided to attack the mountain in stages rather than one long push into the clouds. We on the other hand were clueless novices so pushed on ahead.

As we marched on, we caught up with a group of fellow gaijin[11], who by chance also turned out to be English. Luke was here visiting a mate who was living in Japan and wasted no time in quizzing me on rumours he'd heard about how to woo Japanese women. Sadly, at this point I had no valuable knowledge to impart and refrained from filling him in on my failure with Tomoka, plus I could barely breathe at this point. How ridiculous would it look on my death certificate?

'Cause of death: Used up all his remaining breath on a mountain to fraudulently explain how to woo a Japanese lady.'

I felt somewhat better in my physical exertions when a fit-looking member of Luke's party threw his arms in the air and said, "I can't carry on!" and turned round and began plodding back down the mountainside. We continued in the presence of Luke and the survivors of his group onwards to the top, arriving at the summit just before the sunrise at 5am. It was cold, really cold, and even with my two woolly hats and two pairs of trousers I felt the chill. But worse than this, I felt what I'd feared most. I needed the toilet.

---

[11] Foreigner (literally 'outside person') sometimes considered offensive to foreigners but used widely by foreigners themselves in Japan. 'Gaijin' is a shortened form of the more socially acceptable 'gaikokujin'.

The toilets here at the summit were exactly as I would have predicted. They were the least accessible for cleaners but quite possibly the most needed for the climbers, who would spend a considerable amount of time lounging at the summit waiting for the sunrise followed by an even more considerable amount of time cooing at the break of dawn at the view and then taking copious amounts of photos of it. In short, the toilets were absolutely disgusting. The first time I went in I came out gagging and retching, but eventually, with a great deal of heroism, I conducted my business and was rewarded by the most beautiful of sunrises.

We stared down into the centre of the volcano, a huge crater whose bottom plunged away out of view into the depths below. On the topic of bottoms, thank God the one thing that was not erupting at the highest piece of Japan's real estate was this caldera, just, it seemed, everything else. I was amazed to find a couple of vending machines at the top of this, the country's highest, mountain and I stood for baffled minutes wondering how on Earth they'd got up here. Had they been dropped from a plane? Soon after we began our descent the answer appeared when we passed a little bulldozer eating up the steep gradient heading toward the summit. If they could bring vending machines up by bulldozer, why not a bottle of bleach and a cleaner?

After we'd taken the photos and the videos and given the backslaps, there was nothing for it but to head back down. The mountain we'd taken nearly seven hours to climb we took one-and-three quarter hours to descend at a frantic and reckless pace. We screamed down the steeper paths desperate to return to Tokyo for some decent food and much needed sleep at a speed and lack of control that would suggest we were begging to turn an ankle or pop a knee but somehow, in our ill-suited trainers, we didn't. The lower we raced, the more layers we shed until we had barely anything on. The hats came off, then the coats, the pullovers, then the second pair of trousers, and by the time we reached the coach station I was shirtless, my trousers rolled to the knees and pouring sweat on this sweltering day which turned out to be the hottest Japan had ever experienced. The mercury had topped out at over 40 degrees Celsius.

There are many things you need after over thirty hours without sleep, and we enjoyed gorging on copious amounts of junk food on our return to Tokyo. What we didn't need, and what we definitely did not enjoy, were the far-right idiots shouting at us from their big black vans as we left the restaurant and headed for Shinjuku station. We hadn't slept in thirty-six hours, we were sunburnt, exhausted and bewildered, and as we made our bloated way to the station to head for home they shouted, "Leave our country, you American!" It was an incongruous end to an adventurous day, but my dreams that night were of spritely old men and the volcano's crater and dirty toilets, not racists in black shirts mistaking my nationality.

***

One Friday in late August I was sitting on a train heading off to work when I was greeted by a female voice. Looking up, I noticed it was a temporary receptionist from one of the schools I worked at called

Yuka. Funnily enough I was on my way to work at the school where we'd met. On the day we first met she'd been covering for the regular receptionist who'd been ill, but on this occasion, she was heading for home in the suburbs. This was the train line that went from central Tokyo to the drab, monotonous and seemingly endless commuter belt of Saitama where she lived just north and slightly west of Tokyo proper. She noticed that I'd been reading a 'How to learn Japanese' book which I'd picked up in my local Waterstones before coming to Japan. She seemed to find my earnest study endearing and sat next to me. We chatted for the remainder of my journey and before I got off the train, I gave her my number. I didn't think much of it. As I sat at home that night, I thought I'd give her a call.

We arranged to meet and suffice to say, despite the language barrier, romance blossomed. Before long Yuka moved into my shoebox-like abode. Apart from the odd days when she would return to the city's suburbs to visit her mother or the weekends when we'd go there together, we lived together in my miniscule flat for the next two and a half years. If nothing else, her willingness to live there with me proved that she must have really liked me. Either that or she was a glutton for the purgatory of living in a mouse hole. What had been a nearly impossibly small residence for one became an even tighter fit for two.

***

I may have won a lady's affections, but I seemed to be losing one of the constant battles of the summer months, keeping cockroaches at bay. Whatever your first experience of something in life is tends to set the standard for all that follows, but I swear to this day that the summer of 2007 was a cockroach paradise in Tokyo. I saw more that summer than I have in the eight summers I've spent in the city since and, though smaller than their tropical cousins, they were an unwelcome feature of the hotter months.

One of my students recommended a spray to solve the problem so I traipsed down to the local drug store and bought one with a big picture of a cockroach on the side with a bold red cross through it. Returning home while Yuka was at work, I proceeded to spray the entire flat with it, under the bed, in the air, up the walls, everywhere, until I'd used almost the entire can. When Yuka returned later that night to find me coughing and spluttering, red-eyed and scratching at my skin, she informed me that you were in fact supposed to only use the spray sparingly to target the roaches themselves. I realised at times like this that learning to read Japanese really would save me a lot of hassle.

My closest ever encounter with a cockroach came one evening when doing the washing up. I noticed out of the corner of my eye a small black object about four inches from my face on the wall. I turned and saw the biggest, blackest roach I have ever seen to this day. A woman I saw on a train one evening had a far closer encounter with our little friends, however. It was late at night and we were the only two passengers in the carriage. She was fast asleep opposite me. I saw movement out of the corner of my eye at the far end of the carriage. I watched as a cockroach scuttled down towards us, ran up the woman's shoe, up her leg, then her arm, over her head and down the other leg and onwards down the carriage. Luckily, she didn't wake, and to this day I swear I made the right decision in not alerting her. Like they say, what you don't know doesn't hurt you, right? It would read like a young Japanese woman's nightmare, being woken up to find yourself alone on a train carriage at night with a strange foreign man and finding a cockroach on your face.

I also had an infestation under my bed, a nest if you will, of what I had at first thought to be mosquito eggs but did in fact turn out to be some other form of flying insect. This received the spray treatment too. Mosquitos themselves were a pain. Apparently, they are particularly attracted to people with certain blood types. The Japanese have got a strange obsession with blood types and claim to be able to tell what sort of person you are from blood type alone - it's a common topic of conversation. Unlike the Japanese, I can't tell you off the top of my head what type I am, but there are two pieces of evidence that suggest I am probably mosquitoes' favourite dish. One is the fact that throughout July and August my forearms looked like a swollen, red relief map of the Himalayas and the second is that the wall by my bed looked like a murder scene, flecked as it was with splatters of blood, where I'd whack them as I slept.

***

I was beginning to pick up the lingo. I didn't attend any Japanese lessons as such, and, remarkably, by the end of my four-year stint in Japan the extent of my Japanese 'study' was the pocket phrasebook that had so enamoured Yuka to me on the train carriage that August day. I learned Japanese like a baby. I listened to what people said when they finished their meal in a restaurant and went to the counter to pay, realising that when customers exclaimed, 'Go-chi-so-sa-ma-deshi-ta'[12] it must be something along the lines of 'Thank you for the meal' or 'That was delicious' or at the very least 'I've finished'. I learned that 'Tadaima'[13] must mean 'welcome home' or at least 'Oh, you're back!' because everyone said it to people returning to a house. I observed that the ubiquitous 'daijobou'[14] was like 'OK' and just as versatile, being used to both ask and answer whether someone was alright.

Like an imitating toddler who listens to his parents and older siblings using phrases routinely, I became a mimic. And just like the curious child who gurgles out phrases like 'Here you are' and 'I don't know' as if they were a single word and not understanding the grammar behind their spoken constructions, I repeated what I heard. As I parroted phrases at train stations, in restaurants and in karaoke parlours, I gradually and clunkily learned to get by. I was a two-year-old in a man's body, picking up language to survive. As the saying goes, necessity is the mother of invention.

The long, humid summer was drawing to an end. I had been in Japan for four months by now and only just beginning to feel like I was settling in. Nearly four years later I still wasn't sure I really had.

---

[12] Its literal translation is along the lines of 'Thank you for the meal, it was a feast.' It is used both in homes and in restaurants.

[13] The phrase means 'I'm home!' and is said or shouted to family or housemates on arrival in the house. The response from those already at home is 'okaerinasai', often shortened to 'okaeri'.

[14] This phrase means 'I'm alright' or 'Are you alright?'

Chapter 3

Tom-u Sensei

Becoming a teacher

To teach is to learn.
Japanese proverb

Before the first week of May rolled around, a nagging question lingered in the back of my mind. Can I really teach? I wouldn't have to wait long for the answer. I wasn't entirely sure I was suitably prepared for life as a teacher. I'd only had three weeks' teaching experience at a language school in Bournemouth. I was pretty sure that my new company couldn't be as dysfunctional as the last. The owner of the Bournemouth school was a borderline psychopath. He had technically retired but hung around the building like a bad smell, overshadowing the cowed principal. He'd burst into classrooms unannounced and just stand there. The principal looked like a man on the verge of a breakdown, his every decision over-ridden or countermanded. The supposedly retired school owner had insisted that any of the students caught speaking anything other than English during their lunch break must pay 50p into the 'swear jar' and he prowled the canteen and school corridors like some deranged charity fundraiser, shaking his tin menacingly and waiting for the faintest "Bonjour" or "Hola" to be uttered before pouncing like a maniac. Surely my new company in Japan couldn't be as dysfunctional as that? Surely?

Within the first minute of the first lesson that I ever taught at the Bournemouth school, a young Korean student with a sourpuss expression on her face turned to me and asked, "Teacher, how old are you?"

"Twenty-three," I replied with a smile.

She looked disgusted.

"You are twenty-three?" she repeated. "Oh my god, my teacher's younger than me! I'm twenty-four," and looked away in horror.

It was harder to avoid being younger than all of my new students in Japan, especially Sawako who was ninety-one. Then again some of my new students were as young as two so there was quite a range. I taught students from absolute beginner to fluent, sublimely charming to obliviously rude. I taught CEOs, toddlers, great-grandmothers and surly teens. I witnessed rudeness, hysteria, indifference, over-excitement, jealousy and about every other type of behaviour and emotion in the classroom, from the man in his fifties who sneered at me and leaned across the table in our first ever lesson and said, "We sunk HMS Prince of Wales in Singapore harbour in 1941," to the toddlers running and screaming from the classroom in absolute terror at the strange white man.

One feature of the company for which I worked was that the teachers would teach at a different school every day. I would teach at the same school on Wednesdays and Saturdays and at three others on Monday, Thursday and Friday respectively. Sunday and Tuesday were my days off. As a general rule, the students had one lesson a week. Some were private students, but others were in groups of between two and eight students. My company was marketed as an English conversation school and its USP was that it specifically taught 'British English'. That said, during my time at the company I taught business English and English for people taking a whole range of language proficiency examinations.

My company was by no means one of the biggest in Japan and yet we had approaching one hundred schools in Greater Tokyo alone, with several hundred teachers on our books. Greater Tokyo was divided into districts. I worked in the West Tokyo district, the busiest of all and the area which contained Tokyo's main commercial and entertainment hubs. The word 'school' is quite misleading, it conjures up images of a large building or group of buildings with a playing field and a large perimeter fence. Our company's schools however couldn't be further removed from this. They were on one floor of a tall building on somewhere between the third and sixth floors and consisted of a reception area, a toilet, a kitchenette and usually two or three classrooms. As a result, on average two or three teachers worked in each school per day.

When my first day of teaching finally arrived, I was terrified. I took two trains on a forty-minute journey to Arai school, which I later realised was only a five-minute bus ride away. The school was located on the fifth floor of a building that overlooked the main street. When I walked in, I immediately met a tall man with a cravat, cream-coloured jacket and shoulder-length blonde hair held back with a hair band. He looked like a cross between Lawrence Llewelyn Bowen and David Livingstone. As it turned out he was a massive eccentric and a force to be reckoned with.

"Hi, my name's Liam. First day, huh?"

"Yes," I replied as I stared at his cravat.

"Yah," he said in a plummy public-school accent. "Got a Japanese girlfriend yet?" he asked.

I explained that I hadn't, and he grinned.

"You'll have one soon enough. When it's your lunchbreak I'll show you around the area."

My first lesson went well. I taught four students, all women ranging in age from their thirties to the afore-mentioned Sawako, aged ninety-one. When they discovered it was my first ever lesson in Japan, they cooed motherly sentiments and smiled and gave their support. I don't think they learned a thing. We chatted about me and England and my family and Japan, and before I knew it the hour was up. The next lesson of the day was a lady in her thirties and an obese man with the yellowest teeth I've ever seen and a phone holder on his belt that resembled a gun holster. Yet again though less chatty they were lovely and understanding and I started to feel my nerves lessen. I began to feel that perhaps I could actually do this.

True to his promise, at lunchtime Liam showed me the local sights. He started by showing me the local mall, Nakano Broadway. I use the term 'mall' loosely because Nakano Broadway bears little resemblance to any mall I'd ever been to. It is, in short, a geek's paradise. Among a few clothes shops and jewellers can be found a plethora of anime and manga shops. There are shops selling every conceivable cartoon and action figure in display boxes, all ludicrously priced, rows upon rows from floor to ceiling of cosplay[15] attire, and even a shop that sells replica assault rifles. This was otaku[16] (geek) heaven.

Liam then took me to Don Quixote. I simply wasn't prepared for this place. I have never been in a shop like it before or since. Don Quixote is a discount chain that can be found across Japan and it is truly bizarre. I don't know what's more alarming about Don Quixote, the sheer variety of stuff they sell or the utterly haphazard fashion in which it is piled up unlike the usual orderly neatness of Japan. The shop looks like a teenager's bedroom after an earthquake. Nothing is tidy, things are all jumbled up, but in a strange sort of way that was its appeal. Whatever you could possibly need, it's there. Whether you can find it on the other hand is another matter.

Going from floor to floor we saw cheese, chessboards and chocolate; dishwashers, dungarees and dildos; baby clothes, bicycles and bear costumes. There were diamond watches, sofas, sex dolls, coffee, guitars, suitcases, toothbrushes, footballs, pyjamas, porn, suits, and milk. But my initial impressions of the store were wrong. Far from an outlier I suppose in some ways, although I didn't know it at the time, Don Quixote is a metaphor for Japan, more specifically Tokyo. Like the city in miniature with all its quirks and incongruities, the mundane and bizarre

---

[15] 'Cosplay', deriving from 'costume play', is a hobby which first became popular in Japan, but is now a worldwide phenomenon, in which people dress up as specific characters.

[16] A term used for people with very keen and specific interests, sometimes to the point of obsession. People referred to as otaku are interested in anime or manga. Otaku is sometimes used as a pejorative.

side-by-side; the mad haphazard jumble, the marrying of the surprising with the strangely familiar, Don Quixote was a distillation of my new home poured into and hanging from every nook and cranny of these seven floors of madness.

***

Why on Earth was I in Japan in the first place? Compared to many of my colleagues I was a bit of an anomaly. I hadn't come to Japan for any specific reason. I had in fact not intended to go there at all. In April 2007 I had turned up in central London for an interview. I talked the interviewer through how I would conduct a given lesson and he grilled me on my subject knowledge and motivations. Finally, he congratulated me.

"We'd be happy to take you on. In which country are you interested in teaching?"

The company had schools from Taiwan to South Korea, from Poland to Japan to Vietnam.

"China," I said resolutely.

I hadn't any particular knowledge about China, but it sounded about the most exotic and adventurous place I could think of.

"I taught in Taiwan, China and Japan," my interviewer said. "And I by far enjoyed Japan the most. Of course, the decision is yours."

I thought about it for five seconds, asked for my form back, scribbled out the word 'China' and wrote 'Japan'.

"How soon would you like to get started?" he asked.

"As soon as possible," I replied.

He looked at me with a wry smile.

"Do you really mean as soon as possible?"

Just under three weeks later I was sitting on my bed with the corned beef.

***

The school day usually lasted from 12pm to 9pm or 10pm and so I got used to getting up late and going to bed late. Our lessons were often back-to-back. It was hard to go in the space of five minutes from dancing around the room like a kangaroo, throwing beach balls and playing 'Run and touch the tiger' to teaching a sixty-year-old company executive. Heaven forbid we should need the loo because we barely had enough time to wave little Taro goodbye, peel the magnetic flashcards off the wall, hide the puppets, pack away the plastic fruit and move the table back into the middle of the room before Mr Sakamoto would come walking in briefcase in hand. You had better have the CD for Market Leader Pre-Intermediate teed up in the right place for the listening activity where Paul tries to negotiate a deal with Ian, which your student wouldn't understand, and you'd spend precious minutes of the lesson rewinding to play yet again while the confused businessman asked loudly, "What is Paul?"

The CD would inevitably jam, and it was at these moments of high tension, as you desperately pressed the CD release button with sweaty fingers and one after the other blew, shook and rubbed the CD with your tie to try and get the damn thing to work because Mr Sakamoto was looking at his watch, that you remembered now just how much you needed the loo. Once you'd spent the next half an hour establishing that Paul was just the name of one of the men speaking and not relevant to any of the questions on which the listening activities were based, Mr Sakamoto would walk out happy in the knowledge that at least if he'd learned nothing else that lesson, he could use the verb to 'Paul'.

Great! time for a wee, you'd think, your bladder fit to burst and get to the toilet and find it occupied because Michiko was in there and she was your next student, and by the time she got out you'd have no time yet again because Mr Sakamoto and the great 'Paul' debate had overrun by five minutes. Michiko is happy because her husband's gone away for a week on business and she doesn't really like him and now she can watch that Korean drama she loves every night and, "Aren't you lovely?" and "Have you found a nice Japanese girl yet?" and "Aren't your eyes round?" and "Isn't your face small? Ooh lovely." You've got the textbook out, but Michiko doesn't want you to open it because she'd rather she sat and cooed at you and talked about your mum and "Ooh, I bet she's lovely, what's her name?" And you're secretly delighted because you hadn't the time to plan the lesson and you're far better at talking about your mum to old ladies who smile and nod and lean in to hear what you're saying than explaining that Paul is a name and not a marketing pitch.

The best children, the ones that were fun to teach were not boring but not naughty little buggers. It's a fine balance and one where only about fifty percent of kids fall into that sweet spot. They'd be up for a laugh and some lowly activities like run and touch or Simon Says without being enough of an idiot to just repeat the word Simon and laugh or run and slam the wall so hard that the next-door teacher would complain about you.

"I'm trying to teach in here!"

What did they think I was doing, fracking for gas? Lessons with those nice kids would end, a fun time had by teacher and students or English learned or even better, in those oh, so rare moments, both. It was even worth the next-door teacher moaning that your racket was enough to put his student off finding out how to effectively use the conjunction 'Ian' in a sentence.

There were students who expected it to be a one-way diatribe, those that wished the English to be spoon fed to then with no effort on their part. Well, I'm here, aren't I? Input some English into my brain. There were the students that had been coming to the school for three years, seven years, thirteen years and they'd had many teachers from Manchester and Melbourne and Montreal and, "Somewhere in Ireland I think or maybe it was New Zealand," and many who in that time had not learned a thing. In sharp contrast to this there were the rare and impressive fast trackers who within a short space of time impressed all and took their IELTS exam and their TOEIC exam and their First Certificate exam and passed them in only eighteen months. There were rare, intelligent, motivated students like the woman I used to teach who spoke English almost fluently and Korean and Chinese and French and Italian and was almost as proficient in all of them.

Saturdays were hard days because it was a nine am start instead of twelve pm and Saturdays were the days of businessmen and seriousness and interview etiquette and business vocabulary. Fluctuate, plummet, asset, proposal, portfolio, candidate, share price, gap in the market, currency exchange rate and, "I'm sorry Mr Yamamoto, oh that, no, that's just a British man's name." Saturdays were good though because I taught Reiko and she was beautiful and tall and a model and had eyes so sparkly and a smile so disarming that I would have gladly allowed her belief that 'Paul' was anything she liked, to go unchallenged. We talked of everything and nothing and she's hard to look at because I'm going red and does she know I fancy her? and is it against the school rules to ask out a student? and I could but if she said yes and the date went badly, she could hardly keep coming here for lessons and if she said no, it would be really awkward and then she could hardly keep coming here for lessons, so either way I shouldn't ask and I won't ask and I'll just continue to sit here looking at her and making English noises and smiling and, "Oh, is our half an hour up already? See you next week, bye."

"Hello Kaito, come in. Head shoulders knees and toes."

I began most adult lessons in earnest, clutching the relevant textbook and referring to my notes to discover how far we'd progressed in the previous lesson. The students had to pay for their textbooks, and they didn't come cheaply. The company naturally skimmed a large profit off the top of their retail price. Mind you, lessons, particularly one-to-one lessons, were pricey too. Many of the adults were quite lacklustre in their attitude to using the textbooks. Though our managers pushed us to maintain a pace (so they could sell the student the next textbook as soon as possible), in many lessons the student would smile conspiratorially and say, "Can we just talk?"

I found that the children made far more rapid progress which I suppose occurred for several reasons. Firstly, their textbooks were a lot more fun than the adults', with cartoon animals and rockets and people kicking footballs rather than some bloke drivelling on in some boring listening exercise in Lower Intermediate recording 5b about how he is going to an interview for a job as an accountant or an endless text in the Reading Section consisting of an email to a stationery supplier asking for a quote for A4 paper or toner for the company photocopiers.

Secondly, as is widely known, children soak up the learning far more quickly than their adult counterparts who have heads full of bills, marital strife, leaky guttering and all the other baggage that comes with adulthood. Thirdly, the children, though sometimes shy, were less inhibited in attempting to use the language and less fearful of making mistakes. And finally, while you may end up not touching the textbook during your one-to-one hour-long lesson with Haruhiko because he's been describing to you his responsibilities as senior sales representative for his ball bearings company, what exactly are you going to spend an hour chatting to a six-year-old about?

The textbooks themselves ranged from good to appalling. Although we had access to a wide range of textbooks printed internationally the company had their own in-house textbooks. They could make an even bigger profit on these. Although they weren't universally bad, the references were often dated, the quality low and they came in a ring bound folder colour-coded by level. In some of the recordings you could even hear the background laughter of some of the teachers as the recordings came to an end. I don't know how much the five or six teachers who made up all the recording voices got paid for their work but after four years of listening to the same voices it really got on your nerves.

With their same predictable and repetitive mispronunciations of even the most basic words and the bizarre inopportune pauses for effect it was torture. Like lyrics to a song you hate, but always hear on the radio, you could mouth the dialogue silently in your head while you played each conversation for the umpteenth time to a student. The annoying intonations, the heavy breathing or nasal whistle of those all too familiar voices grated the more as time went on. The illustrations rather than slick photographs in professional textbooks were often badly drawn cartoons. They looked amateurish and slapdash as if someone had knocked them up on a rickety train in five minutes.

The children's lessons were much more fun. In addition to the books and colouring in and dot to dot and CD songs, we used a whole plethora of equipment to ensure the lessons were exciting and interactive. Each school was equipped with a little room of toys and tools. There were beachballs to be chucked around group lessons for drilling animals or colours. There were sticky balls to be launched at the whiteboard at my terribly drawn pictures of tennis or bananas or a badly proportioned cartoon elephant which looked more like an oversized mouse with a tumour. There were magnetic flashcards we used for playing snap which we stuck to the whiteboards, at which the students threw sticky balls, or they could be stuck to the metal walls for often very noisy and occasionally quite dangerous games of run and touch. I pity whoever worked on the floor below my lessons. The whole walls would reverberate as two eight-year-olds jostled to be the first one to touch the 'rabbit' and crashed shoulders first against it, no doubt causing the people in offices below to momentarily assume an earthquake had begun before heartily wishing that damn English school above them would go bankrupt.

Saturdays were good because of the early finish and the night was yours. There were however two things that could scupper our Saturday night. 'Cover' and 'Standby'. A 'cover' system existed to account for those teachers who for whatever reason had to have a day off in advance. The 'standby' system existed to allow for teachers who became ill. Each month a large A3 sheet was faxed to each school with the names of all teachers who were to perform a cover or standby day that month across all of the districts in the Greater Tokyo region. On average you'd have either one standby day or one cover day per month. However, the inconsistencies were enormous. I know of teachers who would routinely teach three a month and others who went months with no cover or standby whatsoever.

At least with cover you knew in advance and didn't build up your hopes. Standby though was hell. The company manual we were all given when we started stated that you must be up and ready for the workday, dressed and prepared to leave your house as soon as you get the call. In reality you played the odds but, like all gamblers, we all got caught out. We all had those nights every once in a while, where we put all our chips on black and the ball landed mockingly on red. If you'd really pushed your luck, you'd been out the night before until the early hours, got steaming drunk and prayed that the call wouldn't come. If the call did come, it came at about seven am because Sunday like Saturday was a nine am start and you might be called to cover a teacher in a school on the other side of Tokyo.

Unlike our regular schools where we were assigned a district of Tokyo, standby could have you travelling to the far suburbs of the city, two hours and several trains and buses away. Surely it won't ring, I'm really hungover and/or still drunk, I've had an hour and a half's sleep and I feel terrible. Inevitably it would ring, and you knew who it was. Who else would phone you at seven am on a Sunday? If by chance you discovered, as I once did, that it was in fact just your phone alarm which sounded exactly the same as your phone ring tone because you'd forgotten to turn it off from the previous day, it was glorious. I plonked my head back on the pillow feeling like I'd just won the lottery and fell back into a comforting deep sleep. Well, almost. Five minutes later the phone went again and this time it wasn't the alarm.

"Jonathan Smith is sick. You need to go to Seibu-Tachikawa which is a long way from you. You'd better leave now to make it on time. I hope you're ready. Are you ready? Hello! Hello?!"

Arriving bleary-eyed in said school you'd be greeted by students you didn't know and who wondered where their teacher was.

"Jo-no-san sensei didn't say he would be away today. Oh, oh my gosh. What a surprise! a different teacher!"

In many ways the children were more polite about it than the adult students and they seemed to implicitly accept that their usual weirdo foreigner had been replaced for the day by a different weirdo foreigner.

***

The manager of Asagaya school where I taught twice a week was an overbearing woman in her fifties called Yuriko. I should have guessed at her annoying tendencies that belied her attractive and youthful appearance early on when Grant, a tall, gay Scotsman greeted me on my first day at the school.

"You'll enjoy it here even though mother hen is constantly monitoring you."

I hadn't understood what he'd meant at the time but soon came to see he was referring to the smothering quality Yuriko had, the incredible ability to make you feel through her words and deeds that she was suffocating you with a blanket. Grant was jaded. He was a good teacher but a talented and stifled painter in the wrong job and Yuriko's blanket was cutting off the oxygen to his soul.

I was a favourite of Yuriko's. The students liked me, I kept them coming back and paying, and new students who took trial lessons with me invariably signed up. The managers of the schools were judged by student numbers so old mother hen was glowing. I went round to Yuriko's house a couple of times, a kind yet intense experience but one which was made worthwhile by the presence of her attractive, if slightly hamster-faced daughter, Misato, who was a few years younger than me. Yuriko also had a son of about my age called Kaito who had clearly inherited her ability to come across as smug and annoying. Sadly, it was Kaito's room not his sister's that I was shown before dinner and it was with him not her that I went for ramen[17] one time, although refreshingly it was to a restaurant where you sit with wooden partitions between diners and are served by a pair of anonymous hands through small curtains. The concept was that you could focus on your food with no distractions. Perfect.

The father of the house was referred to by all as 'Daddy' in English. Daddy didn't get to say anything, Daddy sat tired and wordless at the end of the dinner table, no doubt worn down by years of being mothered by his overbearing wife. I felt sorry for Daddy. He was I felt a hostage. I had a few run ins with Yuriko during the years I taught there. She was oddly furious when she discovered that I was dating a receptionist from another school. It had nothing to do with her and it wasn't against the school rules but nonetheless it incurred her wrath.

***

I felt like a prat in my first week of teaching when the owner of one of the schools took me and the

---

[17] Chinese noodles served in a broth, often served with pork and seaweed. Nearly every region of Japan has its own signature ramen style.

receptionist of that school out for dinner. It was the perfect cliche. The clueless foreigner, fresh off the boat, bumbling, incapable and useless. In that first month of the grand adventure in this far away land I sat there in front of my co-workers and bashfully asked the waitress for a spoon. Not only had the clown that sat red-faced at that dinner table come to Japan unable to use chopsticks properly, I had never even picked up a pair.

As the weeks and months progressed what was new and nerve-wracking became normal and routine. The weekly rota of schools, the buses and trains and bicycle routes I'd need to get to them all, the places I found near to each school that I could stop in for lunch. New students would come, and old ones would leave, but as I settled in and gained more experience of teaching students of all ages and abilities my confidence and contentment grew. I was highly regarded amongst my peers and by the management of the company. I was as keen as mustard, hard-working and punctual. I was willing to go the extra mile, to do my best and give it my all.

After two years with the company, I was promoted to Senior Teacher of Suginami school and my schedule rearranged in order that I could work there four days a week. Only the larger and busier schools had a senior teacher at all which was roughly one in three of them. In theory my position required me to mentor the ten or so teachers that worked in the school. In practice I only had contact with the teachers who worked in the school on the same days as me.

The senior teachers were responsible jointly with the school manager, a Japanese member of staff, for increasing student numbers through promoting the school and organising parties and events. I was also responsible for keeping all of the resources in good condition and ensuring that orders for anything new the school needed, from replacement textbooks to new CD players, were put to the head office for approval. I would have a monthly meeting with an Assistant Director of Studies, the School Manager and the Japanese lady in charge of all of the school managers. I arranged Christmas parties, Halloween parties and Easter parties for the children with games and goody bags and sweets. For the children's Christmas parties, I would dress as Father Christmas, we'd play pass the parcel and musical chairs and listen to Christmas songs. For the adults we had tea parties, quizzes and British food tasting events. I took great pride in my job role and, though the salary was scarcely more than as a regular teacher, I enjoyed the sense of responsibility.

New students to the school were offered a free twenty-minute trial lesson in the hope that they'd sign up for lessons. They allowed the students (and their parents in the case of children) to see what lessons were like and for the teacher to assess their level. 'Taikens', as the trial lessons were called, tended to throw up some odd surprises. For the children's trial lessons, it was normal for a parent to sit in, usually the mum. At the beginning of one such trial lesson I watched in disbelief as the mother, then the father, then two grandparents, a sister and finally an aunt (clutching the full weekly shop in several shopping bags in each hand) traipsed into the tiny classroom and squeezed along one wall. The child felt inhibited with his extended family there and so did I. It can be embarrassing as a twenty-five-year-old man to jump around a small room surveyed by a group of adults while performing the actions to 'Head, Shoulders, Knees and Toes' or 'Jump Like a Kangaroo'. Strangest of all the adults seemed to leave the room happiest of all.

Scared children would be ushered in or equally nervous adults who needed coaxing into the classroom by the receptionist. One trial lesson that springs to mind is that of a seven-year-old boy. I'm not quite sure how or why it occurred, but while his mother sat grinning in one corner of the small room the boy spent the entire twenty minutes of the lesson repeating and mimicking every single thing I did and said, every word, every physical action. He'd stand with my exact gait and when I scratched my nose or adjusted my belt he'd do likewise as if the entire thing was one enormous game of Simon Says. He was confused, I was confused. He was wondering why on Earth he was there and, for a fleeting moment, so was I. 'Simon says, "touch your nose", Simon says, "touch your knees", Simon says, "hop on one leg", and all the time I half expected….'

"Excuse me, Teacher."

"Yes, Akira?"

"What is Simon?"

Chapter 4

The Biggest City on Earth

Living in Tokyo

Wherever you live, you come to love it.
Japanese saying

Tokyo was bewildering and exciting in equal measure. I hadn't really known what to expect. My early imaginings of inner-city Tokyo probably bore far more resemblance to downtown Hong Kong than the eventually realised reality of the city. The famous neon strip, Yasukuni Dori in Shinjuku not far from my home was one of the filming locations of The Killers' 'Read My Mind' music video filmed just a month before I arrived, the moustachioed Americans singing on the crossroads amid the hustle and bustle. It was also the same road that Bill Murray's character travels along in the opening scene of 'Lost in Translation', his face pressed wearily up against the taxi window in a blur of jet lag and sensory overload. I could relate. True, he didn't have a middle-aged woman in the front seat guiding him to his new home, but the discombobulation he felt at suddenly arriving in an alien world was something with which I could readily identify, and he was just there for a week to film a commercial.

It wasn't my first time living abroad. At the tender age of 18 on a pre-university gap year I'd spent the best part of a year on Canada's east coast, but that was a whole different kettle of fish. Tokyo couldn't have been more different. For nine months between 2001 and 2002 I'd lived in Nova Scotia. I spent the first five months living and working in a 'village' of care homes for children. I had my own room in a 'family' of three children and two carers, a wonderful married couple, at the top of the forested 'North Mountain', a picturesque and remote setting.

The view from our house to the North just one hundred metres away was of the ocean, was of whales visibly surfacing from the glittering water of the Bay of Fundy. There was a quaint little wooden lighthouse and little fishing boats moored against a wooden pier. A waterfall, which froze solid in winter, crashed onto the beach from forested cliffs. The North mountain, where in winter we were snowed in for days at a time, tapered gradually on its south side to the wide lush expanse of the Annapolis valley with its farms and apple orchards, where I lived for the following four months. It was fun and adventurous and vaguely 'foreign', but doing maintenance work in the village, working on the farms in the valley, making maple syrup in the forests and working in the sawmills hadn't, couldn't prepare me for urban Japan. Come to think of it, nothing could.

The thirty-seven million people who call Tokyo home live in by far the most populous metropolitan area in the world. Greater Tokyo's population is roughly equivalent to that of Canada or California. To put it another way that is more than half the population of the entire U.K. and it positively dwarfed Australia. Between a quarter and a third of the entire population of Japan live in Greater Tokyo but it hasn't always been this way. Until the 12th

Century 'Edo' was just a small fishing village. The capital moved from Kyoto in the west of Japan to Edo, which was renamed Tokyo ('Eastern Capital') in 1868 at the time of the Meiji restoration[18].

Population aside Tokyo is first in many things. For a start it boasts the largest economy of any city on Earth. Tokyo's economy is only slightly smaller than the entire economy of Canada or South Korea. However, it is when it comes to trains and their infrastructure that the sheer scale and pace of the metropolis are laid bare. Of the fifty-one busiest train stations in the world all but six are in Japan. Over half of those are in the city of Tokyo alone including the top three which are all in west Tokyo and relatively close to my old flat.

Shinjuku station, which with a footfall of over three and a half million per day is the world's busiest, is particularly close to my old home. I felt pretty stupid in those early months constantly getting lost in the subterranean maze of Shinjuku station with its huge labyrinthine concourses and having to ask for assistance just to get out. Considering the entire above/below ground station complex has two hundred entrances/exits I suppose my navigational errors could be forgiven and it certainly made the nine or so entrances of Waterloo, Britain's largest and busiest station, pale into insignificance. Also, in addition to the main 'Shinjuku Station' itself there are five more train stations in Shinjuku which is just one

---

[18] The Meiji Restoration of 1868 consolidated powers under the emperor of Japan. The structures of Japanese politics and society changed significantly as a result. Japan quickly industrialised and took on western concepts and methods of production.

district among many busy districts in west-central Tokyo alone, never mind the rest of the city and its sprawling environs.

One of the many train lines which passes through Shinjuku station is the Yamanote line with its immaculate silver and lime green carriages and onboard TV screens. It is to Tokyo what the Circle line is to London, the difference being that the Yamanote line is above ground. Its roughly elliptical route around the centre of the city links the business districts and financial centres to the main entertainment hubs. If you stand on a Yamanote line platform and just miss a train, you only have two minutes at most to wait before the next one arrives going in your desired direction. During rush hour that two-minute wait is reduced to thirty seconds.

When people talk of Tokyo, they usually refer to the urban sprawl which stretches well past the city limits to the neighbouring prefectures of Saitama, Chiba, Kanagawa and beyond. In this seemingly endless metropolitan space city boundaries and prefectural boundaries are meaningless to the eye. When you get a train from the centre of Tokyo to Yokohama, Japan's second largest city, there is no gap in the buildings. There is no greenbelt, no obvious division.

'Tokyo proper' has twenty-three 'special wards', much as London has boroughs. Each city ward is known in Japanese as a 'ku'. I lived in Nakano-ku in the west of the city. As well as the twenty-three wards and the urban sprawl there's a third definition of Tokyo because Tokyo is also a prefecture. There are forty-seven prefectures in Japan which are roughly equivalent in number and function to English counties, though on average significantly bigger. Most Japanese prefectures would be as unfamiliar to westerners as the names Northumberland or Suffolk would be to the Japanese.

The prefecture of Tokyo, rather fittingly, is shaped remarkably like a fish. Its tail is the city of Tokyo proper with the twenty-three special wards, curving at its end around the western side of Tokyo bay. The head of the fish climbs westwards into the lower reaches of the 'Japanese Alps', the lush green forested mountains with boulder-strewn rivers and sparse hamlets which seem a long way from the neon glare of Shinjuku, but both are Tokyo.

***

The area of Tokyo in which I lived is a quiet little neighbourhood called Nogata. It is quaint and cosy-not in the way that the Cotswolds or a rustic Italian town could be considered as such but with its own intrinsic appeal. Although it is fairly central within Tokyo you wouldn't know it. Away from the skyscrapers, the flashing neon and the frenetic swarms of people in the main hubs of the city, and though it lies just a few miles away, Nogata's quiet streets, such as the one on which I lived, are peaceful and serene. The area has a family aura with young mothers on bicycles whizzing through the lanes, a small infant in a baby seat on the front and another on the back.

Like most of Tokyo, Nogata's streets are a zigzagging jumble of buildings crammed haphazardly next to each other. Apparently designed to confuse invading armies, the winding narrow streets dogleg back on themselves or end abruptly without warning. There is a certain charm to the jumble of buildings that make up Tokyo's street layout, and in those first few months I strolled through my neighbourhood discovering hidden alleyways barely wide enough to walk down that would suddenly open up to fascinating little enclaves.

Nogata's long high street, a five-minute walk from my old home, is bisected by the Seibu-Shinjuku train line and its level crossing. The bright yellow trains, which reminded me of the U-Bahn in Berlin, pass through from the distant suburbs to the centre of the metropolis. Though the high street and surrounding narrow lanes are not pedestrianised, there are so few cars it might as well be. It is a calm, homely little nexus full of friendly shopkeepers and familiar neighbours. The narrow streets which radiate out from the train station are a hotchpotch of closely packed restaurants, cafes, drug stores, fishmongers and grocers. Sometimes I had to pinch myself to remember that I was in the largest city on Earth.

The quietness and the homeliness belied Nogata's location, as close as you could really get to the beating heart of the city without sacrificing the small-town feel, and just like a small town if you were young or elderly, you didn't really need to leave the area. Nogata feels self-sufficient and self-contained, which I suppose has as much to do with the familiar faces and family-run businesses as the fact that it wasn't a place you passed through unless you lived there or were visiting someone. The lampposts are festooned with banners advertising local events and the flags of local sports teams. Speakers on the lampposts, nestled somewhere amongst the high tangled nest of wires, play endless muzak. I love it there. I love the smells and the noises and the colours and most of all the people, and it's silly and sentimental but I am strangely and fiercely proud of Nogata. I have always had a peculiarly strong attachment to place, and it will always be a second home to me.

***

In the evening as the sun set behind distant mountains and the cityscape took on its characteristic neon hue the Seibu-Shinjuku line whisked me in just 15 minutes to meet the Yamanote's central loop around the city. Just before arriving at Takadanobaba the tightly packed jumble of buildings, the haphazard residential mix of gleaming newbuilds and the odd rusting relics dotted amongst them, disappeared. In one long sweeping curve of the tracks, I was no longer at ground level whizzing by apartments closely abutting the tracks with air conditioning units and washing lines strung from balconies. I was suddenly thrust into the city's bustling core on elevated tracks four storeys high above rivers and roads with trains on different lines converging beneath and above me and from all sides that raced by at great speed in seemingly all directions.

I felt out of place amidst the bustle and colour and efficiently busy people travelling quietly and neatly, like a detached observer. The throngs moved with purpose to loosen neckties and sleep and hopefully read their children to sleep but more probably to dine and drink and sing and dance in karaoke parlours with colleagues and the boss. You can't go home before he does, and he's just ordered another round of beers and is busily cueing up 'Let it Be' on the karaoke machine so stop worrying and pick up a tambourine.

At the end of the workday the business districts empty of the besuited masses who head to the buzzing entertainment districts of the city to be fawned over and stroked in hostess bars and maid cafes, and to fawn over and stroke in cat cafes and owl cafes and to whack golf balls into nets and smash buttons in games arcades. Why not send all the stress and the angst and every single atom of pent-up frustration through the microphone and the golf club and the joystick and the owl? Extinguish every care with every sip and drag and bite and song and then get the last train home and then get up a few hours later and get the first train back and do it all over again because, well, that's what people do, and you might get to see your kids on Sunday. You might.

***

Early emails and letters home told of ticket vending machines in restaurants, of neon lights and of the weather. With breathless enthusiasm they related early impressions of a bewildering metropolis and how awe-struck I was by its size, pace and energy. I told of the baseball batting ranges, golf driving ranges and even football pitches situated on the rooftops of tall buildings in central Tokyo. I described the building next to Takadanobaba station which had a neon-underlit waterfall cascading noisily down its slanted roof at which I'd stare as I waited on the platform for the train home. Tokyo was different, so I explained. Whatever you fancied doing you could do it in this land of seemingly endless possibility.

I may not have contacted home as often as my mother would have liked but when I did, I regaled her with anecdotes of strange foods, strange people and nests of insects under my bed. The responses to my emails home told me of the weather back at home and the local news. Amidst the heat and sensory overload of that first long summer they informed me that grandma, and then one week later the cat, had died.

It's the trivial things that stay in my mind as much as the outlandish and the iconic- and heaven knows there were plenty of the latter in my newly adopted home city. One thing I love about Japan is the police boxes or 'Koban' that can be found across the nation's towns and cities. Although they vary, they usually consist of a small front area with one or two chairs and a large metal desk and a single back room. You can't walk far in an urban setting without stumbling across one. The idea is beautiful in its logic and simplicity. The large 'proper' police stations are too few and the staff within them too busy to deal with the daily minutiae of helping the public. As well as directing tourists to the nearest train station and helping grandma to find her missing cat, the officers in these police boxes give a constant and reassuring presence twenty-four hours a day, come rain or shine.

The light in the Nogata police box never went off and it was comforting to know that the police were always there when needed. They'd mount bicycle patrols from the police boxes and one officer would invariably be standing at the threshold to the little building leaning on a swagger stick. As antiquated as the idea may seem, I would love to see the introduction of police boxes to the UK. Maybe I'm naïve to think that the British police would have the manpower or resources to staff them. Maybe the nature of law and order in both countries is so different as to make the prospect untenable. The 'Koban' in Nogata was sandwiched between a drug store and my favourite little fast-food restaurant, which itself was squeezed up right against the train tracks. As I sat in the little noodle shop next door, I'd see the officers cheerily turn up at the kitchen window to order their fried rice and dumplings and chat and laugh with the kitchen staff like friendly storybook village bobbies.

As apparently devoid of other visible foreigners as my neighbourhood was, it would not be entirely true to say I was the only gaijin in Nogata. I once came across an American in the barbers who said he'd lived in Nogata for thirty years. On another occasion I was standing in the street watching a fire. As the firemen poured out of their wailing engines and began to deal with the raging flames spreading throughout the building, and as the young flat owner screamed and argued with a middle-aged man in the street, as if from nowhere suddenly a white boy of about 11 just appeared beside me. He started talking animatedly in English in a thick Eastern European accent about the blaze with an enormous grin across his face. "Beeg fire! very beeg fire!"

I felt like a toddler, constantly seeing, hearing, smelling and tasting things I'd never encountered before. I was transfixed by one contraption parked outside a small family run ramen restaurant just a stone's throw from my flat. The first time I stopped at the little coin laundry next door to the restaurant to use their dryers I gazed at the restaurant's moped. On the back of the bike were these tall metal poles and springs from which a metal platform dangled. It looked like the sort of implausible zany contraption a seven-year-old would produce if asked to sketch a diagram of a new invention. What I didn't know at the time was that this modification was a self-balancing platform that facilitated the speedy delivery of bowls of noodles in hot broth. Even the most imaginative child's flight of fancy wouldn't suggest this was possible, but my students soon enlightened me that deliver hot bowls of takeaway ramen these scooters did, with not a drop spilt. In addition to its gravity-defying delivery system, like other bicycles and motorbikes in Japan, it had stiff gloves permanently attached to the handlebars although I always wonder how dangerous this might be if the rider were to get in an accident.

***

Seeing new things was all well and good, but I discovered a new way to spend my free time which was far more immersive. My favourite thing to do in Japan is to take a hot spring bath. 'Onsen[19]' is a popular Japanese pastime that dates back centuries. All across the volcanic archipelago hot spring water

---

[19] The term is used to encompass hot spring facilities and the traditional Japanese hotel resorts in which they can often be found. Onsen are distinct from 'sento' which are bathhouses for washing rather than places of relaxation.

bubbles up through the ground. Spas have been built on these sites for centuries and some of them are truly a sight to behold. There's a place in Tokyo called 'King of Onsen'. For roughly £15 you can spend as long as you like enjoying a whole range of baths and other facilities.

Upstairs the spa is divided into separate men's and women's sections. You are given a bag containing several towels of various sizes and a robe that you can wear as you wander around the facility. At the front desk as you enter you are given an electronic fob to wear around your wrist. This is scanned as you leave to assess which of the facilities you've used and what you've bought from the restaurant and the various vending machines. As with all Japanese public baths and spas before you bathe you must first scrub yourself clean at one of the wash stations that line the wall. Once you're sparkling clean you can enjoy the facilities without the thought that you're wallowing in other people's filth.

The range of baths and other options on offer is simply breath-taking. There's the standard warm bath, the hot bath, the very hot bath. There's the hot milky bath and the hot bubble bath. There's the electric bath (yes, you read that right, it sends electric pulses through the water to relax the muscles) which I needed a not insignificant amount of coaxing to try for the first time. Then there are the herbal baths over the sides of which hang nets of what look to be tea leaves. There are also the mineral baths which give off a brown rusty colour and smell of sulphur. And there are the cold baths too. Next to the cold baths is a row of stone seats. Hot water constantly cascades from

above your head. I don't know what's more
unnerving about sitting on these stone benches like
some kind of naked, wet Caesar- the fact that the hot
water cascading down your neck and back and then
under your legs creates the sensation that you're
urinating, or that you sit there on your elevated
throne displaying your naked self to everyone sitting
in the hot milky bath?

There's a sauna with an in-built TV playing
baseball games on a loop and there's a steam room. In
an outdoor area there are large hot slabs of slate that
you lie on which are so hot they're just about bearable.
It feels a bit odd at first, lying completely naked on a
huge hot rock in front of lots of other naked men lying
on hot rocks all around you, but it is in fact incredibly
relaxing. Next to this there are a series of individual
tiled areas with a couple of inches of hot water
running across them. You can lie there comfortably
and enjoy the sunshine or the breeze through the
bamboo roof.

Downstairs in the mixed section in your dressing
gown you can meet up once more with your partner
and enjoy a selection of four steam rooms. There's
fifty degrees, ninety degrees, five degrees and
menthol. Then there are five separate rooms filled
with hot pebbles on which you can lie in your robe
with a small pillow. Once again you have menthol,
'warm', 'hot', 'very hot', and 'why the hell would you
want anything that hot?' In the communal area
outside these rooms people lounge on massage chairs
and watch more baseball. There's an area where you
can have your feet nibbled on by little fish, a
masseuse, a restaurant, and countless vending

machines. On several occasions I have been to King of Onsen intending to stay for an hour or so and walked out three and a half hours later.

I felt great but I must have made a strange sight to the locals each time I left there as this light-headed but incredibly relaxed white man wafted off into the Tokyo night like a deflated balloon, barely in control of his trajectory.

Chapter 5

Sensory Overload

Sights and sounds of the metropolis

We're fools whether we dance or not so we might as well dance.
Japanese proverb

Good examples of the breath-taking scale of the city are the crowds at festivals and big events. I am told that the Sumida river fireworks display, to which Nigel and I took the girls, is attended by over a million people every year in Tokyo and it is only one of many in the city. To see such a swarm of humanity in one place is awesome. What is more shocking than the sheer number of people is the lack of chaos. There isn't wild unruly behaviour and hardly any litter is dropped.

It's at the nearby train stations that the crowds are truly a sight to behold. The platforms are packed solid as everyone arrives at once to board the trains. Yet people wait patiently and calmly and put up with the discomfort. They don't shout or push or jostle. There are no stabbings or assaults. People simply arrive and leave in an orderly fashion while monotone policemen repeat their shouted mantra endlessly through loudhailers.

"Take care and stay to the left!"

During the humid Tokyo evenings of August, to the usual summer noises of the whirr of over-working air conditioner units and the hum of insects in the trees were added the drums and cries of the many festivals. There were Bon Matsuri festivals in the grounds of ancient temples with large red and white striped platforms strung with rows of lanterns, upon which a large drum beat out a rhythm that reverberated around the whole neighbourhood. Smiling old ladies in matching kimonos sang and moved as one around the platform in a dancing procession. Whether the strange sweating foreigner who lurked in the dark shadows of the pagodas and sweeping temple roofs eating fried noodles and chocolate covered bananas as he watched the events with fascination detracted from the ambience is up for debate. From the elbow nudges, whispered conversations and stares of the passing festival goers, I always had a vague feeling of paranoia. Were my flies undone? Was there toilet paper stuck to my shoe? Oh god, please tell me I haven't accidentally come out naked in public again!

Some of the festivals were processions; parades of drummers and dancers through narrow streets, stopping outside each small restaurant and pub they came to and then, to my great surprise, continuing the procession through them, moving between the tables and crying out their chants. There were other times when beautiful bright lanterns floated on Tokyo's rivers by night and Tanabata[20] festivals with huge elaborate constructions of papier-mâché and tissue paper hung from the roofs of covered malls.

There were huge portable shrines known as mikoshi, carried through the city streets towards the

---

[20] Also known as the Star Festival, it is a Japanese festival of Chinese origin which celebrates the meeting of the deities Orihime and Hikoboshi.

many temples, upon the shoulders of sweating and exhausted men in yukata[21], their bare legs showing as they screamed out a time by which they'd bounce the giant wooden structures painfully up and down in unison, while being hosed down and having buckets of cold water thrown upon them. Overly amped up young men shouted out, jostled and swapped places when they had reached the end of their endurance, dropping out from under the large wooden limbs beneath the shrine, and my shoulders and back ached just to watch. In the east Tokyo district of Sanja each year, shaven headed yakuza with full body-tattoos, naked save for a small white loincloth and little white socks, added their weight to the already giant burdens of the shrines as they rode upon them through the streets above the heads of the thronging crowds.

Glimpses of the animist traditions of Japan's ancient Shinto past could be seen in the huge ornately carved wooden floats at the Hachioji festival in west Tokyo. While I looked on, men and women teetered atop the unstable-looking structures lit brightly by the paper lanterns which hung from them. I watched the rickety vehicles move down the street upon their wooden cartwheels while I tucked into fish-shaped pastries full of sweet bean paste. Men dressed in terrifying long-haired fox masks and dragon heads emerged intermittently through the curtains of these giant hand carts and writhed around in ancient dances with jaunty, angular, sudden startling

---

[21] A casual summer kimono worn by both men and women at special events such as fireworks displays and festivals.

movements as they snarled and darted out at the crowds to the haunting and piercing strains of flutes.

Wiping my sodden brow, I looked on in amazement and no small amount of pity as I watched smiling young couples ushering their petrified toddlers towards the wicked-looking creatures. The infants clung desperately to their parents, delirious with fear and gasping for breath in a state of abject terror, crying and screaming themselves hoarse, and a few so scared that no noise would come out of their open mouths at all, and instead simply looking all around with red faces, the veins in their necks fit to burst, in wide-eyed raw fear. I wanted to tell the parents to leave their poor infants alone, for surely there is no good luck tradition worth the scarring of such small minds so susceptible to primal dread. It was the essential stuff of childhood nightmares, like confronting for real the so-longed anticipated but often reassuringly dismissed reality of Mr Wolf who stood now, unavoidably and menacingly before you. Unspeakable horror.

The climax of the summer festivals is 'Awa Odori[22]' which takes place each year in a fashionable district called Koenji over two evenings on the last weekend of August. Luckily for me Koenji was just a thirty-minute walk from my flat. Awa Odori is truly the biggest and the best. With over ten thousand dancers and over a million in the audience it is a spectacle for the eyes and ears. Awa is the ancient

---

[22] The largest dance festival in Japan. The dance originates from the ancient Awa region of modern-day Tokushima prefecture in the island of Shikoku. The origins of the dance can be traced back hundreds of years to a combination of Obon festivals of the dead and harvest festivals.

name of a region of Tokushima on Shikoku island, and it is from there that the dance originates. Troupes of performers travel in procession along the high street up to the train line and down through the covered shopping arcade. The brightly coloured women's kimonos denote their troupe- shades of scarlet and purple, yellows and lime, in intricate and beautiful patterns. They are immaculately turned out with wooden geta[23] on their white-socked feet, scarlet lipstick and amigasa[24] hats, like oversized straw lemon slices. As the women dance, they chant in unison the haunting cry of the harvest.

"A- ya-ka-sa!"

They flick their fans in time with the beat. With incredible skill they move as one like a beautiful army progressing in formation. They balance on their toes and thrust their fingers out in front as the flutes, the drums and the symbols beat a thundering rhythm.

Behind these rows of immaculate ladies come the burly drummers. The noise of their thunderous drums reverberates around the buildings. The crowd feel themselves moving involuntarily to the beat as the drummers, with sweat pouring from their sodden brows, strain every sinew as they pound away. The raw magnetism of the drums and the energising rally of the symbols contrast perfectly with the gentle rhythmic tune of the flutes. And then there are the male dancers with bandanas tied under their noses,

---

[23] A traditional Japanese sandal (worn by both men and women) with a flat wood base raised up on two or three wooden struts and a fabric thong. Geta are usually worn with yukata (a casual summer kimono worn by both men and women).

[24] Traditional, 'wedge-shaped' Japanese straw hats, typically worn in folk dances.

the female dancers with their bandanas perched on their heads in little halos who dance bare foot save for their thin white socks on the tarmac, and who pay not the slightest attention to the rain if it falls.

Children as young as two can be seen amongst the dancers, being ushered along as they waddle open-mouthed past the rows of clapping grandmas. Dotted amongst the troupes are the fools, old men who gurn grotesquely at the crowd. They joke and elicit laughs and whelps as they sidle up to people on the flanks of the road and pretend to flash the audience, although we all know they've got cycling shorts on beneath their yukata. They dart off tittering and waving their fans and the next troupe begins, signalled by their frontman or lady, a smiling leader at the head of each clan who strains to hold a tall bamboo staff many times their height in both hands, at the top of which sit rows of white lanterns. The beautifully inscribed characters upon the ornate lanterns denote the name of the next troupe in the gigantic procession.

It's enchanting and bewitching and there's something magical and timeless in this combination of sound and colour. Though it is the harvest dance and here in central Tokyo the fields and mountains and steep-sided valleys of Tokushima feel a world away, we are reminded so close to Obon that everyone is from somewhere else originally. Strangely in this celebration of the changing seasons I feel at home as if the harvest dance were a Wiltshire one and maybe we are not so different at all, separated as we are by continents and seas. Whether it's druids and henges and crop circles or wooden clogs and fans and lemon slice hats, perhaps the irresistible rhythm that calls to us is universal.

It is my favourite festival in Japan, and it only serves to emphasise what a crazy topsy-turvy world this is because the atmosphere is that of Rio during carnival. The drums feel strangely African, and the crowd are verbose and excited in a way that you just wouldn't associate with this country. The dour businessmen of yesterday wear their dancing robes for two nights a year, the silent commuter on the train dances their heart out and everyone is everyone else's friend. Because the event is so joyous you accept the crowds, six deep and only room to sit at the very front on a narrow blue ribbon of tarpaulins on the road. You forgive the struggle to get out at the end and you accept the fact that all the bars and restaurants are completely full at the end of the dance as you leave on a wave of euphoria with ringing ears.

***

To escape the oppressive summer heat a mixed group of English teachers and our Japanese friends would head west on the train to the mountains. Mitake was technically part of Tokyo prefecture but with its gorge flanked by thickly forested green mountains and a crystal-clear river, it was hard to believe. We'd barbecue sausages and fish over an open fire amongst the rocks by the river and strip off for refreshing dips in the cool water. The more adventurous would climb the huge rock face on the opposite bank and launch themselves into the water. We'd greet the groups of kayaks and canoes who'd pass by on course for the white-water rapids further upstream with waves and cheery smiles.

Families and young couples dotted the flatter sections of the riverbanks with swimming trunks and picnic rugs. With our speakers among the rocks and a guitar or two that someone had brought along, we'd sing and dance as night fell and drag more logs from the forest to keep the fire burning. If it rained, we'd crawl into the lee of the large boulders, trying to avoid the spiders that hid amongst them and wait for it to pass. We felt we needed to escape the city every now and then, especially those of us who'd grown up in the countryside. Even for the native Londoners the crowds were intense, and the sheer scale of Tokyo could be oppressive.

***

Although the cliché of Tokyo as a modern, bustling neon metropolis of bright lights, electronic chirping, high-speed trains, robots and vending machines is borne out by reality, there are places within the city itself to escape. It is one of the city's great triumphs that surprisingly close to the skyscrapers and the bustle and the lights, in quiet corners, and against all the odds, stillness and tranquillity can be found. The historic Asakusa district in the east of Tokyo with its ancient temples and tiered pagodas, which you approach along old streets lined with cherry trees under giant red paper lanterns hung from huge wooden gates, is beautiful. To stand amongst the ancient structures, to smell the incense burnt in the giant urns wafting in clouds from beneath the temples' awnings, to see the pink carpet of fallen cherry blossom and hear the tones of the temple bells is so incongruous in this city as to almost trick you in to thinking you are not in Tokyo at all.

This is surely not that same restless city home to the noisy karaoke parlours and games arcades. But it is. So much of Tokyo's historic districts were bombed into oblivion that those pockets which do remain are more beautiful and enchanting for their rarity.

But I find the most peace not in the old districts that attract throngs of tourists by summer but in the hidden gems dotted around the city. The little temples and shrines on side streets set back from the main roads, the little-known complexes hidden by the boughs of trees are little oases of calm. To step into one is to step through the wardrobe into another world where noise and time seem to disappear. When in these secret places I feel welcome and accepted. They do not expect any commitment from you, no faith or prayer. To emerge once more to the outside world is to almost never have left it. The little shrines and temples hide away once more, not immediately visible but always there for you when you choose to return.

***

Living in central Tokyo as a twenty-three-year-old man with very few commitments was wonderful. I liked the fact that I could go out in Nakano and play electronic darts in darts bars where if they didn't have your favourite brand of cigarettes, they'd send out a member of staff to buy them for you. I liked the fact that you could run into a couple of punks, one a Japanese woman with dyed red hair and a lip ring, the other a Brazilian with a Mohican who works in a car factory in Nagoya, and then go for dinner with them.

I liked the fact that you could spend hours in restaurants sharing tiny dishes of seafood and pork and fresh vegetables where they know your name. I liked the fact that as you ate you would recognise the old man who'd just arrived. Wasn't he the guy with whom you sang Hall and Oates' 'Private Eyes' at three am last Friday in the underground 80's jukebox bar and with whom you laughed when he tried and failed his best moonwalk across the bar? And you remember it was him because of the sound of his laugh and can already picture him in the trilby, the sunglasses and poorly fitting suit he was wearing at the time and how your friends all cheered, and how the music played.

And boy, did the music play! Everywhere you turn in Tokyo there are jingles. Speakers on train station platforms blare jolly tunes each time a train stops at them. Each station has its own distinct jingle, played in the brief period before the automatic doors close, the purpose of which is to alert sleeping passengers to which station they have just arrived at by dint of the music alone. It was all so Japanese. Many of the tunes were from favourite childhood Japanese cartoon series like the 1960's 'Astro Boy' theme tune played at Takadanobaba station, no doubt providing nostalgic relief to weary commuters. Good idea I thought, but I couldn't imagine South West trains following suit.

"Basingstoke, this is Basingstoke! We're off to Button Moon......!"

"Woking, this is Woking! Pugh, Pugh, Barney McGrew, Cuthbert, Dibble, Grub."

At five pm every day I thought of bread. I was instantly transported incongruously from Tokyo streets to the steep cobbles of Gold Hill in Shaftesbury, Dorset. Why? Because the speakers around my neighbourhood broadcast the song played in the old Hovis ad, the one where the boy pushes a bicycle up a steep, winding hill. I heard that tune thousands of times in Japan. No doubt, if that advert was re-released on British TV today, I'd instantly think of little Japanese boys and girls scurrying home from school at the end of the day, because that was its purpose, to call children home because the day was done. There was something comforting and familiar in the warmth of the music and its regularity.

Electronic music blared out of high-tech games arcades, the pedestrian crossings chirped and the restaurant vending machines beeped at me when I made an order. In those early days I would keep my fingers crossed when entering a restaurant that the vending machine would have pictures on the buttons. If not, I would press a button at random, choosing some friendly-shaped Japanese characters, maybe ones with rounded edges not sharp and pointy because that's as good a system as any, right? I'd sit hungrily at restaurant counters desperately hoping for some steaming bowl of deliciousness which, as luck would have it, is what turned up nine times out of ten, and not the rare but occasional unwitting purchase of pigs' innards or bird bones.

In many restaurants you summon the waiter or waitress with an electronic buzzer. All the different convenience stores have their own jingles which play when you enter through the automatic doors. Some of them even have lyrics to go with them. Come to think of it, even the ladies in the convenience stores chirp their own little jingles. "Irasshaimase!" (welcome) they cry aloud when you enter, when you leave, when you approach the checkout and once you've bought something. To be honest, they also shout the phrase at random points intermittently throughout the day. I admire their diligence. I should think British workers would mutiny if they were required to shout welcome three hundred times a day. But the workers here oblige and are seen to be doing their jobs the better, the louder and more heartily they shout it.

In Harajuku and Shibuya, the fashion districts much beloved by Tokyo teens, a seemingly endless procession of music lorries drive slowly around the streets. The sole purpose of these trucks is to blare out the whining strains of boy and girl bands at maximum volume. The lorries are plastered with giant images of the latest in-vogue group next to details of their latest album and its release date. This is advertisement as I'd never seen it, no subtlety, no craft, just in-your-face shouting about it, consumerism laid bare.

Once every few months in Shinjuku I'd see the little black vans of the far-right adorned with Japanese flags cruising the streets. These were the idiots who'd hollered at Nigel and me the morning after our Fuji ascent. From huge loudhailers atop the vehicle, they warn the public of foreigners and moan on about Chinese indiscretions and how the war dead at Yasukuni shrine should be honoured as heroes and patriots. The extremists are largely ignored by most, far more at least than the slow-moving lorries blaring out the latest hits of whichever smooth-skinned boy group is currently topping the charts.

The sights of the metropolis are as beguiling as the sounds. By night on the edge of tall buildings long narrow, brightly coloured neon signs with characters written vertically light up the busier thoroughfares. They advertise restaurants and bars, karaoke, live shows, ice cream parlours and 24-hour shops. On quieter streets, the more subtle beacons away from the neon glare, are the beautiful lanterns, atmospheric on quiet nights and blowing gently in the breeze. In Spring above the fallen cherry blossom petals, the rows of gentle pink lanterns strung along the city's riversides reflect serenely on the water's surface. Down narrow alleys lanterns outside late night establishments light up the dark and beckon the weary worker. Red lanterns indicate drinking establishments, known as 'akachochins[25]', whereas white lanterns outside denote a restaurant. On cold nights in winter these serve as beacons of light and warmth, little oases of raucous laughter and a rich fug of smoke as the food smells waft out of the sliding wooden doors each time they open. On warm summer nights businessmen with loosened neckties sit on upturned beer crates around ramshackle tables outside these establishments drinking lager and eating yakitori[26].

---

[25] Non-chain 'izakayas' (Japanese style pub). These bars traditionally hang a red paper lantern outside.

[26] A type of Japanese skewered chicken that is grilled and usually served in izakayas or outdoor food stands at festivals and other events.

On the gradually cooling evenings of early autumn near my home upon the moonlit pavements, or on colder ones under the cover of the Sun Mall, an old lady would sit at a small table with a little rectangular lamp. She was a fortune teller. One evening as I sat before her she gazed at me and scribbled on some paper. I should have been relieved that she didn't foretell the litany of bumbling mistakes I'd make in the months to come. She instead told of excitement and adventure and good things in store. For the price of the generous donation which I gave her as she bowed and bade me safe passage, it was the least she could do. Behind her in the alleyways of the Nakano Sun Mall, too narrow for humans to access, litters of stray cats poked their heads out and darted back in with high pitched meows each time someone came too close. On dim evenings when the shops of the mall closed, and the footfall petered away the cats ventured out more boldly and the mall was theirs.

**

Early on I discovered a restaurant that I really liked in Nogata. Sadly, it's gone now, replaced by another restaurant. 'Fukushin' is a chain. They are tiny, cheap, greasy spoon sort of places, no frills, no etiquette, no fuss, but I absolutely loved it. Its bright blue sign with its logo, a little square white face with a tongue licking its lips, was like a beacon to me. My usual order was the 'B set', a delicious combination of soy sauce ramen and a side of egg and pork fried rice and I'd often order some delicious fried pork dumplings on the side for good measure. I became such a frequent visitor to Fukushin that they almost knew my order before I'd opened my mouth. It was open until 2am every night and I could often be found strolling the ten minutes there from my flat. Yuka and I developed a nickname for the guy that ran the place, 'Uncle Japan', and so most evenings I would be roused from my lounging with the refrain, "Shall we go and see Uncle Japan?" to which my response was invariably "Yes."

I also loved the Cocoichi curry house also on the High Street. I became a regular and the owner quickly became a firm friend. He talked of his family and we chatted about England and holidays. Through his pidgin English and my even more pidgin Japanese we built a rapport, and in the years after I left Japan when I'd visit in August he'd look up in pleasant surprise when I'd stop in for a curry and a catch-up. The place opposite was another curry place I loved where the guy would endlessly top up your glass with cold green tea on warm summer nights from the huge metal kettle filled with ice or steaming mugs of the same brew on chilly winter evenings. Further down the street still was the beef bowl shop, open 24 hours, serving beautiful slices of thinly cut fatty beef or pork on a bed of fluffy white rice, served with pickles and hearty miso soup and salad, all for a ridiculously low price.

My diet left a lot to be desired. Though Japan is known as a nation of healthy eating, my restaurants and dishes of choice, particularly those served by Uncle Japan at Fukushin, were by and large fatty, oily and full of salt. You aren't supposed to drink all of the soup that the huge bowl of ramen noodles comes in, especially not if it is the very salty shoyu (soy) variety which is what I like best. If you do, it is a once-in-a-while blow out, not a five-times a week routine. You aren't supposed to then go and order the greasy pork dumplings to go with it or the huge side bowl of fried rice. And you definitely aren't supposed to order the 600-gram portion of rice at the Cocoichi curry house instead of the standard 300 grams and then order an extra fried chicken cutlet and the sausage and the cheese to go on top.

I suppose I had sleepwalked into my bad food habits. Perhaps I was no different from some of my students who didn't put in any effort. You know, the 'Well, I am here, aren't I? Input some English into my brain' brigade. Maybe this was no different. Was it possible that I'd imagined that simply by dint of being in Japan the pounds would magically stay off? that I could eat what I liked because you can't get fat in Japan? I loved the counter-style dining and the ability to do it regularly. I loved that I could afford to do it in a way that would rinse my bank account back at home. I loved the food and the atmosphere and the ease. I loved the ambience and the people with whom I'd talk and, as time went on, I felt more and more part of the fabric of the place.

In April 2008, a year after I had arrived in Japan, my mother came to visit. She may have been expecting many things. She may have expected me to be fairly proficient in Japanese by now. I wasn't. She may have expected me to have taken up some rarefied and impressive martial art. I hadn't. She may have expected that living in the Far East I was now able to view life with some zen-like enlightenment. I couldn't. But there was one thing she definitely wouldn't have expected with her son living in Japan for a year. She definitely would not have expected when she met me in her hotel lobby on that April day to suddenly notice that I'd become really quite fat.

Chapter 6

White Gloves

Craftmanship, service and the pursuit of perfection

Better to be proficient in one art than to smatter in a thousand.
Japanese proverb

An abiding revelation for any visitor to Japan is that nothing can be done by halves. This doesn't just apply to people's jobs but to their hobbies too which are taken very seriously with people decked out in all the right gear. The ten-pin bowlers bring their own balls in bags on wheels which they polish before putting them away; the blokes at the local pool hall often bring their own cue and wear their own special glove, and people turn up at the electronic darts places with their own custom-made darts that they keep in a special leather pouch on their belt. It seemed that everything was done the right way, all the time, nothing slapdash and nothing half-hearted. I'd left the land of the casual kickabout or the relaxed game of pool at the local over a couple of pints behind. These guys meant business.

I suppose the doing of things the 'proper way' is all about ritual. And if there's something Japan knows about, it's ritual. From the hallowed tea ceremony to the immaculately raked stone gardens and precision clipping of bonsai trees, ritual is important, and ritual is art. The craftsmanship of the potters and the woodworkers and the swordsmiths is second to none. I knew this to be true even before coming to Japan. I knew that Japanese attention to detail was of the highest order. My girlfriend's mother's neighbour however clearly thought I hadn't quite got the point. He'd clearly thought the foreigner needed a little initiation into *real* Japanese culture. He came over to the house drunk with his samurai sword, which was genuinely a beautiful piece of craftmanship. I was slightly perturbed however given his level of inebriation, when he unsheathed the sword and, as he wobbled around the living room off-balance, began swashing it through the air uncomfortably close to my face. I made impressed noises while surreptitiously taking small shuffling steps backwards until I almost fell backwards over the sofa.

In Japanese crafts you find the pursuit of perfection. The immaculately dressed ladies in the department stores will wrap boxes of chocolates or biscuits or grossly over-priced cases of premium fruit for you as gifts with the level of precision and dexterity you would expect from a brain surgeon. The delicate process is a wonder to behold and the results beautiful. The trivial and the mundane are turned into an art form. People don't scoff at doing the small jobs, they don't shirk at being cleaners or waiters or dustmen or bus drivers but instead do these jobs to the absolute best of their ability and with a dedication to their duty. The gloves of the taxi drivers are an immaculate white and their peaked caps sit pristinely on their heads, and I shall never forget how quickly and cheerfully my order was taken the first time I walked into a Japanese McDonalds. It felt like a formula one pitstop with burgers instead of tyres and smiles instead of a refuelling pump. The uniforms of the bullet train maids who rush in for their five-minute cleaning of the carriages are neatly pressed and spotless. In the brief window of time after the train arrives in Tokyo from Osaka and is about to go back again, they bow at the train in unison while waiting patiently for all the passengers to alight before performing their duties quietly and efficiently at breath-taking speed. Train guards and drivers perform their ritualised checking system. They chant their safety checks as they point in white-gloved hands at the items they are ticking off.

"Doors closed, yosh[27]! Lights on, yosh! Platform clear, yosh!"

It is art and it is theatre all rolled into one. The beauty comes in doing the best you can do and in being the best you can be.

***

The customer service often went beyond expected duties. People were willing to go the extra mile. The taxi driver in Shimane prefecture in western Japan that whizzed me from the train station to a historic village through the picturesque countryside went the extra mile. I had paid for him to drive me from A to B, not to be an impromptu tour guide, but his wealth of local knowledge and eagerness to fill me in on the local delights were a real bonus on my trip. He waited for me while I trekked around the historic village and offered to do everything short of shining my shoes.

---

[27] A spoken term used for 'right', 'ok', or 'yes', used often by someone making sudden movements or exertions or performing checks.

He filled me in on the local area with interesting facts and recommendations. This area, so he said, had many wild boars. Apparently, they could be seen darting along at great speed parallel to the main road at the foot of the mountains. His depiction of these hogs racing through the ancient landscape conjured up a romantic image in my mind. He then added that they could also be found in great numbers skulking in the shadows of a concrete-roofed carpark in the nearby town, which I must admit hadn't quite the same air of romance.

As we passed a pretty rural scene with the crystal-clear, boulder strewn river sparkling beside us and the mountains rising behind rice paddies and tiled roof houses in the distance, the driver pointed.

"Do you see that house over there?" he said. "It burned down a few years ago, then the owner rebuilt it, then it burned down again, then he rebuilt it. Can you believe it? It then burned down for a third time. He's just finished rebuilding it again."

***

My girlfriend's father was an intriguing man. There were hushed rumours that as a younger man he'd been involved with the yakuza[28]. With his bald head and moustache, the shades he seemed to wear everywhere and his tough features I could easily picture it. Now in his sixties he ran a bar in Chofu in

---

[28] Highly hierarchical traditional Japanese crime syndicates whose rough equivalents in the West are the mafia or other gangster organisations. The name derives from the worst possible hand in the card game 'Oicho-Kabu' which is '8-9-3' (ya-8, ku-9, sa-3). Yakuza are marked for life. Therefore, they are seen to be playing a losing hand in life. The number of yakuza, their activities and influence has dwindled in recent years.

Tokyo's suburbs. When he showed us the bar it looked nice enough, if a little small, but he then ushered us through to a hidden room behind a secret door. It opened up into a large area with plush black leather sofas, electronic dartboards and a karaoke machine. This only added to the man's intrigue. But the bar wasn't his real passion.

His real passion was paper cutting. On the walls of this back room and in Yuka's home were some of the most beautiful and intricate pieces of artwork I have ever seen, from incredibly delicate and intricate flowers to elegant women and dragons. There was no ink, there were no pencils or paint. This was the ancient art of kirigami[29]. The breath-taking designs were cut with remarkable precision out of black paper and mounted on a white background. I'm not sure how many hours a single piece took, but with tigers emerging from thick leaves, tangled vines and ladies' long flowing locks, I can only imagine it was a long and painstaking process to say the least, not to mention one that required the utmost of artistic vision, patience and a steady hand. One mistake and the whole thing would be ruined.

When Yuka first came to stay in England, as a thank you for my parents putting her up for ten days, her father kindly gave my family three of his most beautiful and ornate pictures. The one question was, How on Earth would we get them back to the UK without them being damaged? In the end I'm glad to say, we did. Our voluminous padding and careful packing ensured they made it to Wiltshire in one

---

[29] A variation of origami that includes the cutting of paper.

piece where they hang today on the walls of my house.

***

How in this topsy-turvy land should we reconcile two elements of modern Japan that are at such odds with one another? On the one hand, the white gloves and the immaculate, beautiful performing of tasks; the precise woodwork and metalwork, the delicate beauty of Japanese art and the flower arranging. On the other, the ugly tangle of overhead utility wires that characterise city streets, the lack of conservation of old buildings and the wholesale destruction of the Japanese landscape?

Perspective. Perhaps no country better exemplifies the old adage that 'beauty is in the eye of the beholder'. The jungle of wires that threads its way like a nest above urban Japan is one thing. It's easy to accept because no one could ever truly claim that Tokyo or Osaka were beautiful in the first place, not after the war anyway. But the endless pylons and concreted riverbanks and deforested hillsides and hundreds of dams that are built and planned to be built, where's the beauty in that?

When in April 2008 my mother and a friend of hers came to Japan to visit me I met her in a hotel in central Tokyo and found her grinning from ear to ear.

"Oh, they're so lovely," she beamed in the lobby. "The Japanese are so lovely!"

I showed my mum the sights of Tokyo, Kyoto, Nara and Hakone. I say I, but we hired tour guides and they were great. My mum wanted to do it properly, wanted to really soak up the Japan experience. She was as bowled over by the bullet train as I was, and Tokyo left her breathless. She was shocked at the size of my flat and amused by the craziness, the busyness and the general hubbub of Tokyo life. If my mother was awed by Tokyo, she positively adored Kyoto where we toured the city's famous sites. When we stopped for a moment, I decided to grab a quick drink from a vending machine by one of the temples.

Our hugely proud tour guide commented, "Look, if you put your money in that vending machine, you'll get exactly the right change. Go on, try it. You'll see."

I entered 120 yen and a cool bottle of water came out. He stood over me watching in suspense. He visibly quivered when he heard the faint metallic clinks of my change dropping behind the plastic flap.

"Go on, check it. Is it right?"

I turned and nodded and, as if he'd just found the cure for cancer, he faced the assembled crowd and assured them, "See, I knew it would be correct. I just knew it! Japanese vending machines always give the correct change."

We visited Gion, the ancient geisha district of Kyoto with its historic wood buildings and drooping willow trees beside quaint little streams spanned by tiny little stone bridges. We took photographs of a young maiko (trainee geisha) in full regalia, drank green tea and generally had a wonderful time. We then headed to Nara where we toured the even older temples and fed the mangy deer and, by the end of the few days we had spent out west, even my mum had to admit, "It's nice, but you do get a bit, you know, 'templed-out'." It was all very touristy, a pre-packaged, sanitised view of Japan but it was great.

I'll never forget my mother's face when we stayed in a ryokan[30] in Hakone near Mt. Fuji. She sat opposite me in the yukata that had been provided for her as the maid entered the room with a large tray of our dinner. As the maid began to lay out the dishes on the low table my mum looked on in horror at what she was expected to eat. She smiled politely and cooed with enthusiasm so as not to offend the lady but once the maid had gone, she looked at me and then at the giant raw fish head in the centre of her plate with panic written across her face.

"Tom, I can't eat fish heads!"

In desperation, she picked up the flower that had been placed as a decoration amongst the little plates and dishes and, looking around to make sure no member of Japanese staff was looking, ate it whole.

***

The pursuit of perfection was certainly on display in the public baths. To be perfectly clean was deemed a virtue. It was the old men in particular in the bathhouses who seemed to scrub themselves to within an inch of their lives. Then again it was mainly old men that filled the bathhouses at all. They would sit on their tiny stool lathering their little white flannels and scouring their skin until it was red. It was another example of taking things to the extreme. No part of their bodies escaped scrutiny. Every gap

---

[30] A traditional Japanese hotel with tatami-matted (straw-covered mats) rooms and usually containing public baths. In some ryokans, dinner is brought to your room and served to you by a maid at a table at which you sit cross-legged on the tatami floor.

between the toes was probed. They lathered and wiped and scratched and scoured until I thought they'd bleed. Most people in the West probably go through their entire lives without ever seeing the general public wash. I wasn't complaining. In fact, it was a mighty relief. As I watched them yank their flannels back and forth between their legs, as if cutting cheese with a wire, I'd silently thank them for cleaning themselves so thoroughly before sharing a bath with me.

I enjoyed chatting to the old men in the baths. I once had an hour-long chat with one toothless old man in a black-coloured mineral bath. I don't really know what he talked of, but he picked up no indication that I didn't understand. I think it was something to do with his wife, but the hand gestures were more elaborate than a puppet show. There comes a point in a conversation where you can't let on that you haven't understood much because it would just look rude. I nodded and laughed when he laughed and shrugged when he shrugged, and as he got out of the water I bowed slightly and said a silent thank you that his arse crack and testicles were more highly polished than the black ball at the Embassy snooker tournament.

Bathing at home had moved on since the hey-day of the bathhouses. Modern Japanese technology had revolutionised the bathing experience. I was slightly alarmed when standing in Yuka's living room for the first time when an unfamiliar female voice chirped up just a couple of feet away from my face and informed me that my bath was ready. The voice had come from a panel on the wall. This was not some expensive luxury but a standard piece of technology in the modern Japanese home. All you need do is type in exactly what temperature you want the water to be, and you needn't even run the bath yourself. You can get on with whatever you're doing and ten minutes later the speaker will chirp into life informing you that the bath is now full, the water is exactly 42.5 degrees and will be kept at that temperature for as long as you like.

***

It will come as little surprise that Japan's pursuit of perfection is perhaps nowhere more evident than in the culinary department. Tokyo has by far the most Michelin-starred restaurants of any city on Earth, considerably more in fact than London and Paris combined. Sitting in a tiny tatami-floored[31] room in an otherwise deserted hotel in the north of Honshu somewhere near Morioka, as I looked out of the window to the distant peak of Mount Iwate, the last thing I expected to be presented with for dinner was a bees' nest.

Of course, it wasn't a bees' nest but the object my lunch was served in had the exact shape of one. The ornately carved ceramic structure I was presented with came in five layers. Lifting off the lid, I was presented with a layer of fresh seasonal vegetables immaculately carved into little creatures; a hedgehog made of carrot, a mouse made of cucumber. Removing the top layer, the second and slightly

---

[31] A type of woven straw mat which cover the floors of traditional Japanese rooms. Tatami mats are a standard size. In Japan the size of a room is often measured by the number of tatami mats that it takes to cover the floor space.

wider layer of the bees' nest was a delicious selection of raw fish. There was tuna and salmon and shrimp and squid all beautifully sliced and displayed on a shiso[32] leaf. The next layer down yet was wafer thin ham folded into an impossibly delicate flower and cooked egg and onions. There were two more layers whose contents I can't fully remember, but I do recall that each was more delicious and delicate and beautifully presented than the last. Best of all, I didn't get stung once, not even in the wallet, as yet again the most delicious and beautifully presented of meals was unbelievably cheap. Indeed, it is a triumph that it is financially viable to eat out regularly in Japan and I would eat out five or six nights a week.

***

No matter how hard a company or a nation and its people strive for perfection, nothing and nobody can be perfect all of the time. Japan's culture of duty and shame at not fulfilling said duty are all-pervading. Both the Japanese and the British are considered reserved. Whether you see lager louts, punk rock and naughty Brits abroad as proof that Britain's reputation as such is false, whether you view it as a consequence, a rebellion against the repression, or simply an outlier from the norm, an exception from the general rule, is a matter for debate. But Japan was different. The evidence of keeping feelings and emotions in check was everywhere. It was almost certainly as a result of these unnatural bedfellows (a desire to be perfect at all things and at all times on the one hand, and the suppression of outward emotions

---

[32] A leaf of a herb in the mint family. Shiso leaves are often displayed in sashimi collections and with other dishes.

on the other) that there are so many tears. I have no doubt Japan would rank very highly among the answers if you were to ask people around the world who they'd least expect to cry in public. But cry they do.

Baseball teams stand in a row after defeat in series finals, each player wailing and screaming uncontrollably. They scream apologies to their teammates, their coach, their families and their hometown. During my time in Japan one of the many female pop idols, who are supposed to remain virginal and pure for the benefit of their male fans, shaved off all her hair in penance when the media discovered she was having a physical relationship with a man. She then cried on national TV among a flurry of bows and repeated apologies, her career likely over, as if a twenty-one-year-old woman having a boyfriend is a crime. Politicians and high-flying businessmen cry when found guilty of misconduct or embezzlement. Actors cry, teachers cry, everyone cries. Perhaps one of the most famous crying Japanese politicians is 'Ryutaro Nonomura' whose floods of tears and wails of repentance have garnered hundreds of thousands of views on Youtube worldwide.

There are now even group crying events known as 'rui-katsu' or 'tear seeking' that take place in major Japanese cities. These have sprung up as a means of catharsis, to enable people to show their emotions in a culture where hiding one's emotions is considered a virtue. These events, much like the act of crying itself, are a sort of release valve, a way of venting the built-up stress and emotion. The irony is, the more a society represses people's liberty to express their emotions, surely the more likely it is for those feelings to suddenly explode in a most extreme way. It was more a case of seldom and huge rather than little and often.

Were the English any different? Roughty-toughty looking types with bulging muscles might burst into tears and hug a mate after nine pints when Southgate or Batty missed a penalty, and what about Gazza's famous cry? But would they break down in such a manner when their performance in the third quarter at work had been found to be below par? In many Western countries mental health is one of the 'in' phrases of the day, and rightly so. If nothing else, these extreme Japanese crying outbursts proved that occasional eruptions aside, feelings in many were being pent up for much of the time. Japan may lead the world in many things but, as I was to witness during my time there, in taking mental health seriously it lags woefully behind.

Chapter 7

Massive Wrapped Apples

My students

Gold coins to a cat.
Japanese proverb

My students were as varied a group of individuals as you're ever likely to meet. I taught professors, chefs, hairdressers, policemen and university students; I instructed dancers, models, sports stars and rock stars. I educated over-excited toddlers, senile great grandmothers, surly teens and high and mighty CEOs. Among the people I endeavoured to educate there were the bright, the dull, the drab and the eccentric, alcoholics, workaholics, perverts and priests. Some were not particularly noteworthy and most I have forgotten in the mists of time. However, a few readily come to mind.

One of my long-term 'private' students was Yuko, a refined lady in her thirties who was obsessed with Britain and all things British. She looked like a long-lost member of the Royal Family in her Hunter wellies and her Barbour wax jacket. She wore Burberry and tartan, she sported jodhpurs, cable-knit jumpers and always carried an umbrella with a wooden handle polished to an immaculate shine. She'd talk longingly of Edinburgh and York and the Cotswolds. When I showed her pictures of the cathedral city near my home, she positively melted. She dreamt of cream tea and roast beef and walks in the Welsh mountains. But most of all, she desperately wanted a British husband. Our lessons soon descended into her leaning in conspiratorially and asking me for tips on how to snare one. Unfortunately, I wasn't best placed to help her, but I'd be interested to know if she ever found her British Prince Charming.

There was a woman of about sixty called Noriko who was absolutely smitten with me. She came in every Thursday afternoon at three pm like an excited little toad with a smile from ear to ear. She would enter the classroom, panting so much she'd become breathless, leaning against the wall for support and letting off little gasps as if the whole affair was about to overwhelm her. I don't think she learnt a spot of English with me. She cooed and cackled and giggled like a thirteen-year-old with a wrinkled hand covering her mouth in embarrassment. She'd always angle to sit next to me at the Christmas parties and was possessive over me in our class which she shared with three other women who just couldn't get a word in edgeways.

There was a woman obsessed with Jason Statham and another who entered ballroom dancing competitions in Blackpool every year. There was the couple who were constantly inviting me out to drink with them, whose invitations I later felt glad I'd always declined when I passed them collapsed on a side street drunk one night throwing up in the gutter. There was the old woman who grinned and told me she was descended from samurai, and the man who asked me, "Do you like prostitutes?" before pointing out of the classroom window and saying, "I go to a

Chinese woman in that building there every week. She's very good."

Many other weird and wonderful students come to mind. There was the woman who came into my class each week and simply repeated everything I said and went home again; the three-year-old boy who would come into the class and grin as he tried to hit me while his mother watched through the window and cooed, "What fun!" There was the extremely polite and formal woman in her late twenties who took a couple of minutes just to say farewell, shuffling out of the room backwards in a crouched posture while facing me in a flurry of repeated 'bye bye's' and bows. She would deftly open the door behind her by touch alone and continue to reverse out in a humble crouch until the door had shut behind her. I had an eighty-two-year-old student whose mother was still alive and a girl of fifteen who had once been to my tiny home city. When I asked her if she'd liked it, I expected a comment on the cathedral, the museums or the Tudor buildings.

"Yes, it was great, it had an HMV."

***

With alarming regularity, the middle-aged ladies I taught would inform me how they loathed their useless husbands. Invariably, once the children had grown up and the husband had retired, she'd come to realise how little they now had in common and consider him a nuisance. I however was lovely-handsome, young, clever, kind and just generally lovely. Of course, I was and am none of these things but that wasn't the point. They believed it because I was exotic. I was a gentleman from a land of gentlemen, refined, sophisticated, cultured and oh, so different from their mundane husbands.

The middle-aged ladies bought me so many gifts that I barely had room for them in my pokey flat. Gift-giving, or 'omiyage' as it is known, is of huge importance in Japan. It is customary, the expectation being that whenever you travel to a different part of Japan or abroad you bring home gifts- gifts for your family, friends, boss, co-workers and for your English teacher. Over the years I received endless gifts from my students. I received mugs, decorative chopsticks, keyrings, trinkets and good luck charms. I received a fabric rabbit, a fabric ball, an ornately carved wooden box, teas, alcohol, chocolates, biscuits and a whole plethora of bookmarks. I got fans galore, antiques, dishes, calendars, stationery, place mats, toys, books and a whole host of other items, most of which I will never use or display in my home. But most of all I got fruit.

I can't imagine ever giving someone fruit as a gift. Local areas of Japan however are famed for different foodstuffs and the people of each region are immensely proud of the quality of their produce. They might have prized apples or grapes, melons or rice. Most strikingly of all, Japanese fruit is enormous, and it is very expensive. I would quite commonly cycle home after work with a huge beautifully ornate display case of massive apples from Aomori province, each cradled in a polystyrene cup and wrapped in cellophane. I received expensive melons from Gifu and impossibly bright oranges from Kyushu. I received huge bags of rice and bean paste cake and cookies. I was bestowed with bottles of sake which came from such and such a region of Japan because the water that ran through its mountains was the purest, which meant the rice was the best, which in turn meant the sake there was of the highest quality too.

I might have imagined in those early days that we teachers were worthy of gifts because our very presence was a rare gift in itself. The truth was this was just part of Japan's gift-giving culture and as 'Sensei' we were assigned a certain respect and veneration. The imagined lives of teachers occupied the fantasies of the old ladies.

"Have you got a girlfriend yet?"

"Can you use chopsticks?"

"Do you like raw fish?"

We were surely free-wheeling and carefree. We had left our families, all tall and blonde and blue-eyed and decided to grace Japan with our presence and perform the honour of educating the Orient.

My students brought their knitting to show me. They brought things they had built, books they had bought. They showed me DVDs and CDs and photographs of idols, pictures of their children, their grandchildren, their dogs and their cats. Children showed me photos of their pet beetles (which are a hugely popular choice of pet for Japanese children, partly due to lack of space) and then frowned at me when I posited the idea that they were just posh cockroaches. I was shown albums of foreign holidays which would invariably follow the same theme: Smiley wife and sour puss husband doing the V sign next to the Eiffel Tower; Smiley wife and sour puss husband doing the V sign at The Grand Canyon;

Smiley wife and sour puss husband doing the V sign at Horse Guards Parade, the picture snapped by a kind passer-by capturing the moment the Japanese couple jumped in shock when told to, "Make way for the Queen's Guard!"

***

As well as the usual husband-hating and questioning of how much you like Japanese girls, there were odd moments of surprise and genuine intrigue. I taught a young man who insisted in our first lesson that I teach him English slang.

"I like to go and hang out in East London," he announced proudly. "You see, I'm into hip hop and grime."

I bumped into him about two years after I'd stopped teaching him. He enthusiastically informed me of the two weeks he'd recently spent hanging out in Newham and Tower Hamlets.

"Yeah, it was fuckin' sweet bruv, get me?" he proclaimed in his best urban London accent as I tried to keep a straight face.

One of my students was a rock star called Yusuke. Well at least, he said he was a rock star. His swanky apartment in a sought-after district, his low rider Harley Davidson with the really long handlebars and his designer clothes indicated that he probably wasn't lying. He also claimed to have been a faster swimmer than Kosuke Kitajima, a boy who had been in his year at high school. Well, he looked fit enough so that wasn't beyond the bounds of possibility. I went swimming with Yusuke after we became friends, and he *was* very fast. So why was it that I still doubted his claim to have been a faster swimmer than this

Kitajima fella? Well, it might have been the fact that this was 2008 and just a few weeks prior to our trip to the pool, Kosuke Kitajima had won the gold medal in the 100m freestyle at the Beijing Olympics.

Yusuke was a good-looking bloke and wasn't shy in approaching the ladies. He had a fiancé, but he quite happily and regularly slept around. He had a particular penchant for foreign girls, so I often wondered when he enrolled with the school if he had been disappointed to discover that his teacher was male.

"I met a blonde girl in the park the other day. She was nineteen and very tall and from Canada. I took her to a hotel, and we had sex."

I didn't know quite how to respond. I didn't know if that Canadian girl had recently competed in any 'endeavour not to have sex with a Japanese man I've just met' international competitions recently or, if she had, whether she'd won the gold medal for it, so unlike Kitajima and the swimming, I arguably had less reason to doubt the veracity of the anecdote.

Yusuke took me out on his Harley a few times. It was a chopper which made a wonderful sound, and we would spend lazy summer days scooting around Tokyo's more fashionable districts and zooming over Tokyo Bay on the famous Rainbow Bridge. I felt a bit sad for the fiancé when I met her. She was sweet and kind. I didn't mention the Canadian girl in the park or the Chinese prostitute or the other untold conquests to which he'd alluded. She was very real and pretty but, for whatever reason, he had a wandering eye. I don't know if they're still together. Maybe she discovered his infidelity. Perhaps it would be fitting if she ever did for her to have a little rendezvous of her own. She could pick up a Belgian in a zoo or maybe a Filipino at a car boot sale.

***

There was a charming middle-aged man I would occasionally teach who took enormous pleasure in coming out with incongruous phrases at the end of lessons. He'd grin and make as if to leave before turning on his heels and, after a pregnant pause for effect, say something like, "It was my pleasure" or "Take it easy!" One day I thanked him before sending him on his way and he looked at me and said, "Not at all" and broke into a broad grin. On another such day after we'd said our goodbyes he leant back into the room and stuck up his thumb.

"Tom-u sensei, I just wanted to say, thanks a million!"

It was sweet and his unbridled enthusiasm and eagerness to please made all the tedium of the husband-hating housewives well worth it.

One of my more lovely lessons was the one with the eight five-year- old children I taught on a Friday. There were five boys and three girls. The girls were respectful and eager to learn whereas the boys raced around laughing whenever I spoke English and positively falling around in hysterics at each other when any one of them so much as attempted to speak English. They launched sticky balls at the large whiteboard at my badly drawn pictures of lions and pineapples and family faces such as the baggy, wrinkled, vaguely spherical approximation of 'grandma'. When it wasn't sticky ball games, it was run and touch the magnetic flashcards I stuck to the walls or 'snap' or run and draw on the whiteboard.

It was my favourite lesson of the week. The children came together for one hour each Friday to stare at and parrot and giggle with the bizarre little foreign man. The eight mums would pop out for a quick half hour coffee and return to view the last part of the lesson, peering through the window before their children emerged, the daughters to smile at their mothers and the sons to punch theirs, my incredulity at this always surpassed by my mixed feelings towards the mums who'd try to pacify their, until now, angelic but suddenly and inexplicably aggressive, little tykes, almost apologetically.

"Please don't hit me Yutaka, please. What will Sensei think?"

***

I often wonder if strange moments linger in the minds of my students as vividly as they do in mine. Each week at Naka-Itabashi school I taught a boy called Hayato and a girl called Kako, both aged 6. One day during their lesson I noticed a small lizard on the far wall of the classroom. I was a little bit stunned by this and I froze, not knowing what to do. The children continued their game of 'snap' with the flashcards at the front of the room, not noticing that I was now totally distracted and edging towards the far wall to inspect the creature more closely. I had to catch it and remove it from the classroom. Although it was no more than four inches in length including the tail, it could be dangerous, and I was responsible for these children.

A series of questions raced through my mind. Are lizards dangerous? Do they bite? Are they poisonous? With the muffled cries of, "It's a sheep. Snap!" vaguely registering in my ears as the children continued to play, I picked up a plastic pen holder and slammed it on top of the lizard, except my aim was off. I had in fact accidentally slammed the rim of the container down on to the lizard's tail. Worse still, I'd sliced the thing's tail clean off! The severed tail was stuck to the wall, very much separated from the body of the now tail-less creature.

Alerted by the noise, the children watched on now in horror as I panicked. Realising that the creature would surely die from blood loss and having not attended for at least several years any courses in trauma management for reptiles, I decided that the most humane thing to do would be to just fling it out of the window to die quietly in the bushes. I picked it up, a little too firmly as it turned out, for its eyes bulged fit to burst, and I realised that as I wandered to the window to fling it out that I was in fact strangling it in my firm grip. The children stared at me incredulously, all innocence lost. Who was this barbaric monster who stood before them? Surely not the same person as the familiar smiling man with whom for the last two years they had played, danced and hopped around the room to the strains of, "I am a Fluffy Rabbit"? Kako's victory was irrelevant now. The excitement of revealing the winning 'sheep' card had now turned to stunned and empty silence. They stood open-mouthed and solemnly watched me as I closed the window and turned back to them.

At least it couldn't get worse than this. At least I couldn't get any lower than murdering reptiles in front of crestfallen infants, my judges, jury and executioners, whose faith in me had disappeared in one swift act. Alas, I was wrong. At the end of the lesson, I waved goodbye to the quiet and subdued children, and as they disappeared out of the door, I mentioned this incident to the school receptionist. She calmly informed me, as if it was common knowledge that, "lizards shed their tails when in danger. Don't you know?"

No, she must be wrong, I thought. She's just trying to make me feel guilty. When I got home, I dutifully researched this on the internet to put my mind at ease, but it turned out she was right. Shedding their tail is a defence that some lizards employ, with the hope that the attacker will focus on the discarded tail and allow them to escape. So, to my horror I now realised that I may have unnecessarily hurt or murdered a reptile and potentially scarred for life these poor little children. And you think you had a bad day at work?

***

In the summer of 2008, a hundred or so children and a dozen teachers boarded coaches and headed off from Tokyo to Fukushima for an English kids' camp. The name 'Fukushima' meant little to me at the time. I was vaguely aware that it was somewhere up north in the cuds, a good several hours' drive from Tokyo. What I didn't know was that Fukushima was one of the largest prefectures in the country, about the size of Northern Ireland and the southernmost of the six prefectures that make up the 'Tohoku' region of Japan.

What I certainly did not know, could not know, was that three years later the name 'Fukushima' would suddenly and tragically become synonymous with the third and final episode in a triple disaster which would rock the world. Today the word 'Fukushima' comes in tandem with images of clouds of radioactive smoke billowing out of one of Fukushima Daiichi's damaged reactors. Radioactive waste filled the air and the sea and Japan stood on the precipice of even more dire imminent crises as the officials in Tokyo one hundred and sixty miles to the south pondered evacuating the largest city on Earth. But that was all three years in the future.

Amidst the excited chatter of the children, many of whom were staying away from home for the first time, there were a few dotted around the coach who were clearly quite travel sick. It was a relief no doubt therefore when we stopped midway at a large blue suspension bridge that spanned a forested gorge and I watched anxiously as the children stuck their heads recklessly between the metal girders and leaned precariously over the guard rails. We then merrily continued our several hours long journey to Fukushima which appeared through the windows of the coach a rural paradise. The further north we went, the narrower the roads became. The rustic villages were quaint and the mountains quiet and peaceful.

At last, the hotel complex appeared seemingly in the middle of nowhere perched on its own little hilltop isolated and incongruous after the quaint villages we'd passed, full of little winding valley roads and wooden houses. We settled in for dinner and evening activities. After snacks by the campfire the next day began with a flurry of English activities. The children played team games, solved puzzles, did English themed arts and crafts and in generally got all Englishy.

The hotel felt like it had been abandoned a long time before and had a cold unlived-in aura and a sterile feel to it. We were its only guests. The empty corridors and the enormous dining hall were strangely haunting. By day, the cavernous function room in which we played party games like 'pass the balloon down the line only using your knees' or make a tower out of rolled up newspaper' (all good fun with some tenuous link to English) had felt fine. By night, once the children had gone to bed, away from the teachers of different Tokyo districts getting to know each other in one of their rooms with drinks and easy chatter, the place felt eerie. It was one of those buildings in which for some intangible reason you don't feel comfortable. Maybe it was the smart and strangely statue-like hotel worker who had stood waiting for us silently by the front doors as we pulled up in the coach as if he had been standing there forever. Maybe it was the entire hotel staff who made little conversation and seemed to exist solely for the once yearly weekend influx of Japanese children and their English teachers, or maybe they didn't exist at all.

The first night tears and longing for Mummy (by the kids not me), the struggle to get to sleep and the wishing to just go home for those few children that were immediately homesick was more than likely because it was their first time staying away from home. On the other hand, it might have been because they had unwittingly stepped onto the set of a bizarre Japanese sequel to The Shining. That said, the weekend was a success.

On the last night upon the huge wooden stage of the function room we had a big ceremony for the children with certificates and prizes and lots and lots of clapping.

If it wasn't for the bizarre video at the front of the bus of Harry Potter unconvincingly dubbed into Japanese which kept me awake on the long journey back to Tokyo "Watashi wa[33] Harry. Wizard-o desu[34]" I could almost have imagined the whole weekend had been a strange dream. Maybe there was no group of children and English teachers. Maybe I was dreaming, and I was still back in that empty hotel alone forever because maybe I wasn't a teacher at all but the caretaker. Come to think of it, maybe I had always been the caretaker.

When we returned to Tokyo the children gratefully debussed into the arms of their parents, back into a world where they could speak their own language in familiar, cosy and distinctly un-haunted homes, homes which felt decidedly lived in and in which you didn't half expect that any second a tidal wave of blood might cascade down the corridor. The relief on the faces of the children, if not the parents, was clear for all to see because when you are only seven, a weekend is a long time, and all English and no Japanese makes Hayato a confused boy.

**

---

[33] 'I am.'

[34] The verb 'to be' which unlike most English sentence constructions appears at the end of phrases and sentences.

In many ways I preferred teaching the children to the adults. One of the school policies was that before children entered the room, they'd do a sort of entrance drill. They'd have to wait at the door while you went through a set of basic questions. If they gave satisfactory answers, you were then supposed to let them in.

This was all well and good when you had one or two children, but with a class of eight pupils it could take up ten minutes of the lesson, especially since they often took ages to remember the adequate responses and then got them in the wrong order.

"Hello."

"Hello."

"What's your name?"

"My name is six."

"How are you?"

"I am Takumi."

"How old are you?"

"I'm fine thank you."

The levels of enthusiasm shown by the children of various age groups ranged from the completely apathetic to the impossibly keen. On the one hand there were mothers who clearly used us as an expansive creche in which to leave their offspring for an hour while they shopped or lunched with friends in peace. The children of said parents would often look incredibly bored and in some cases completely bewildered as to why they were there at all. They would look on impassively with a mixture of boredom and pity as some recent British university graduate hopped around the room to the strains of a scratchy recording of, 'We like to dance,' on a threadbare tape cassette.

There were even the children so lacklustre that they completely refused to take part in some activities all together. Oh well, many teachers thought. I'm getting paid regardless and the mother will think the child's having a wonderful time so who cares? The enthusiastic children like Shoji came in breathless with big smiles and such an eagerness for even the most mundane of activities like 'Head, Shoulders, Knees and Toes' that if they were kids back home, you'd have just assumed they were taking the mick. Then there were the tired students ferried to their weekly English lesson sweating on summer evenings from one train to another after long days at school and inevitable hours of homework after they left me.

The teenage students were the hardest- too old to be throwing beach balls around or singing songs but too young to be having earnest conversations about grammar. They didn't have husbands or jobs to complain about. In truth they didn't have much to say at all. I suppose you don't have much time for boyfriends or girlfriends when you are at school all day and then cram school and English school in the evenings. Unlike back at home, the 15-year-olds I taught did not smoke behind the bike sheds, did not camp in fields with a bottle of famous Grouse and two packs of Lambert and Butler. They didn't have the time, and Tokyo wasn't that sort of place.

There were shy teenagers whose parents short-sightedly believed they'd get the most out of English lessons if they did them one-to-one rather than as part of a group and a pained half an hour would be spent eliciting barely audible one-word answers. By contrast there were also those who came to group lessons as the outsider- a clique of three fourteen-year-old girls and then the terrified new girl who would invariably have to suffer the stares of the others as she introduced herself to the class. Some of the five-year olds I taught would now be adults. Should they ever bump into me when I'm on a summer holiday in Japan, or while they're on theirs in England, I wonder if they would recognise the older version of the man that danced around the room to, "Touch the Watermelon" and high fived them when they correctly identified 'grandad' or the colour blue.

There were certain errors which students would repeat whose origins were hard to trace. On more than one occasion, adult students of mine would say, "But my teacher in High School taught us to say it like this". A good example of this was that my adult students, nearly without exception were unable to use the word 'almost' correctly. They'd say, "Almost Japanese people eat rice", when of course what they meant was, "Almost *all* Japanese people eat rice". They were so baffled when I corrected them that they looked totally crestfallen, as if they'd been lied to all their school lives. I did on occasion try and add a little bit of wit and light relief to my corrections, explaining that "if almost Japanese people eat rice, who were they? Not quite Japanese?" How droll.

For all my inner chuckles at the oft repeated mistakes and commonly held misconceptions, one fact remained unavoidably and uncomfortably true. For all that I was master of all the English I purveyed in the classroom, whenever I was outside of it, I was painfully aware of just how limited my Japanese was. Hypocrite.

Chapter 8

Trains, Planes and Automobiles

A country in transit

Like a barrel of potatoes.
Japanese proverb

The Japanese are known the world over as a people who bow when greeting. They don't shake hands or touch much at all. I suppose in this way it is the opposite of some of the Mediterranean cultures. I have mixed feelings about the Japanese no-touch etiquette, recognising that it is simultaneously hygienic and unobtrusive while also being cold and impersonal. However, it was in Japan every week that I got closer to strangers and touched intimate parts of their bodies more than I could have done anywhere else- involuntarily, I might add. I sniffed teenage boys' sweaty armpits in the summer, my knees thrust against those of businessmen, and I could tell with incredible accuracy who wore deodorant, who had missed a bit while shaving and whose suit fabric felt cheap to the touch.

I am of course talking about the experience of Tokyo trains during the rush hour. I say rush 'hour ' but I refer to any time between six and nine in the morning and between the same hours in the evening. What most surprised me was that I never broke a bone although I hear that people did on occasion, a couple of ribs or maybe an arm. I should imagine that physiotherapists and chiropractors do a roaring trade in Japan, as much for the awkward and painful contortions people must perform in the train to work, as the endless hours they must spend sitting in uncomfortable office chairs when they get there. The one good thing about being on an incredibly packed train is that you cannot fall over. You can't in fact sway or wobble at all. I did often wonder what would happen in a crash or an earthquake, although perhaps none of us would be the slightest bit injured, bubble wrapped as we were by the hundreds of bodies holding us together as an immovable mass.

People who have taken the underground in London, Paris or New York think they've travelled on crowded trains, but they have no idea. The difference is that in those cities when it becomes clear that no more people can fit on a carriage the people on the platform stop trying and wait for the next train. In Tokyo however, they push hard, their legs outstretched behind like the number 8 at the back of the scrum. There are different methods to getting on a train that is so full you shouldn't get on it. My favourite is backwards. You take a step on to the ballet rope-thin space by the doors, clamp your fingers on the inside of the top of the door and then push with your bottom, hoping that when the automatic doors close, they don't clamp shut on your nose or your genitals or stupid, long, 'fashionable' shoes. And once you're in, you're in. It's a bit like the old expression beloved of mothers. 'If the wind changes, you'll stay that way.'

I grew wise to this, knowing that if I got in with my hands down by my side, I had no way of covering a sneeze or cough as you simply wouldn't be able to raise them to your face. If, as the doors closed, you found your hand pressed on a businessman's bottom, then there it would stay. Being pressed up against the sliding doors as last man in, or indeed the first man in, was a mixed blessing. On the plus side you'd be the first to tumble gratefully out onto the platform when you arrived, but you also bore the weight of the bodies behind you, and besides this strategy only worked if the next station was the one at which you intended to alight. Being male the drawback of the crush was merely physical discomfort, whereas for female commuters the busier trains sadly provided plenty of opportunities for the wandering hands of perverts, of which stories abounded.

The hazards of train travel are of course not limited to the twice daily commuter crush. Whether it was due to the crowds or whether he was just distracted by his phone my memory doesn't relate, but I once saw a man fall down the crack between the platform edge and the train. He was jammed right in up to his waist. Horror flashed through my mind as I contemplated what might happen if the train were to set off at that moment but luckily, he was spotted by the driver doing his checks and train guards rushed over and pulled out the man who fortunately seemed completely unharmed.

Sometimes the trains are so packed that guards at departing platforms will gather together three or four at a time to push extra passengers on to carriages. They make an odd sight, immaculately dressed in their pristine white gloves and peaked caps, like skinny sumo wrestlers with the laws of physics their opponent rather than a fat man in a nappy. Now imagine this is how you get to work each day before spending gruelling hours at your desk and then returning home on an equally packed train, before snatching a few hours' sleep and repeating the whole process again. Hell. For all the whinges of our nine pm finishes, we English teachers were mostly spared the rush hour commute. We existed almost in a parallel universe I suppose - in Japanese society but not of it, residents but not citizens, visitors but not tourists.

Despite the stresses and strains of the rush hour commute, it is an inescapable fact that Japanese trains are incredibly punctual. They are so punctual in fact, that on the rare occasion that a train is delayed, passengers are issued little slips of paper by the train guard to prove to their boss that this was the real reason they were late for work. Without the slips of paper, they are simply not believed.

In Tokyo it's easy to know which line you are on because the trains are colour coded. A coloured stripe or sometimes the entire train is painted to match the train map key. Sometimes, during promotional campaigns, the trains that shoot through the metropolis are plastered with images of Pokemon characters or Hello Kitty or Transformers. The interiors of Japanese trains are generally immaculate. One of my colleagues did however send me a photo of a half-naked man he'd found lying in a pool of his own vomit on the train home one night. And contrary to your imagination, it was his top half that was clothed, not his bottom half (in a Power Ranger outfit if you're wondering, and he was holding a briefcase).

Though the individual train lines were easy to decipher, catching the right train itself offered more potential for mishap. Trains running to and from the city's suburbs did not always stop at all the stations on the line and sometimes hardly any at all. This I found out on many occasions to my cost staring anxiously out of the carriage window watching the words 'Nogata' or the destination of whichever school I was covering at that day flash past in a blur. Take my local Seibu-Shinjuku line for instance, along which ran seven types of train, which in order from most to fewest stops were the Local, Semi-Express, Express, Commuter Express, Rapid Express, Haijima Liner and the Limited Express. If when heading home I accidentally hopped on to the Semi-Express, I only had to get off two stations further down the line and go back. Mistakenly get on the Limited Express however and you couldn't get off for 30 miles.

***

During my time in Tokyo foreigners seemed slightly over-represented on the posters inside train carriages. There were foreigners advertising insurance and satellite navigation systems, foreigners advertising make-up and hair products and foreign children doing bizarre foreign things too. There was also a significant number of foreigners advertising English schools. In those early days I had never imagined my half-wit gap-toothed smile would also eventually adorn the interior of Tokyo's trains. At some point in 2009 a few of the teachers in my company were offered the opportunity to appear on our company's promotional material. Half a dozen of us trooped down to a school in central Tokyo and, in our best suits and with our fakest smiles, we pretended to teach. The models who played our students were impossibly good-looking and even more impossibly keen. I'd have spotted them anywhere as imposters a mile off. After all, they weren't telling me how much they hated their husbands or drivelling on about 'Paul'. Most disappointingly of all, they bore absolutely no fruit (which I sincerely hope is not a metaphor for the results of my teaching).

We struck a variety of different poses, most of which were a variation on the theme of me pointing at something and the students looking on with interest and huge smiles. In one I point at an article in a newspaper while 'businessmen' and 'businesswomen' crowd around nodding. A large arrow drawn on the whiteboard in the background simulates a graph. In another a pretty young lady bats her eyelids at me as I look animated and mime an object with wide eyes and a breathless grin. Yet another shows me with my hand stuffed inside a dragon puppet and a little Japanese cherub feeling its nose. I suppose these shots were intended to entice the customers and who doesn't want their teacher to be pointing out articles in the Financial Times or offering a puppet's nose for your 3-year-old to touch. The funny thing was for all the keen poses and picture-perfect models not one of them could speak a single word of English.

I'd never realised just how widespread the resulting banners and posters would be until I found myself standing one day on a packed train with my face pressing up against my own crotch. On overground trains at the end of long days of teaching, in idle moments amidst familiar i-pod songs, with the brightly lit neon streets of the megalopolis fluttering past me in the dark night, I'd fantasise. What if the young office lady half-dozing on the seat opposite should look up and recognise the suave, handsome Englishman on the poster, or indeed his far-less glamorous short, grinning colleague next to him, and then glance my way with a sudden flash of recognition? Hey, are you the man in the poster? Would you give me your friend's number?

Sometimes idle fantasy translated into brave moments, attempts at being cool. On one such evening, in an effort to impress an attractive young lady in my train carriage, I caught her eye and half-upward nodded and half raised my eyebrows in the direction of the poster above me. It could have gone brilliantly, she could have fallen breathlessly into my arms amidst sensual pleas for me to whisk her the hell away from this big, bad city, or longing whispers that she wished to slip into something a little more comfortable, but it didn't. She frowned at me probably thinking I was just insane or that I had a strange nervous tick involving my neck and my eyebrows and she instead just returned to the safety of her paperback.

One day when I was about to catch the train, I spotted a nearly empty carriage towards its rear. Great I thought as I entered it and sat down. There were only two or three other passengers in the entire carriage. I sat quietly victorious, thanking my luck that I was clever enough to notice a carriage that the other commuters crammed uncomfortably into the ones in front clearly hadn't. As I idly pondered the pretty pink colour of the carriage's interior and how it matched its exterior, too pleased with myself to question why it differed to the rest, the carriage slowly began to fill up with passengers. Strange, I thought, they're all women. Fanciful notions began swimming through my mind that I had drawn them here by my raw magnetism. Perhaps it was my new aftershave. Or was it the poster? Had these female office workers been enticed by the man whose image they'd so often gazed at on their daily commute? I was definitely getting plenty of looks. In fact, they were all looking at me. Hello ladies!

As the music on the platform began to play, indicating that the doors were about to close, I spotted a large pink sign on the window containing a message in both English and Japanese.

'Women Only Carriage'.

Idiot! If there is one thing more embarrassing as a man than accidentally riding in a women-only carriage, then perhaps it is the act of desperately leaping out of one breathless and flustered and getting trapped in the closing doors. I managed to free myself but not to avoid the stares of passengers and the consternation of the train guard. But at least I didn't have to suffer the indignity of alighting from the pink carriage at my destination to the disapproval of those waiting to board. I did however miss the train.

***

I had expected the trains to be different. Even the most clueless of foreign visitors, a cohort to which I firmly belonged, is aware of Japan's incredible train network before they set foot in the country. The buses were pretty impressive too. To take one look at the drivers with their pristine white gloves, peaked caps, waistcoats and immaculate white shirts with razor sharp creases, you could be forgiven for thinking you were about to step into a limousine rather than onto a bus. Quite why Japanese bus drivers announce each stop you arrive at with such soothing tones as they do, I am not sure. So relaxing are their almost whispered announcements through the head-mic, I find myself battling just to stay awake. More impressive than the drivers' voices, though not as hypnotic, are the bus payment machines. There's no need to slot the coins in one at a time, you can just dump a fistful of change haphazardly into the hole and the machine will sort it in seconds, culminating in a satisfied ping and the appearance of your ticket.

The thing about cleanliness, much like the propensity to follow rules, is that it is contagious. It's a well-known fact that litter begets litter to which every over-flowing bin on any street or beach in the world is testament. Yes, if you add your small piece of rubbish to the wasp-swarmed piles on top of or around the bin instead of taking it home like you should, you're a dickhead. That's not up for debate. But somewhere in the minds of the sheep-like and cretinous surely there's a nagging voice, 'but everyone else is doing it!' And so, I think it must be with the immaculate buses and trains.

Decent people aren't going to trash a place regardless, but for the morally apathetic I'd imagine there'd be an especially keen feeling of guilt if you stuck your gum under the seat in front or carved your aspersions as to what Carly likes to do with Lee behind the bike sheds in an otherwise pristine environment. Maybe this logic stretches to your very behaviour. Having said that, I'd like to think the fact that I never once kneeled on the backseat of a Tokyo bus making rude hand gestures to the lorry driver behind was more a mark of my good character than simply indicative of the fact that the vehicles in which I travelled were far cleaner than the 10:35 to Swindon.

***

In common with much of East Asia, Tokyo is a city of bicycles. The chorus line of Katie Melua's famous song states that 'there are nine million bicycles in Beijing'. Well, there's a damn sight more people in Tokyo than in the Chinese capital and by my reckoning more bicycles too. That's probably a fact. I realised very early on in my time in Japan that I would need one as well. It would make my commutes to work easier and it would be handy for shopping and just for getting about in general. More to the point, everyone had one and I didn't want to be left out. I headed down to the local bike shop and having rehearsed the phrase all morning, after cobbling together words from my English to Japanese dictionary, I announced, "I'd like your cheapest bike please."

The owner smiled and pointed at a grey 'mamachari'[35]. The mamachari is ubiquitous across Japan. They are usually grey or silver with upright handlebars and a small basket at the front for carrying

---

[35] Literally meaning 'mother's bicycle'. A standard cheap road bicycle with a basket at the front. This type of bicycle is by far the most commonly found across Japan and is useful for carrying groceries.

groceries. It was very uncool and cost me the princely sum of 10,000 yen or about £50 at the time, brand new. I had never realised that purchasing a bike would involve a level of security clearance roughly equivalent to joining the CIA. I was asked for my name, my address, my nationality, my place of work and my phone number. These details were dutifully scribbled down in a big, thick hardback ledger. I showed him my 'Alien Registration Card[36]' (colloquially known to one and all as a 'Gaijin Card') which foreign residents are required to carry on their person at all times. He read the card with great care as he copied from it my passport number and other details.

It might seem odd that such an enormous amount of invasive detail is recorded for the purchase of a bike, but in Japan the rules regarding bikes, as with much else, are strict. Perhaps because bike ownership is so common and there are so many of the things, the local authorities keep a very tight control. Every day in any part of the city you will see old men with green baseball caps and green armbands around their shirt sleeves walking around with clipboards checking bikes and recording their serial numbers. Bikes parked illegally on pavements or outside shop fronts are carted away in trucks and stored where they can be released for a fine by their owners. The trouble was I wasn't really au fait with all these details at the time, which was soon to cost me.

---

[36] Foreigners staying in Japan for more than 90 days are required to register for such a card. Its purpose is to record information about Japan's foreign residents.

I went off one day on a shopping trip for groceries only to emerge from the shop to find my bike had disappeared, so I did what any clueless foreigner would do. Indignant with anger and ready to explain to the local constable that my property had been stolen, I fished my Japanese phrasebook from my bag to arm myself with the correct terminology and presented myself at Nogata's police-box. The officer on duty eyed me with suspicion as he leant on his swagger stick and gazed at me beneath the peak of his cap. Luckily for me, one of the policemen in the back of the police box, younger and a little more forgiving, informed his less welcoming colleague that he recognised me, and he took over.

"My bicycle has been stolen," I said, entirely forgetting the Japanese phrase I had just read and instead I just spoke in English more slowly and loudly than usual.

This didn't quite register, so I resorted to mime. The passers-by must have found it rather amusing and I'm sure the police did because the older policeman to whom I'd first spoken fetched another officer from the back to come and watch the freak show. I mimed a man with a swag bag stealing my bike. The very act of me miming, hopping up and down on the non-existent 'bicycle', I have no doubt, was enough to convince the commuters on that weekday morning that gaijin were indeed a bizarre breed. Eventually, through a mixture of Japanese, English and my Monty Python-esque sketch show, the younger policeman managed to ascertain that I'd had my bike nicked.

"Please wait-o," he said and made a phone call.

I saw him punch in a number and, after he'd relayed my name and address to the person at the other end, a broad grin covered his face. I knew that grin, it was a grin that said, 'Idiot'. Why? Well, as he went on to explain, the idiot standing before him hadn't had his bike stolen at all. He had in fact parked his bike in an illegal location and it had been carted off on one of the trucks to a holding area with all the bikes of other idiots who had parked where they shouldn't have. I was instructed to go to the main police station a twenty-minute walk away where they would question me further.

When I arrived at the large police station, a plain clothes detective sat me down at his desk, littered with piles of papers.

"Why did you park your bike illegally?" he asked.

I explained as best I could that I hadn't known I couldn't park there. The questioning went on for about ten minutes before I started to wonder what an interrogation would be like for an actual, genuine crime.

"You will have to pay!" he said gruffly, and I shrivelled in my chair, hoping desperately that he was using the phrase in its literal sense and not in the style of a comic book villain.

Luckily, as it turned out he was. He gave me directions for the bike depot and sent me on my way with a handwritten note and a warning that next time my bike would be confiscated for good. I turned up at the depot and sure enough there they were in their green armbands looking all officious and judgemental. I handed over the note the policeman had given me and watched as they muttered between themselves.

"Not here," one said finally. The others immediately swooning over his good use of English.

"But the policeman said…" I began.

"No, not here," he repeated.

What followed was a frantic meeting between the three colleagues. They fashioned a sketch map of the actual place I needed to go to retrieve my bicycle. I strode off frustrated and eventually stumbled across the location. I received a hearty telling off, which was delivered once more in a mixture of English, Japanese, hand gestures and bizarrely, even a little French. I then handed over 4,000 yen, the irony not escaping me that I had just paid as a fine 40% of what I'd paid for the bike itself.

**

I'm glad I got my bike back because as it turned out cycling was one of my favourite things to do in my free time. I would go to the Myoshoji river that flowed less than 100 metres from my house, turn left and follow it, keeping it to my right the whole way and head east towards the heart of Tokyo. On the return journey I would then simply follow the river back. What I saw on my river rides was a completely different Tokyo. The city you navigate by train is entirely different to the Tokyo you travel by road. Likewise, riverside Tokyo had a life and culture all of its own. By day and by night I whizzed through the neighbourhoods of Numabukuro, Arai-yakushi, Nakai and Shimo-Ochiai, onwards to the central Tokyo districts of Takadanobaba, Iidabashi and beyond.

Futons[37] hung out to air over balconies and t-shirts on miniature rotary washing lines billowed in the breeze. Cats stared at me and babies gurgled from open sliding doors. Televisions and radios hummed while old men in white vests sat smoking in their back porches. Housewives momentarily paused amidst their frantic front step sweeping and threw a curious, if not wary, glance in my direction. The river weaved erratically under weirs, past rusty green chain-link fences, inaccessible for fifty-metre stretches at a time where it would then promptly re-emerge beside me. I passed by play parks and kindergartens, old people's homes and rusty little garages with people tinkering away on a whole assortment of machines. I passed builders perched high on bamboo scaffolding in their flared trousers and split-toed boots. I cruised by groups of a dozen toddlers on nursery outings being pushed in an enormous trolley, their mouths open as they stared at the strange foreign beast with wide eyes beneath their little yellow caps.

I whizzed by the high-netted or chain-linked baseball parks and the groups of elderly doing group aerobics by the pond. I freewheeled down narrow winding alleys passing French doors which were flung wide open revealing couples arguing, children playing and babies crying. I shot along the back of buildings, behind the kitchens of tiny restaurants whose open doors in the summer heat revealed sweaty chefs toiling amidst billows of steam and shouted orders. Past the playparks I dodged the angry stares of the enormous crows and the curious

[37] A traditional Japanese style of bedding, a thin mattress that is laid out on a tatami floor and can be stored away each day.

gaze of teenage boys who shouted at me from swings when I had got a safe distance away. This wasn't the Tokyo of the brochures or the tourist districts, there was no polish or show. This was everyday life where people lived and slept and worked and it was fascinating.

As much as I enjoyed cycling, I never mastered it, not in the way the Japanese had. Their bike-based multi-tasking was a sight to behold. They were able to have full-blown conversations on their mobile phones, eat, smoke and drink, all while riding. But perhaps most impressively of all they'd mastered the art of cycling while holding an open umbrella. It's a tricky enough balancing act on an open country road but the way businessmen, schoolboys and grandmothers alike weaved through the narrow city streets without getting plastered to a lamppost by a passing bus, I'll never know. The problem is when you have to turn sharply or come to a sudden halt you've only got one hand. Naively, I had thought after several months that I too had mastered the umbrella bicycle trick, albeit with my added touch of flair. Finding it difficult to open or close an umbrella mid-ride, I would have my umbrella at the ready with the catch unclipped and I would hold the sliding mechanism. All that I need do in the event of rainfall was release it. Genius.

However, one day I learned a pitfall of this technique. You might cite my cycling on the pavement as irresponsible and to blame for the crash that summer's day and you may well be right. Cycling on the pavement in Japan is illegal but everyone does it including the police, so it is a fairly redundant law. I often wonder what the Japanese couple made of the sweating white man that ploughed into the side of their car bonnet that morning like a modern incarnation of a medieval knight as they pulled out on to the main street. Granted, my steed was metal, and my lance was plastic and transparent, but I felt the incident had a joust-like quality to it. After my bike dented their fender, the momentum carried me onwards over my handlebars and had me stabbing at the passenger side window with the outstretched ferrule of my umbrella. I landed spread-eagled half on their bonnet and half in the front basket of my mamachari. As I examined their car red-faced, the dented panel looked miniscule compared with the one to my pride.

***

For all the high speed, dead on time trains and high-tech buses; for all the taxis with automatic doors and the drivers in their immaculate white gloves, not all of Japan's movement is intentional. Every evening a small green-grey toad would wait outside of my sliding patio doors on the narrow strip of green moss which ran behind the equally narrow strip of patio, all that separated my flat from the building next door. Yuka would sit smoking with the balcony doors open at night.

"I know you don't stone," she would say in her faltering English, which nonetheless put my inferior grasp of Japanese to shame, to the amphibian which sat motionless, camouflaged amongst the small rocks that surrounded it beside the whirr of air conditioning units.

One evening as Yuka sat smoking and as our nightly amphibian visitor sat amongst the stones and moss, a flock of squawking birds flew overhead and out of sight. She studied their unusually frenetic behaviour with interest for a moment.

"There'll be an earthquake in a few seconds," she said looking back at me impassively and taking another drag on her cigarette.

I dismissed her comment as a joke. I mean who was she, Mystic Meg? Nonetheless, it was incredible to think that here in the centre of the largest city in the world, right below where we sat, four tectonic plates met. This was the famed 'Ring of Fire[38]', the volatile region of earthquakes and volcanoes that span the Pacific Rim[39]. Tokyo sits on one of the world's most fragile fault lines. Sure enough, moments after she'd spoken, the windows rattled, and the Earth began to shake.

---

[38] A volatile tectonic region around the rim of the Pacific very prone to large earthquakes and volcanic eruptions. This area encompasses Japan, the west coast of the USA, the west coast of South America, the Philippines and New Zealand among other countries.

[39] The land on the rim of the Pacific Ocean.

Chapter 9

Gaijin

The capsule hotel from Hell and bathing with the yakuza

Unless an idiot dies, he won't be cured.
Japanese proverb

My first ever experience of staying in a capsule hotel came in Osaka and it was by far the worst. I've stayed in several capsule hotels since and as a general rule they're not nice but then again, they're not intended to be nice. Their purpose is convenience and the fact that they're cheap. For little more than £15, you can have a safe, dry, clean space for the night with access to toilet facilities. They are ideal for the businessman out drinking late with his colleagues who misses the last train home, which is what they were originally designed for of course. These days you're also quite likely to find backpackers from around the world using them as cheap and novel alternatives to a hotel room, in addition to your common or garden drunk businessman. Staying in a capsule hotel is part of the whole 'Japan experience'.

I can understand why to some people the idea of climbing into a coffin-shaped plastic chamber on your hands and knees and then lying entombed with barely enough room to roll over is unappealing. It's not as if you can just sit up. Well, you can, but you'll hit your head. Since it feels like a mixture of being in a grave and a washing machine, it's definitely not for the claustrophobic. One particular problem for me is that I'm not very flexible. If there are no capsules available on the bottom row, I have great difficulty climbing the rungs to the second or third rows and then launching myself inside, and I have even greater difficulty getting out the next morning. I can't count the number of times I've returned to the hotel late and received irritated grunts and bangs on the thin plastic walls as I bang and thud up past people trying to sleep. In an ideal world I get a capsule on the bottom row and at one end, then I only have two neighbours as opposed to potentially four, and I can simply get down on my hands and knees and crawl in.

I knew I was in for an ordeal when I arrived at the capsule hotel in Osaka. We've all been to places where, for some intangible reason, we just feel we're not welcome. This was one of those places. The staff were hostile, and the other patrons looked at me as if to say, "What the hell are *you* doing here?" I couldn't put my finger on it at the time. Perhaps it was the famed rough around the edges Osaka manners or was I perhaps just being paranoid? Things soon started looking up when I discovered that this wasn't your standard capsule hotel. This was an enormous complex with a restaurant and a large hot springs area. Perfect.

Something was slightly amiss however and, try as I might, I just could not identify what it was. I felt a bit of a prat wandering around the large, carpeted hallways in my hotel-issued robes and ill-fitting slippers. I've always been one of those people who can't really walk properly in slippers. I don't think I've got the right type of feet. Sandals are bad and flip flops are purgatory for me. Why anybody would want to wear them baffles me.

It was like a constipated ostrich that I, this hairy pale oddity, came down the central staircase into the communal relaxation area. It was a big room with perhaps fifty people in it and everybody stopped and looked at me. The scene might have almost had a Titanic feel to it (you know, where Jack and Rose descend the grand staircase) had I Kate Winslet on my arm. Alas, I didn't, and I have the ruddy complexion and squat stature of a farm hand and none of the refinement of Di Caprio. Any pretence of movie star glamour vanished completely when I temporarily lost my footing on the stairs and, as my right slipper slid off, stumbled cursing and red-faced to regain my balance, performing a wobbling pirouette and nearly careering face-first into a wall.

With all dignity lost, I strode up to the front desk and asked where I could find the hot springs. As I then walked back through the staring faces it suddenly dawned on me that everybody here was male. From the impatiently tutting men queuing up behind me at the reception desk while I took ages to book a room in my pidgin Japanese to the audience in the relaxation room to my clumsy clown act down the stairs, they were all men. I ambled on through the vibrating massage chairs, past the TV blaring out the ubiquitous baseball game and into the bath area. I got undressed and placed my hotel branded robes into one of the small wooden compartments which I'd failed to notice were numbered. A sopping wet man came up to me and, surrounded by his sopping wet companions, grunted as he moved my clothes out of the way and put his down. Oh no, it was done by room number and I'd messed up yet again. Could things really get any worse?

Yes. Nervous now and on edge, I proceeded to lose the rubber band with my room number on it, scold my testicles with the hot tap in the wash area and stub my big toe. Great! Something was still niggling me and it wasn't just that everyone in this gargantuan hotel was male. It suddenly dawned on me that they were all here in large groups of men who knew each other. I couldn't have stood out more. This was obviously some type of hotel complex where company groups go to stay together. There were groups of ten to fifteen men lounging around in the hot baths and then I, Little Ole' Scolded Testicles with the throbbing big toe, get in.

Of course, they stared at me. The more they stared the more I became self-conscious. I have never ever wanted to just fit in as much as then. Groups of joking colleagues dipped in and out of the various baths, all jocular back slaps and banter and innuendo. I'd been to team building events back in England and it was usually something like 'build a structure out of marshmallows and dry spaghetti' or maybe 'solve the hypothetical conundrum of how to transport a fox, a chicken and a bag of corn across a river', not 'get naked, bathe together and sleep in a plastic cuboid'. But here they were, and here I was.

I finished my bath and gingerly dried my reddened testicles watched by the HR department from Yamamoto printing supplies, then I headed upstairs in my robe, back through the men in the buzzing chairs and enquired at the desk if I could eat at the restaurant. I could. Fantastic. The restaurant was a large affair and consisted of long low tables that you sat at cross-legged on the floor. Agony. The pain of my knees and back at least masked the embarrassed feeling that I was occupying one massive table all to myself.

None of the company groups wanted to assemble around and chat about the new secretary or their New Year's bonus with a strange gaijin with scolded testicles who couldn't wear slippers properly plonked in the middle. It just wouldn't do. The elderly maid came out, I ordered my food and she hurriedly returned and served me my curry rice. I knew what she was thinking because as another large group of company executives fresh from the hot baths came to the top of the stairs, she made embarrassed gestures and apologetic nods and waved her hands in my direction. She no doubt whispered that as soon as that hairy, pale gaijin who's got the scolded testicles and shouldn't be here is out of the way they could sit down and eat. The men of Nakamura air conditioners or whoever they were tutted and chortled in equal manner. I didn't enjoy the meal, it was barely warm, but at least the lack of heat allowed me to wolf it down and get my silly foreign behind to bed where I wouldn't be smirked at and remarked upon like some freakish circus exhibit.

One of the more curious features of the complex was that in the corners of the restaurant, in the relaxation room and in many other communal areas, men lay on the carpet and slept. I may have been a red-testicled, slipper illiterate, swollen-toed, pasty little foreigner, but I wouldn't be that silly. But then again maybe you were supposed to. But I'd displayed myself as a freak show enough for one day and skulked off to my capsule for a night's sleep.

The trouble was there were at least five floors of capsules and on each floor at least a hundred capsules all divided into two or three rooms and, of course, I'd lost my bloody capsule number. Cue me traipsing back to the reception desk and by now they were sick of me. And I was sick of them. I was tutted at again and roundly humiliated by a man queuing up who I'd thought at first was helping by translating, but instead used the opportunity to make his friends guffaw. Although my Japanese was not proficient enough to bore through the thick dialect of the receptionist, I had enough to understand the rude jokes that Mr Translator was telling his little group of pals about me. I had had enough of playing the good little polite gaijin and was on the verge of forming the syllables on my tongue to tell him in front of his stupid little friends to sod off but, like the coward that I am, I didn't. Instead, I satisfied myself with the thought that my scarlet balls were hidden beneath my robe so at least you can't joke about those, mate. Ha!

In the end, the room number was found in the system and I skulked off to bed on the verge of tears. I wasn't a company member, I wasn't one of the team, I couldn't talk about the new secretary or the New Year's bonus or the horrible boss because I didn't work for Yamamoto printer supplies or Nakamura air conditioners. I vowed to not stay there a single night longer. To this day I wonder if I was the first foreigner ever to stay there. I was certainly one of very few people who didn't come as part of a large company group. I was male, barely after the tap incident, so at least I fit that demographic, but I felt like every prat in the world rolled into one. I was Frank Spencer, I was Curly Watts, I was Rodney Trotter, a bumbling idiot.

It was at this point that I found my capsule and realised to my horror that it was on the top row. I climbed ungracefully like a drunk monkey to the top, not caring now about the irritated grunts of disapproval from all the company bods in their pods around me. I pulled the door shut on my little coffin. I would be buried away from the prying eyes for several hours. I did sleep eventually with difficulty, finally drifting off after hours of trying. The nearby sounds through thin plastic walls on all four sides were those of company-sanctioned coughs and company-sanctioned farts. Men in their little plastic tubes next to my little plastic tube rustled suspiciously in their sheets to the in-capsule adult channels. I finally got to sleep and got five glorious hours of dreaming- in my own company. And after my bold promise that I'd never spend a single night there ever again, I huffed down to the reception desk in the morning......and booked in for a further two nights.

***

Living as a foreigner in such a homogenous society was interesting, funny and occasionally annoying. I had very few truly negative experiences, but one does come to mind. I was walking home late one evening talking on my phone near my flat. A middle-aged man approached me and told me to keep the noise down. I hadn't thought I was speaking particularly loudly, but in fairness to him it was one am. What did annoy me though was that he was talking equally loudly on his phone. I pointed this out which angered him before he launched into a tirade about me being a rude American. I think the fact that he assumed I was American angered me more than anything. When I pointed out that I was in fact British his immediate refrain was that "All Anglo-Saxons are racist." Anyway, one thing led to another, he called the police and proceeded to chase me down the street while on the phone to them. As well as being racist, Anglo-Saxons must be pretty good at hide and seek since I got away with the most basic dog-leg manoeuvre.

Perhaps it was my indignant rage at having been tarnished with the same brush as all my fellow Anglo-Saxons or perhaps I am just an upstanding citizen, but a few days later I decided to do a good deed. One day as I walked to the station, I found a woman's purse on the road. It had her identity card in it and a few coins. I did what I thought was the honourable thing and for the second time availed myself of the services of the police box in Nogata where I handed it in. They eyed me with suspicion, I can only think because it had so little money in it.

"Where did you get this?" asked one of the policemen.

"I found it on the road."

He looked at me warily which is strange because surely the least suspicious person is the one who hands in a purse. Before I arrived at the police box, as ridiculous as it sounds, I'd thought that perhaps I should actually pop a little more cash in it, maybe ten pounds worth of notes to make it look as if I was not in the wrong, which of course I wasn't. It had almost occurred to me as I stood looking at it that perhaps I shouldn't touch it at all. The initial suspicions of the police gradually turned into confused curiosity as another officer was coaxed out of the back room to come and see the oddball handing in a purse. Eventually the police tentatively thanked me, and I went on my way, sensing their quizzical expressions and bemused stares following me down the street.

It was after crashing my bike into the car that I began to be stopped by the police on a fairly regular basis. I'd usually see the police mounting bicycle patrols in ones and twos around the local area and sometimes they'd also wait at the bridge of the Myoshoji river near my house. The reason they stopped me was entirely justified. The mechanism for my bike light, which ran off a dynamo and shone when you pedalled, had been bent completely out of shape by my little prang and I hadn't bothered to get it fixed.

I didn't mind being stopped by the police. They were always firm but friendly. In my every encounter with them I found them to be professional, polite, and not in the least threatening. At their request I would produce my Gaijin card. Once they'd checked the details on my card such as my nationality, job, and the status of my visa and had asked me a few rudimentary questions about what I was up to and where I was going, they were quite chatty. They'd ask questions about British culture and, upon discovering I was an English teacher, adopt a slight but noticeable reverence for the 'sensei' in their midst. They'd invariably then apologise in Japanese that their English was poor, which of course is ridiculous as I was in their country not vice versa and I should have been the one apologising to them! It's hard to argue against the notion that to learn the native language of the country to which you have moved as quickly as you can is as much a sign of courtesy and respect to its people as a necessity for getting by.

***

Being visibly foreign most definitely had its benefits. No matter how crowded a train carriage is, the last seats to fill will be those either side of you, if they fill at all. I have sat on packed carriages with passengers squeezed on the bench seats, people standing up pressed against the doors and still I have an empty space on either side of me. This was quite nice, a privileged way to travel that no Japanese person could enjoy. The trouble is I think it's contagious. No one wants to be the weirdo who breaks the unwritten rule and those who do must feel like real adventurers, like Steve Irwin getting uncomfortably close to a wild and unpredictable beast.

It would be wholly incorrect to suggest that the Tokyo of 2007 bore any resemblance to the London of 1967. When my friends and I turned up at a central Tokyo bar one night, upon seeing us the bouncer uncrossed his arms and, to dispense with unnecessary chit chat, simply pointed at a big yellow sign on the door. The large notice written in English in capital letters did not read 'No dogs, no blacks, no Irish', the message in front of our eyes was far less specific. 'NO FOREIGNERS ALLOWED'. I'd come across this sort of thing once or twice before and I would come across it later. At least we knew where we stood and there were other bars to go to whose welcome was incredibly warm. Finding a home on the other hand was not as simple. Many landlords would not let to gaijin, that was just a fact of life, their refusal to do so not plastered on big yellow signs but in the small print of contracts and phone calls filled with sighs and polite apologies. Luckily for me, my company provided a flat as part of the package, the rent for which was taken directly out of our wages each month.

The 'foreigner mask' (yes, that was the literal translation on the packaging) I once found on the fifth floor of that ubiquitous emporium of chaos, Don Quixote, was a pale rubber mask with a long, pointed nose, blue eyes and a mop of blonde hair. Statistically speaking, the vast majority of non-Japanese humans on Earth are not white, far fewer still are blonde with blue eyes, and when you factor in the long nose, it becomes clear that the mask represented an incredibly small demographic, so this off-the-shelf image of a generic or default 'foreigner' was curiously unrepresentative, but not surprising. Maybe I should have been offended but I wasn't. In fact, perhaps I missed a trick. I should have brought it in to school to dispense with lengthy explanations for listening exercise 3a and watched my students' faces light up.

"Ah, so this is Paul?!"

The 'tall noses' thing was quite an icon. There's a brief video advertisement for a Japanese English conversation school I found in a dusty corner of YouTube a few years ago. A blonde-haired British man walks into a football changing room with a whistle and says, "Come on guys, it's time to play." Two little Japanese boys turn around to face him and they are wearing long fake plastic noses. "Ok," they say, "let's go!" How very droll.

Admittedly, the ad is a little dated now. It's mainly guilty for being unfunny. I did not, and still don't, take this sort of thing to be evidence of wicked racism. Ignorance? Sure; a fetishizing of the West? Probably. The novelty value of 'foreign' looks in a largely ethnically homogenous nation? Yes. My reaction therefore to the foreigner mask was amusement. In the end I didn't buy the mask. I didn't need it.

It was certainly true that many types of equality lagged behind in Japan as a whole, but outdated attitudes came across not as those of the vicious bully boy looking for trouble but the occasionally ignorant grandfather who is behind the times and who doesn't realise that you're not allowed to say those words anymore and doesn't mean any offence, but anyway, enough of this PC stuff, is my dinner ready yet dear?

Undoubtedly it could be argued that this type of unwitting discrimination is no less harmful for its lack of intent, and whether or not I would hold such forgiving opinions were I female or of another nationality or race, I have no idea and obviously can never either. What I do know for certain is that the 'being foreign in Japan' thing could not, cannot be considered a one-size fits all experience. It would be naïve and disingenuous of me to suggest that as a young white British man, the category of 'gaijin' to which I was perceived as belonging (by some people) in no way differed to that of other 'gaijin'. It would also be as presumptuous of me to attempt to speak for the experiences of others as it would be narrow-minded of me to assume that people are always treated solely on their superficial characteristics. At least I hope that's the case. It would be grossly unfair for all gap-toothed little white men to bear the stigma of my bumbling and idiotic ways.

Just before coming to England for the first time to meet my family, Yuka was very nervous. I found her the night before we flew out in tears and asked her what was wrong.

"I'm scared that when we go to London everybody will stare at me."

Her comment spoke volumes about one major difference between London and Tokyo. To her this was a legitimate concern. After all, everybody in London would be white and she'd stand out for being East Asian. Obviously, to anybody even vaguely familiar with London this is slightly amusing. Being East Asian, or indeed of any race or ethnicity, would not warrant even the most cursory of glances in such a hugely multiracial city. Her comment served as much to inform me of how little she knew of London as they did to unwittingly highlight how different the two cities and two countries were.

***

One day in the late Spring of 2009 Mark Taylor and I were walking through Nogata when outside a dingy public toilet, we came across a middle-aged white man with his shirt off smoking and shouting out at passers-by and generally acting like a raucous hooligan, so naturally we befriended him. 'Al' was English and incongruously had been educated at

Harrow but spoke like an East End geezer, with a voice like sandpaper from his two pack-a-day habit. When Al wasn't shirtless, he was wearing his signature brown leather jacket. He was an alcoholic and would lounge around local parks smoking and drinking. He was a strange enough sight for Mark and me to behold so what the locals made of this man, who despite having been educated at one of England's most prestigious private schools, came across as somewhere between a football hooligan and a tramp, I shudder to think.

On a sunny weekend, Mark and I took Al to the park to kick a rugby ball about. Between hoofing the ball into the air and fits of coughing and wheezing laughter he pointed into a stand of trees and told us that that was where he'd had an intimate encounter with a young woman he'd met on a train. Apparently, she'd fallen asleep on his shoulder and let's face it folks, what young Japanese woman wouldn't be attracted by the idea of copulating with a middle-aged vagrant with the face of old leather and the breath of a chimney when offered a tryst in the corner of a ramshackle park? And they say romance is dead. Al told us that his son was a famous racing driver in Formula 2, and after some due diligence Mark and I discovered this to be true. Sadly, Al informed us that his son disowned him, and looking at the state Al was in I wasn't entirely surprised. After a few weeks I didn't see Al again and neither did Mark. He seemed to have just totally disappeared.

***

It was while at the public baths one day that the thought occurred to me that there is one unlikely group of people in Japan to whom gaijin are quite similar. I've tried many of the bathhouses in Tokyo. I enjoy using different ones although I do have favourites to which I often return. Some of them are ornate with wood-panelled changing rooms and historic carvings of dragons and tigers on their walls. One I went to had old scrolls of sumo tournaments and images of the wrestlers hanging from the wall. Many have the common tiled mosaic at the far end of the bath area itself of Mount Fuji, while other tiled mosaics show the cherry blossom, a heron or a sparkling lake beneath a ridge of mountains. There's something wonderful about the bathhouses and their history is fascinating. I like the fact that they did not come into being as some fad, not as locations for a spa retreat weekend where people lol about with cucumbers on their face while they have a manicure, but as a necessity. In the era they were built, the houses of old Edo had no baths and so people of the community would come down here to bathe and chat and socialise.

The baths served as more than just washing facilities. They were the focal point of communities. People would get together and joke and catch up. They were, if you like, the local pub. I say 'were' because even though the public baths are still dotted around Tokyo and around Japan, they are dying a not-so-slow death. Every year across the country many old bathhouses across Japan close forever. It's sad because of what they represent, it's sad because of their beautiful tiled and wood-panelled interiors and decorative chimneyed exteriors- and surely, they'll just be replaced by some tatty strip-lighted coin laundry or noisy games arcade.

There is nothing better at the end of a long day than wallowing in a selection of hot steamy baths. They let tired people unwind, loosen muscles and relax the mind. You can feel the knots of stress loosening and you walk out feeling fresh and relaxed-something much needed in a city like Tokyo. You feel sad when the three-hundred-year-old pub down the road shuts its doors and I feel sad at the decline of the bathhouses. Of course, obeying true Sod's law, it is the oldest and the most decorative that close fastest, history and heritage literally disappearing before our eyes. I shall enjoy the bathhouses of Japan on my every visit until the very last one closes, and I shall lament their loss.

Most 'sento[40]' in Japan operate a strict no-tattoo policy. This is because tattoos are traditionally associated with the yakuza, Japan's organised crime gangs. But there are a select few sento that do accept people with tattoos. After all, gangsters have to wash somewhere. I hadn't realised one summer's day that I'd stepped into such an establishment. I was sitting on the ubiquitous 6-inch off the ground tiny plastic stool, a feat for which I almost need the hot bath alone. I strain my back muscles just to get down to that level and then when I do, I must perform a bizarre Punch and Judy show with my testicles to avoid sitting on them.

I was happily scrubbing myself and looking at my sunburnt face in the mirror when a hulking figure

---

[40] Public bathhouses found across Japan and distinct from 'onsen' which are hot springs and primarily used as resorts for retreat and relaxation.

appeared to my right. I glanced in the mirror next to me to see the tallest, most muscular tattooed yakuza type sitting next to me and glowering at me. Why, I thought had he decided to sit at the taps next to me? There were loads of places free all around the washing area. Perhaps he wanted to intimidate me.

As he scrubbed, I glanced at him covertly. He had long, dyed shoulder-length hair and a large ring through his nose. His mouth was curled into a permanent crooked snarl and his eyes were those of a cruel emotionless brute. His muscular body was covered with an enormous green and scarlet dragon that curled its way from his bottom in twisting curves up his back and over his shoulder. The rest of his body was covered in elaborate designs of samurai battling with enormous blades, tigers and geisha in kimonos under parasols, great multi-coloured carp and cherry blossom petals. Amongst the shades and shadows were ancient Japanese ghouls and demons amidst burst of brightly coloured chrysanthemums. It seemed that no inch of his body was free of ink. Great I thought I've just become the next instalment in a manga series. 'Hapless gaijin murdered in the sento as the bath runs red'.

I quickly rinsed off, taking great care not to splash any of my soap bubbles on to him and headed off to the hot bath which I found a little too hot, so then I skulked off to the cold bath in a secluded corner. Unbeknownst to me, the gangster had stopped washing and was heading in my direction. Oh no! With a snarl, he entered the frigid water and sank in up to his neck. He shrieked like a little girl and let out a feeble grin. Could it be that this roughty-toughty thug was scared of a little cold water? He laughed and looked at me meekly.

"Gosh, it really is cold, isn't it? Where are you from?" he said in a friendly voice.

We chatted for a brief while like a couple of old grannies and he hobbled off to one of the warmer baths with a cheery "take care" and I smiled to myself. Never judge a book by its cover.

Walking home that night a thought occurred to me. Maybe it wasn't so surprising that the man had talked to me. The yakuza by their very definition were outcasts from society. Branded for life, they were a sort of gaijin, an instantly recognisable 'other' that people fear and from whom people steer clear. Indeed, the very name 'ya-ku-za' (8-9-3) derives from the worst possible combination of cards you can have in the traditional Japanese card game 'oichokabu[41]'.

The yakuza were deemed outlaws from society and marked for life by their full body tattoos and often missing fingers[42] for indiscretions. If I'd thought being visibly foreign made me stand out, I hadn't a clue. Far removed from the Japanese and foreign portrayals of gangster glamour in media and popular culture, these men by dint of their life choices had quite literally decided to belong to a caste of men 'dealt the worst possible of losing hands in the card game of life'. With all this in mind, I thought that

---

[41] 8-9-3 (yattsu, ku, san) is the losing hand in oichokabu, a traditional card game which is played with a deck of hanafuda 'flower cards.'

[42] Yakuza members are expected to atone for serious offences by chopping off their finger to show remorse for their actions, an act known as 'yubitsume'. The first finger to go is usually the little finger. As a result, men missing fingers are easily recognisable as yakuza or ex-yakuza members.

perhaps he was happy that he'd found a fellow circus exhibit to wallow with, even if it meant braving the cold.

Chapter 10

Lost in Translation

Communication problems

If you understand everything you must be misinformed.
Japanese proverb

Getting used to Japan was about more than just adapting to the local cuisine and picking up a bit of the lingo to get by. There was a whole plethora of dos and don'ts to get used to, from the obvious (taking your shoes off at the door, bowing, etc) to the far more nuanced and subtle intricacies of daily etiquette. The first time somebody gave me their business card I said thank you and stuffed it into my pocket. Cue a Japanese friend of mine giving me the evils and whispering in my ear that, "That's not the way to receive a business card". He went onto explain that what I should have done was received it with both hands, studied the front of it carefully, turned the card over, read any information on the reverse side, bowed and said thank you. The giver of the card must also offer it with two hands. I immediately blushed a deep shade of scarlet, but it was too late now to retrieve the card from my pocket and, besides, it was probably now crumpled at the edges and covered with pocket lint.

Interpersonal relationships, especially professional ones, were a particular minefield. I studied the social interactions of the public from cafe windows, on train journeys and on my wanderings around the city. What I saw instructed me that when with someone, the more senior to you they were the deeper and more time consuming your bow must be and the more of them you must do. Colleagues of roughly equal status to you or lower would get a shallow bow whilst those well below you in the pecking order may get a perfunctory nod or nothing at all.

Junior members of staff would bow to their bosses so extremely that they seemed to be trying to touch their knees with their noses. They would fold right over at the waist like a contortionist from Cirque du Soleil about to climb into a suitcase. Bowing wasn't confined to work situations though. The convenience store ladies bowed at me when I entered their store, when I left their store and even when I approached the checkout. I was bowed at by students when they entered and left my classroom, by bus drivers when I got on and off their bus and when I paid them, and by every other proprietor of a company whose business I was patronising or may potentially patronise as I walked by.

The nasal whine of the shop staff called out 'Welcome' and 'Thank you' and 'Please come again'. The Japanese call it 'omotenashi'. Omotenashi is a Japanese code of conduct whereby the self is subjugated in service of the guest or customer. It is deemed right that the customer's every whim and need is catered for, even to the point of catering for needs he or she wasn't aware they had. This manifests itself in many ways. Waiters and shop assistants will jump up and shout, "Yes!" when given a task by a senior colleague or manager and rush at maximum speed to perform tasks. Waiters are summoned by buzzers at the table and there is a barely noticeable momentary pause between the 'ping pong' registering after you push the buzzer, to the shout of "Hai[43]!" from one or more members of staff before they rush to your table or counter to fulfil your request.

This incredible desire to please and attention to detail, this exemplary customer service is a double-edged sword, however. When visitors to Japan or foreign residents of Japan return home, they then have to put up with the disappointment of inferior customer service. When visiting a restaurant on my yearly trips home at Christmas, as I craned my neck and made eye contact with the waiter to get his attention, I remember thinking as he strode idly up to the table, why is he not rushing up to me in eagerness? What the Japanese must think when they go abroad, I can only imagine. But, if nothing else, I have no doubt that they take comfort in knowing that their country does it better.

Cynics would claim that omotenashi is devoid of genuine sentiment, that the robot-like cries of 'thank you' and 'welcome' are not genuine but pre-programmed and therefore meaningless. This may be true, but to a customer in a hurry who wants quality service, it could equally be argued that 'good service is good service', whether the hearts of the people giving it are in it or not. Who cares about the level of sincerity attached to it?

The potential for cultural misunderstandings is everywhere. I, myself was guilty in those first weeks

---

[43] Yes.

in the country of failing to understand omotenashi. What about the smiley girl in the convenience store to whom I'd given my phone number? She didn't have any genuine interest in me, she was just doing her job. As the years went by, I would see clueless foreigners, just like I had been at the start, misinterpreting the welcome smiles of the shop workers and shy laughter and fawning attention of the bar girls and club promoters as genuine warmth and flirtation.

A few years ago, while on holiday in Japan, I was in a sushi restaurant in Shinjuku, a busy, bustling, quite impersonal sort of a place, which by no means all such establishments are. As I was eating, a young American man walked in with his girlfriend. He was wearing baggy jeans and had his baseball cap on backwards at a jaunty angle. The couple came and sat within ear shot of me. He was clearly a tourist. I gathered from snapshots of an overheard conversation that he'd been to this restaurant before, and the person he was with clearly hadn't. As the sushi master cried out his customary "Irasshaimase!" (welcome) as the pair entered, perhaps misinterpreting this highly ritualised gesture, the American guy in the baseball cap shouted out in English, "Yo, my man! How ya doin?!" so loudly that half the restaurant turned around, and then he proceeded to swagger over to a table. "Yeah, that dude's great, he's so cool." the man said to his partner. There was nothing wrong with the American being so jovial towards the sushi chef, he was no more out of touch with Japanese etiquette than I was when I'd given the convenience store girl my number. In fact, less so. What I did was surely far more presumptuous and inappropriate.

Merely three weeks before I moved to Japan, I had no idea that I would be going there at all and I knew very little about the country. Perhaps therefore I could be forgiven for not knowing about 'honne' and 'tatemae'. 'Honne' are people's true feelings which they only express in private. 'Tatemae' are the behaviours and opinions you display in public. The word 'tatemae' literally translates as façade. Like most people, I'd known the Japanese were reserved but wasn't aware that such a recognised dichotomy existed between private and public personas. Perhaps, coming from a fairly reserved country like Britain had led me to believe I was somehow equipped to understand the reserved nature of the Japanese. After all, I came from a land of politeness and the stiff upper lip. Weren't we Brits a similarly shy, reserved people known for our manners and etiquette?

The eyelash-fluttering girl in the shop had been treating me according not only to the expected omotenashi, but also adhering to the tradition of tatemae. She might think someone was the most repulsive cretin, but her job and her public face required that she hide those feelings. And the sushi chef, goodness knows what his true honne was with regards to the brash American. To the casual observer, especially reading a Westerner's perspective on Japanese cultural traditions, it may come across as overstated. It isn't as if outside of Japan people just routinely go about speaking their minds and blurting out how they feel deep down.

People of all nations put up artificial fronts depending on the context. We all have public and private selves. What makes Japan stand apart is not that it is only true of them, it isn't - it is the degree to which such concepts of omotenashi, honne and tatemae permeate every aspect of human relationships outside of the home.

I'm not entirely sure how the behaviour of the drunken man with the bald head and silver moustache that my friend Jake and I met in a Koenji noodle bar one night and I again the following day was indicative of the honne and tatemae dichotomy. It seemed our presence was a greater delight than a visiting circus. Once he'd hugged us and sung to us in the karaoke bar to which he took us, he then whisked us off to another bar where he and his overly made-up lady friend danced with us while he touched our faces and declared we were his best friends in the whole world. We were bemused no doubt but, having lived in Japan for years by this stage, we weren't at all surprised.

What came as more of a surprise, but on reflection shouldn't have at all, was the way he completely blanked me when I bumped into him in the street and said hello the following afternoon. He stared at me vacantly before looking the other way. Surely, no matter how drunk he'd been the night before, he must have recognised me. My foreign face stood out pretty clearly at the best of times and, besides, it was the very same face he had been fondling mere hours ago. But ignore me he did as, sober now, he walked off po-faced down Nogata's high street towards the station.

I'd thought at first that he might have been embarrassed at having let his guard down when drunk, or simply drunk so much that he'd completely forgotten the events of the previous night, but as I watched him and the person accompanying him wander off into the distance it suddenly occurred to me that the woman by his side was not the lady of last night. Perhaps to have acknowledged me, the man who just a few hours before he declared was his closest companion in the entire universe, would have been to reveal to his wife, who I can only presume this new lady was, where he had been the night before, what he had been doing and with whom he had been doing it. "Yoshi, you told me you were working late at the office!"

***

When I was at secondary school there was a childish and inane saying that if you opened your packet of crisps the same way as a member of the opposite sex in the same room then you fancied them. This childish belief saw year-sevens opening packets upside down, back to front, from the side, even in the middle. It is hardly surprising that over the centuries Japan had developed myriad weird and wonderful ways to open their collective packet of crisps, and it wasn't because they were eager to be seen to not fancy the West.

Japan had essentially been a closed country to all outsiders for two hundred and fourteen years. The only contact made with foreigners during this period was with a select few Chinese, Portuguese and Dutch merchants. These were the only nationalities permitted to trade with Japan and nearly all trade was conducted on a tiny artificial fan-shaped island known as Dejima in the centre of the city of Nagasaki. Dejima was separated from the Japanese populace of the city, both metaphorically and literally, by a canal which the foreign traders were forbidden from crossing to leave the tiny island. Likewise, save for a select few traders, translators and prostitutes, the Japanese were forbidden from crossing the canal to enter the island, lest they be exposed to the malign influence of these strange foreigners, their Christian beliefs and other insidious ways.

In the mid-1600's, the Shogunate suspected the Portuguese were involved in a Christian rebellion against it and therefore banned them from trading. The Dutch provided weaponry to help the Shogunate end the uprising, and they were consequently granted exclusive trading rights with Japan. As a result, extremely few Japanese people would ever have clapped eyes on a foreigner, East Asian or otherwise.

It was only in the mid 1800's that Japan opened its doors once more to the outside world, its fashions, its technologies and its social, cultural and political influences. And just like that weird bloke who lives in that house in the woods, comes out at night and only talks to badgers, near-complete isolation from all others can lead to some rather unusual habits. It was during this period that so much of what is now understood to be 'traditional Japanese culture' developed. The fact that Japan is so starkly different to everywhere else is in no small part due to this self-imposed national isolation.

Some differences in culture go back much further in history. Take reading for example. In most of the Western world we read from left to right and across the page. The Japanese, on the other hand, read from right to left and down the page in columns. Unlike the West, the Japanese address people with their surnames before their first names. And then there are the addresses which are back to front starting with the country then city and then the district.

In approximately one-third of the countries and territories in the world people drive on the left, a significant number of these are former British colonies which explains why. It came as somewhat of a surprise then to find Japan among their number. Wasn't it the right-side of the road Americans who had taken the Japanese surrender and then occupied the country until 1952? A glance at Japan's parliamentary system, modelled on the British and not the American's, gives a hint that Japan mixes and matches its influences. But the left-side of the road issue runs deeper. It goes back to knights and samurai, most of which being right-handed would need space to draw their sword to engage an enemy whether in Wessex or Wakayama. Hence travel on the left.

***

If I had had a better handle of Japanese, perhaps I would have discussed the intricacies of Anglo-Japanese relations with my neighbour as he lay with a broken leg on my patio. He lived above me, was about my age, and was constantly and loudly putting his various lady friends through their paces in his apartment. To say the walls and ceilings of my apartment building were thin is a massive understatement. Well, he was either a serial killer or was having good fun up there. My only contact with him was passing him occasionally in the street. When he'd play his music too loud, I'd take the vacuum cleaner attachment and smash it against the ceiling, and he'd return this gesture by smashing against his floor. Unfortunately, this backfired one evening when I prodded the ceiling so hard that I put a hole straight through it.

All differences were put aside one summer's evening when I came to his aid. I could tell he was drunk by the loud singing coming from above. I heard him on the balcony and then, as I sat on my bed (which doubled as a chair because I didn't the luxury of having enough space for an actual chair), I heard a groan, followed by the shadow of an object hurtling to the ground outside my patio doors, which itself was followed by a thud and a scream. I went outside onto my patio and found him writhing around in agony holding his shin and groaning.

Now the thing is I hadn't the faintest idea what the emergency number in Japan was. The last thing you need when you're in critical pain and may have really hurt yourself is a stupid foreigner, one that you've been feuding with, standing above you, waggling a phone at you and asking what the emergency number is. He beckoned me over and dialled in the number himself. I took the phone back off him and as the ring tone chimed, I suddenly realised I hadn't the vocabulary to explain what was wrong, let alone give the address. A man answered and I blurted into the receiver in English, "Please help, my neighbour hurt his leg, Nogata." The man babbled something back at me, of which I could make neither head nor tail. At this my neighbour groaned and reached for the phone yet again and proceeded to make his own emergency call.

When the ambulance arrived, I greeted it in the street and beckoned the paramedics through my flat to the man. He was ferried away, and I uselessly stood above him and muttered a few feeble good-luck messages in English. He came hobbling back to our building a few days later and gave me a begrudging nod of what I presumed to be thanks, as he made his way slowly upstairs. Putting our differences behind us, I bought him a six pack of lager and knocked on his door. I expected the grand ceasefire, the coming together of nations. After all, I'd saved him, hadn't I? He opened his door, muttered a grumbled and barely audible 'thanks', grabbed the beer and closed it again abruptly in my face. It then occurred to me that surely it should be him buying me the beer. The cheek! Before long, he moved out and was replaced by a woman who I never saw, only heard. The noises now, though just as voluble, were of constant crying. I almost hankered for the return of 'broken leg man' and I certainly hadn't the heart to smash the floor below a distraught woman with a vacuum cleaner.

If I'd thought my relationship with my immediate neighbour was trying, I simply wasn't prepared for the cantankerous old grouch-bag that lived on the corner of the street. The disposal of household waste in Japan is a meticulous and rule-bound affair. There was 'burnable', 'un-burnable', 'compost' and many other weird and wonderful categories into which your rubbish must be sorted. The only bin bags you could buy were transparent which of course was useful for two reasons. Firstly, it ensured that miscreants didn't breach the rubbish sorting rules and stuff their eggshells in the same bag as their broken umbrella. The second, and surely far more important benefit of the clear bags, was that 'Ole' Grouchy' could stare at, prod and then sift through my rubbish like a customs official who's just happened upon a kilo of heroin in a suitcase.

He did it openly, no doubt to prove a point, bent double in his white wife-beater vest and growling under his breath like an ill-tempered dog. Perhaps I wouldn't have attracted the attention of the old man if our rubbish was left outside our individual dwellings, but as is the norm in Japan, the accumulated rubbish bags of the street or cul-de-sac are centralised at one point. The pile is then covered with a blue net to keep the pesky crows at bay. It just so happened that the rubbish point was right outside Grumpy's house so perhaps he was somewhat justified in his ire.

It was a pleasant surprise to find that the old lady who lived opposite me was much nicer. She'd smile and say hello each time we bumped into one another. She didn't seem in the least bit perturbed that I was foreign. She was so jovial in fact that I half expected her to invite me in for a cup of tea. However, I am glad she didn't, because whether it was a pet or not, I would often see a large rat scuttling along inside the kitchen window.

***

In my first year in Japan while my inability to read Japanese proved a mild irritant in restaurants with vending machines or at train stations, I quickly learned the spoken get-of-jail-free phrases to bypass the necessity of mastering any one of Japan's alphabets, let alone all three. However, while, "What do you recommend?" or "Can I have a ticket to X please?" were useful, they didn't help me in the slightest when on my days off I stood ashen faced in front of my washing machine and decided which random combination of buttons I would press this time. Given that I did one or more loads of washing weekly, it is statistically quite possible, if not probable, that on at least one occasion I hit the right buttons in the right order. But random, stab in the dark washing machine options could hardly produce that much angst. I mean, what's the worst you can do, accidentally press 40 degrees instead of 30, 'rinse' instead of 'spin'? It wasn't as if there was a button for 'destroy the clothes', or 'self-destruct'. No, for a real nail-biter, I reserved my illiteracy for medicine.

Buying medicine was a bit like Russian roulette. It usually went like this: I would turn up at the drug store and mime an ailment to the perplexed member of staff. I would then pray that I received something appropriate. Sometimes I'd simply go by the pictures on the packet and hope for the best. I've no doubt by now at some point or another I've used sea sickness pills for my headaches, thrush cream for aftershave and deep heat for deodorant, but at least you can't confuse a cotton bud with a toothbrush. In 2009 my family back in the UK decided to go on holiday to Egypt and invited me. I gladly accepted and flew from Tokyo to London, then to Luxor, back to London and then back to Tokyo in the space of ten days. Before I went, I needed vaccines but hadn't the time to get them in England, so I turned up at a Japanese hospital with some mess I'd scrawled on a piece of paper from google translate and with my fingers tightly crossed. I'd hoped to leave the hospital protected against malaria, typhoid and yellow fever, but after three injections from confused looking nurses, for all I know I might have been injected with some experimental new drug or unwittingly have begun the first stage of my gender transition.

If my physical health was lucky to largely avoid the negative consequences of my poor Japanese skills, then my wallet was less fortunate. Standing in a bar one night I asked a nice young lady if she'd like something to drink. She mumbled something incomprehensible with a wide grin on her face. My friends all began tittering in the background as I nodded to the barman and said, "Yeah, get her one of those." To my everlasting horror, the barman returned with the bar's most expensive bottle of champagne. By now my friends are rolling around on the floor in tears as the barman proceeds to pour the smiling girl a glass. 10,000 yen (£70) later, I had learned a costly mistake. Always get the translation accurate before you agree to anything.

***

The mess ups, though occasionally costly and usually amusing, were sometimes painfully embarrassing. Perhaps my king of mess ups happened one day in a local video game arcade. You will find huge multi-floor video game arcades across the country decked out with all the latest electronic fads you'd expect in shooting, driving and dancing, as well as rows of old-style machines with a bulb-headed joystick and just three faded buttons offering such retro favourites as Street Fighter and Sonic the Hedgehog. I enjoyed the old-style games, tapping away frantically on the blue button for 'kick' on Mortal Kombat and trying to get Jax to 'Finish Him' as if it were a Saturday evening in 1994 all over again, with 'Blind Date' and 'Gladiators' on the telly in the background and inevitably putting off my Maths homework until the last possible moment the next day. Flawless Victory.

Amongst the modern games my favourites were the driving ones as I don't have a steady aim and I've got two left feet and a bad back. 'Midnight Maximum Tune 3' was the latest must-play game for all budding Lewis Hamiltons. The race route was a simulation of Tokyo's famous Wangan[44] highway, a favourite haunt of Japan's bosozoku[45] street racers. There was a row of four or five such machines in my local games arcade.

I became quite addicted to the game and spent countless evenings and my days off pushing my Subaru to its limits through the neon glare of Tokyo's streets. It was bizarre really, the huge blade-runner-esque metropolis and city streets that made up the

---

[44] The Bayshore route of the Shuto Expressway, a 43-mile-long stretch of toll highway in Greater Tokyo. It is a major route that runs between the islands of Tokyo bay.

[45] A Japanese youth sub-culture which peaked in the 1980s, mainly associated with violent motorbike gangs who ride customised motorcycles but also a term used to describe the illegal street racing scene.

racetracks in the game were the same buildings and streets as those of the city in which I lived. As my face became recognised among the others that played the game incessantly, I got on nodding terms with a group of men who regularly frequented the games centre and were expert at the game. Now you might be picturing these guys as spotty teens, high school kids or twenty somethings but, in reality, they were all middle-aged. They were lovely and welcoming and kind and shamelessly spent their evenings chatting, smoking, playing and showing the clueless gaijin how to modify his car and access the various game modes without ruining up one of their prize machines.

As it turned out, I didn't ruin one of their prize machines. In the way only an idiot like me could do, one evening after getting to know the group quite well and enjoying the hallowed status of being on speaking terms with them, I miraculously managed to ruin all five machines in a row, I think forever. Now I shall plead ignorance here. Whenever various Japanese writing would flash up on the screen, I would just paw wildly at the buttons hoping that whatever choices I made would fare me well in the race. On one such day I entered my racing card, a small credit card sized piece of card with my details on - car type, race points etc, and it spat it out again. In frustration, I kept shoving the thing in until eventually the machine seemed to self-destruct, taking the other four in a row with it. The only thing the scene lacked was smoke coming out and a flashing red siren. I skulked away, leaving the machines imploding and the faces of the other men in disgust, and never ever walked back into the game centre ever again. What a fool!

My mistakes were endless. I remember on one occasion trudging up to the fifth floor of a building in Tokyo to join a large group for dinner in a restaurant. They were all Japanese except for Nigel, the only person I knew, and he was guiding me there by phone. I was pretty sure I'd found the right venue, so I walked in.

"We're on the table in the far-left corner as you walk in," Nigel informed me.

"I've just arrived. Yep, I've got it" I replied.

I caught the eye of the maitre d' and gestured towards the far table. He nodded and allowed me to pass. Sure enough, there was the large group at the far table in the corner. I approached, greeted everyone and introduced myself, before sitting down cross-legged on an empty cushion. I couldn't spot Nigel at first which didn't worry me as he was no doubt at the far end of the table obscured by other diners.

As I began contemplating the assortment of delicious-looking dishes on the table that the diners were sharing I noticed I was receiving unusual looks. As a gaijin this was not particularly noteworthy, so I thought nothing of it. I'd been there a few minutes and was busily chatting to the young lady sitting next to me when my phone rang.

"Tom, where the hell are you?"

It turned out I wasn't just at the wrong table. I was in the wrong restaurant in the wrong building.

***

Thankfully, the mistakes were not all mine.
'Japanglish[46]' is an endless source of mirth. Given my
sluggish progress at learning Japanese, I should stifle
my inner chuckles at Japanglish like a self-conscious
Japanese woman with a hand over my grinning
mouth. I have no doubt that the elderly grandmother
shopping with her grandchildren in my local
shopping mall had no idea what her t-shirt said. It
was in English and therefore stylish so why worry
about the meaning? It was a strange appropriation of
the foreign. The fact that vain Europeans might think
they have 'brave' or 'tiger' tattooed in Chinese
symbols on their biceps when in fact it says 'idiot'
could be embarrassing. Nonetheless, I hope for the
sake of the granny I saw in that mall that she never
discovers that in large bold neon pink capital letters
her t-shirt told all around to 'FUCK OFF'.

There was a clothing shop in nearby Nakano called
'Boutique Psycho', and a bar near my home claimed
to be 'for royal drunkard' (which I can only presume
is a horridly unfortunate mistranslation of a Japanese
phrase trying to convey the regal sophistication of its
clientele). I once came across a masseuse service in
Western Japan called 'Body produce' and a duty-free
shop in Kobe whose sign read, 'We Knight creates one
wind'. I found a selection of t-shirts in a shop in
Tokyo that I simply had to buy for my brothers as
Christmas presents. There's a picture on one of a
stick-man rushing to the toilet with the slogan, 'The
body feeling is emergency. Must release, Now is
happiness'. What I love about the Japanese

---

[46] Sometimes known as 'Engrish', 'Japanglish' is a slang term for the
misuse of English words and phrases by the Japanese.

appropriation of English is how they pick ever so slightly the wrong thing. Somehow this is funnier than if they massively mistranslated.

The word 'mansion' conjures up images of huge stately homes in acres of land with maybe a national trust shop, or even like Longleat, a safari park. However, in Japan a mansion is a different prospect entirely. This is a case of Japanglish at its most extreme. The word has been so lost in translation I'm surprised it doesn't mean radish or scrotum. Incredibly, with no hint of irony, the Japanese have adopted the word mansion to describe tiny urban apartments. Near my home I passed a 'mansion' called 'Stoke on Trent' and another called 'Milton Keynes'. There was also a hotel in a Tokyo back street I came across called 'Somerset'. Priceless. I suspect some poor junior worker had panicked and stabbed a finger randomly on a map. If that is their method of apartment-naming, I can only hope one day I stumble across 'Loughborough' and 'Gloucester', not for any intrinsic comedy in those names, but in the hope that I'll hear Japanese people pronouncing them.

One of the most popular isotonic drinks is called 'Pocari Sweat' and there's a famous band named 'Bump of Chicken'. You could fill volumes with 'Japanglish' and it is a never-ending source of childish amusement which I challenge even the most high-brow visitors to Japan to rise above.

**

Maybe it's appropriate that so much was mistranslated on all sides. The language, the faux pas, the misunderstandings and bumbling errors were mainly mine. Of course, in a culture as alien as

Japan's, things were bound to get misunderstood. After leaving Japan I watched for the first time Bill Murray and Scarlett Johansen confused and bewildered in Tokyo. As I watched, my thoughts drifted back to 2007. The film neatly summed up my feelings, particularly in the early days. It was released merely a few years before I moved to Tokyo and its opening scenes are the same bustling neon streets near my home and the part of the city in which it was filmed and was set was where I lived. The film chimed true in some ways because for me so much, like in the film, was 'Lost in Translation'.

Against all the odds, as the months turned into years my Japanese language ability increased. I'm always reminded to be careful what I say in English in Japan because you never know who in the vicinity may be able to speak it well. It is wise council that perhaps the two middle-aged ladies who sat opposite me on a bus one day ought to have taken. I'd been in Japan for about three years by then. The women commented on my clothes and how annoying it was that they had to sit on a bus with a foreigner like me. As they whinged and moaned and slagged me off, I pressed the button on the handrail and stood up to get off at the next stop. As I passed them, I leaned down and quietly explained gently in Japanese with a little smile and a condescending voice that I had understood every word they had said. I gave them a little wink and hopped off the bus. I shall never forget the look of horror that covered their faces, and I can guarantee that their habit of slagging of foreigners on public transport was abruptly curtailed from that day forward.

Chapter 11

Love Hotels, the Robot Restaurant and a Skewered Penis

Only in Japan: The bizarre and the ridiculous

Time spent laughing is time with gods.
Japanese proverb

I knew living in Japan was going to be an unusual experience from a single anecdote I was told by the man who interviewed me for the job in London. He said that his parents were visiting him for a week while he was teaching in Japan and while out with him drinking one evening, a drunken salaryman[47] had wandered over and proceeded to weave toothpicks through his father's eyebrows. The story seemed unbelievably ridiculous then but having lived in Japan, it doesn't surprise me at all.

For many people, a typical Saturday afternoon consists of mowing the lawn or watching the local footie team lose on a rainy afternoon followed by a few pints in the Rose and Crown before roast beef, parsnips, The Antiques Roadshow and bed. Well, I had no lawn, good luck finding parsnips in Tokyo, and when I turned on the TV it wasn't grandma's brooch being valued in the grounds of a stately home

---

[47] A Japanese salaried white-collar worker. Typified by businessmen in black suits who work in offices, commute to work by train and work incredibly long hours. Salarymen show great loyalty and dedication to their jobs and traditionally have spent long careers working for the same company.

but a game show with two screaming men in nappies trying to waft a chicken-shaped balloon into each other's goals by farting, all the while being tickled by feather dusters and hit over the head with foam hammers and having eggs thrown at them from the side-lines by a giant teddy bear.

Well, as they say, when in Rome, so perhaps it was fitting that I should spend one Saturday afternoon in a hedgehog cafe (a place to pet hedgehogs, not eat them) with a man I'd met in the street only five minutes before, feeding millet worms to the wretched beast, who thanked me by defecating on my lap (the hedgehog, not the man). Next time we vowed we should try the ferrets or the micro-pigs, but after walking out into the city streets and bowing to my new-found companion we both wandered off never to see each other again.

Besides, the closest 'British pub' to me was not the Rose and Crown but a place in Nakano that no longer exists called 'British Spirit', a large wood-panelled bar and restaurant with two or three electronic darts machines at one end. Being a fan of darts, I went regularly with friends and got to know the staff well. There was Hayato, a short guy with dyed spiky blonde hair, a gold tooth and 'South Coast' tattooed on his belly in English (I'm guessing it referred to Kanagawa rather than Weymouth). There was Ryu the bar owner, a tall guy with a beard and ponytail, and then there was Taro, a shaven-headed self-confessed yakuza thug who fancied himself as a bit of a tough nut. He indeed must have been tough as I came to discover one night while I stood at the bar with a few of my friends and he got on to the topic of sex. It never took long for the topic of sex to come up whenever in the presence of Japanese blokes. Some things I guess are universal. The formula was always the same.

"Do you like Japanese woman?"

"Did you try Japanese woman?"

It was a little tedious and missed the fairly blatant point that since I was in Japan, unless I wasn't dating at all, I would be dating 'Japanese woman'. The usual conversation had been initiated when Taro leant into our group and explained that he had something special for "attacking Japanese woman". Now, I'll give him the benefit of the doubt that his use of English verbs is rusty at best. He then went on to demonstrate with some elaborate hand puppetry exactly what he meant, but quite frankly his little rendition of Finger Mouse left us rather non-plussed.

To dispense with hours more of this X-rated version of charades, he ushered us five or six guys into the men's toilets, pulled down his jeans and pants and pulled out his penis. To our horror, he pointed at two large spherical bulges under the skin of the top side of his shaft each about the size of a large garden pea. His penis looked like some bizarre goggle-eyed amphibian. Back in the bar, and thankfully with his penis back inside his pants, he went on to explain that they were pearls and that he himself had inserted them beneath the skin of his penis. The obvious questions were then inevitably asked by the open-mouthed members of our group, who I noticed like me had sub-consciously placed their hands, as if to protect their manhood, in their laps. "Why? How?" and most pertinently, "Did it hurt?" to which he laughed and answered respectively, "To increase the sexual pleasure for women", chillingly, "with a metal skewer," and "Yes, a lot".

Apparently, this was not unheard of in Japan. Some hasty googling on our phones at the bar revealed that he was indeed right, as image after image of knobbly penises filled our screens, some positively covered with them like the warts on some horrific witch's nose. The risk from infection was surely huge and I've no doubt that we all went to sleep that night, legs firmly crossed, marvelling at how desperate some Japanese men must be that enhancing women's pleasure was worth taking an ice pick to your own cock, sticking a couple of pearls in and then waiting agonising weeks for the thing to (hopefully) heal. I'd love to say this was the most bizarre evening spent in that bar but that would simply be a lie. Some things I simply cannot disclose as they are beyond the bounds of decency (as if a skewered penis isn't).

There were other characters that I associate with that bar. The name 'Papa' conjures up an image of a venerable Italian grandfather being greeted by his adoring grandchildren or perhaps, if you were born before the 90s, the father of the pretty French girl in the Renault Clio advert. The Papa I knew could not have been further removed from this. I first met him when I was playing darts in British Spirit with my friend Jordan Chivers. In strode a man of five foot four with long combed back silver hair and a silver handlebar moustache that went down to his chin. He wore the tightest white t-shirt I've ever seen, tucked into a pair of jeans with a Union Jack sewn onto the back pocket. On his feet he wore pointed cowboy boots. Without saying a word, he strode up to Jordan, squared up to him as if he was about to punch him, and tweaked his nipple.

After that of course, we were mates. I got the impression that Papa owned the bar, but I never found out for sure. What I did know is that he held a position of power in the local area, and everybody seemed to know and respect him. Strangely, he had a beguiling charm and always seemed to have a different young lady on his arm every time I saw him. Each was twenty years or more his junior and fawned all over him. Papa would invariably signal his arrival by slapping us on our bottoms or blowing us kisses. Despite this, I don't think he was gay.

***

Faux British pubs with their wood-panelled walls and Guinness on tap probably don't conform to most people's images of Japan. Japan's food culture on the other hand is well known globally. It is when it comes to dining that the Japanese truly go overboard. I didn't particularly like Japanese food when I arrived but with time grew to love it. Themed restaurants stay in the memory more than most. When you think of a themed restaurant you might picture a 1950's American-style diner in London or a place with movie star memorabilia but Tokyo, as you might expect, took the concept to a whole new level.

The prison-themed restaurant I once went to with a group of teachers was terrifying. It was less like a prison than an insane asylum. On arrival we entered into a large dark room and were immediately handcuffed and led by a 'psychiatric nurse' to a cell into which I was unceremoniously shoved with my friends. I wondered for a moment if we hadn't accidentally attended a horror-themed restaurant, as almost immediately the screams of petrified customers mingled with the howls and maniacal laughter of actors who raced around, jumping out upon the customers. After some ten minutes struggling to read the menu in the darkness, our cell door was opened, and our orders taken. The drinks when they arrived were in test tubes and smoking beakers and mine had to be administered with a syringe. We were all on edge, a sensation that was only heightened by the ear-splitting sirens and flashing lights that pierced the darkness every few minutes as if there had been a breakout.

As we waited for our food to arrive, I noticed that a hitherto unseen figure had crept into our cell among us, and I turned with horror to find a deranged looking clown with a big painted red grin staring at me mere inches from my face. It was ironic that after many boyhood years spent convincing myself that Pennywise didn't really lurk beneath my bed as I tried in vain to sleep, he had in fact been waiting for me in a restaurant-cum-lunatic asylum in Tokyo instead all along. I should have known. As another siren went off his ghastly face was illuminated by the glare of the lights which in turn cast a hideous silhouette of his friends lurking beside us in the shadows, a crazy axe man and a doctor covered in blood. Our food was dyed black and served in bubbling cauldrons and every few minutes we'd be disturbed again by a madman climbing over our cell walls or a man with a plastic chainsaw trying to break through the metal bars and screaming like a banshee.

Some of the themed restaurants were more sedate but no less bizarre. One restaurant we went to saw my friends and I using fishing rods and nets to catch our own fish which swam around the 'river' which meandered through the restaurant. The seating area was designed as a large wooden boat. We handed our catch over to the waiter who then shouted out what we'd caught to the whole restaurant and banged a big drum while chanting. He asked us how we would like each item cooked or whether we'd like it prepared raw as sashimi[48]. A couple of minutes later our food arrived at our table perched high up in the bow of the vessel. This was about as fresh as you could get. The only drawback was you had to eat whatever you caught, and with huge lobsters and stingrays swimming freely amongst the smaller fish, with one wrong move of the fishing rod, and just like buying a lady a drink when you speak little Japanese, it was easy to make a costly mistake.

The ninja restaurant was fun. A Japanese friend and I were met at the entrance by a silent man dressed all in black whose face was obscured by a black mask. He silently led us through narrow corridors, through trapdoors and over a little rope bridge until we arrived at our table. There were walls you leant upon that spun you round into secret rooms and, with an incredible disregard for health and safety, even missing floorboards you had to jump across. It was

---

[48] 'Sashimi' usually refers to thin slices of raw fish but can also refer to thinly sliced raw meat.

all very fun until it was time for me to use the toilet. When I left our table, I was directed by at least three members of staff to the gents but time and again, after taking one wrong turn after another, I found myself back at my table dying for a wee. Was this part of the whole experience? Was I supposed to somersault through the air and then contort myself through a narrow twisting passage just to relieve myself?

However, none of these experiences prepared me for the strangest restaurant of all, the robot restaurant. The robot restaurant was all the crazy neon madness of Tokyo distilled into a single large room. Upon entering, you are first taken to a bar area to wait. I surveyed my surroundings, walls covered in mirrors and glitter balls and disco lights hanging from the ceiling. I was seated at a table next to the sparkling stage on which a robot jazz band were playing. The gold metal costume of the band's front man looked like a bad replica of a muscular C3PO. Whether the real C3PO is anywhere near as good on the saxophone, no Star Wars script to date has cared to relate, but this guy was going for it, gyrating his hips so suggestively that even R2D2 would have blushed.

We were soon taken down to the restaurant itself, a large open room flanked by tiered rows of seats. I hadn't known what sort of clientele to expect, but I was slightly surprised by the middle-aged ladies and besuited groups of businessmen all around me waving huge brightly coloured glow sticks. As overly cheerful young women wearing hot pants and huge grins began warming up the crowd with chanting and rhythming clapping, the lights were dimmed, the music was cranked up and the show began.

I sat open-mouthed as a huge metal triceratops ridden by bikini-clad women with toy axes and swords fired green and red laser beams from its horns and did combat with a T-Rex. Naturally, this scene was broken by a rampaging cow ridden by a panda which suddenly emerged from behind a curtain to frenzied mooing sound effects and smashed both adversaries with a large foam hammer. There were more dinosaurs, whose species I fail to remember, but I do recall that one dragon-like beast had huge chrome multi-barrelled machine guns sprouting from under its wings.

Somebody must have heard I was coming because yet again to my horror there were clowns. Robot clowns. Everywhere. They came twirling, juggling, dancing, riding on unicycles and one raced up and down the room driving an electric flashing neon monowheel recklessly between the battling dinosaurs. By the time the final clown robot appeared, I'd almost lost my coulrophobia[49] completely through sheer exposure. He whizzed around the room on roller skates, wearing a rainbow wig with a flashing blue police light on top. I can see how people end up in asylums.

To my enormous relief, the clowns disappeared and were replaced by the far more calming and reassuring presence of a large brightly lit tank which suddenly emerged and trundled across the room covered with grinning ladies draped over its barrel suggestively, wearing knee-high leather boots and diamond encrusted bikinis. I'm not sure the bright neon tank and bare-skinned ladies were in line with

---

[49] The fear of clowns.

conventional military practice. There was not much camouflage and even less concealment.

There were floats of barely clothed women (there's a theme developing here) in animal masks thumping huge drums; there were marching bands of women in miniskirts playing trumpets and trombones. A gigantic fifteen-foot-tall snake burst on to the scene with two women in leather underwear clambering upon it, the braver of the two climbing right into the serpent's mouth and finally killing the beast with a thrust of her sword. There were raptors and spiders, and giant over-sized goodness knows what who each appeared in turn through a puff of smoke, a flash of light, deafening music and lights and sound and enough laser beams and strobes to turn anyone epileptic. No matter what creature emerged next you could guarantee it would have laser beams coming out of its eyes, machine guns for claws, and more certain than the sunrise, it would unfailingly have scantily clad grinning young women clambering all over it.

For the finale two giant robots almost as high as the ceiling emerged with great fanfare and proceeded to do battle with one another. Atop the giant robots, which rather unnervingly had oversized plastic women's heads, sat two real women operating the machines and battling it out. Throughout the hour my mouth didn't close once. I left the robot restaurant over-stimulated, confused and feeling that nothing I would ever see from that day forward could ever shock me. After the sensory overload and the surrealism of the place, I wouldn't blame people for believing that the enormous Godzilla head bursting out of a nearby hotel roof was real. It's quite fitting I think that the exit to the street from the robot restaurant is lined with full length mirrors. Perhaps the most entertaining part of the experience is catching sight of your face as you leave because it doesn't look at all like the face of the person that innocently entered just an hour before.

**

For all the robot restaurants and lumpy penises, by and large, after some time, life in Tokyo took on a regularity and familiarity like life back at home. It was all very different to life back home of course, but familiar in its own way, like two parallel universes. When you move to a foreign country you often picture yourself doing all the touristy things, visiting temples, going to festivals and seeing the sights. The more prosaic truth about moving to a new country is that in reality you spend most of your time doing all the mundane things you would back home, just in a different place and language - buying a carton of milk, going to the gym, posting letters. It wasn't exotic, but I suppose it is amongst the routine and the everyday that you truly get under the skin of another culture.

Feeling adventurous, with my hair in need of a trim, I decided one day to dispense with my normal discount barbers, where the sign above the door stated in English '1,000 yen cut- it's reasonable', and try an old-fashioned place tucked away on a back street with a striped awning and barber's pole. In addition to a haircut, I decided to have a barber's shave, which I'd never had before. Sadly, as a result of the following experience, I'm not sure I'll ever have one again.

"So, you'd like a haircut and a shave?" said the respectable-looking man.

I smiled and nodded and then he called through to the backroom. The man who came out was wearing incredibly thick glasses. Fine, I thought. Lots of people wear thick glasses.

I knew something was wrong when this new bespectacled barber began searching for the necessary implements of his trade by pawing at the porcelain counter. A question crossed my mind with trepidation. Just how bad is this guy's eyesight? Well, I suppose in many ways the proof was in the pudding, which was my face and when I walked out nearly an hour later it was a very sore and rashy pudding indeed. If I had to judge the quality of his vision by the pain of my raw cheeks alone, I'd be generous to give it a two out of ten. Having paid the equivalent of £20 my face was still covered in large tufts of hair. I wasn't best pleased, but to be honest it could have been worse, I still have my lips and ears. Suffice to say, I stuck to my usual barbers after that. I inwardly mused that the slogan of my regular barbers was quite apt because it indeed is perfectly reasonable to expect the person sliding an incredibly sharp cut-throat razor across your neck to have decent eyesight.

***

Vision-impaired barbers and lumpy penises were unexpected surprises, and let's face it you'd seriously have to question your lifestyle if they weren't, but surprises also came during dinner at students' houses. Chieko, a lovely lady in her fifties with a husband and teenage children, had kindly invited me, Harry and his Japanese fiancé to her house for dinner. The husband was a little over-familiar and I was never quite sure when he was joking. As he helped me to another portion of fried prawns, he made an announcement.

"Tom-u sensei, you are single. You can try our daughter."

I didn't know if he was joking or not. Later in the day he insisted that Harry, his girlfriend and I go over in the summer sometime to try out the hot tub.

"You can look under the door of the changing room while we are getting dressed," he announced with a smile. I nearly spat out my food but just smiled weakly and stared at my plate.

***

Away from my quiet neighbourhood, Harajuku was one of the districts of Tokyo that was a little more off the wall. Harajuku on a Sunday was a sight to behold. From the rockabilly dancers Nigel and I had seen in our first couple of weeks in Japan to the man I once saw dressed as a little girl playing a tiny plastic toy flute. There was a woman I saw walking her rabbit and guinea pig on a lead through the park and an endless procession of people in cosplay. It is where people go to see and be seen, a place for the trendy, the show-offs and the voyeurs and you can buy almost anything there.

Harajuku is a mecca for all trends and bizarre fashions from maid costumes to bondage gear. While I was in Japan one style in vogue was the 'dolly kei' look, inspired by antique or vintage fashion with women in multiple layers of lace and doll-like accessories. Spin-offs of this style saw teenage girls dressed like European peasants of the middle ages. Another popular style was the overly brightly coloured 'decora' trend, characterised by clothes with Hello Kitty and other childish cartoon characters. The over-the-top 'cutesy' styles of Harajuku were encapsulated by 'The Harajuku Girls', a group of back up dancers who performed in several of Gwen Stefani's music videos in the mid to late noughties, and after whom the singer named a song released in 2004.

There were punks with brightly dyed mohawks and endless piercings. There were goths with black lipstick and people who sported the bohemian look complete with flowers in their hair. There were the rockers in leather jackets and black boots and even a sizeable element who seemed to be going for the L.A. Chicano[50] saggy jeans, goatee beard and bandana around a shaven head look. The youth fashions are a way in which people can express themselves creatively, an outlet for their own persona in a culture that too often seems designed to encourage conformity and stifle individuality.

Harajuku's main street, Takeshita dori, is a long, narrow, winding pedestrianised street that wends its way between row upon row of bizarre shops. It almost feels like a dream as you pass by shops with such names as 'Listen Flavor' 'Paris Kids' and 'Cute Cube'. I scratched my head over the mind-boggling array of neon pink, overly 'cute' rubbish. How

---

[50] A Mexican-American identity/subculture with its own distinct fashion, geographically centered in southern California.

ridiculous, I thought, to use the American spelling of flavour.

'Cute' it seemed was in vogue. It had been for quite some time and there is no end in sight to its popularity. To be cute, to look cute, to have cute things are all desirable. While in the West the more conceited or insecure members of society book in for treatments for larger bottoms and breasts and puffed out fish lips, many Japanese ladies just wanted to be cute. I could never have imagined the myriad bizarre ways in which this would manifest itself, from the strange high-pitched nasal whine of the shop girls who called out their welcomes in a timbre that was somewhere between a gurgling baby and a bleating lamb to the over-the-top, gaudy and garish child-like fashions. There was an uncomfortable fascination for all things childish. The bizarre and disturbing trend of some teenage girls and young women wearing school uniform in their leisure time to look 'cute' was one thing but that was only scratching the surface.

'Yaeba' or 'double teeth' describes canines that are particularly sharp with a fang-like appearance and they are deemed youthful and attractive. While in the West men and women increasingly strive for a set of perfectly straight gnashers, in Japan crooked and pointy teeth are not only not deemed unattractive but desirable. Teenage girls are even known to undergo surgery to cap the upper canines for the fang like effect. It was all strangely unsettling and bizarre.

Medical concerns for me were far removed from my gappy teeth. For a couple of years before coming to Japan I had been suffering from a bad back from an accident and stomach pain. The source of my stomach pain remained unknown. One doctor I had seen in the UK had suggested it might be a stomach ulcer, another had said it was muscle damage and yet another had cited a problem with my nerves. Whichever it was, I'd learned to live with it until one day while teaching, the pain suddenly and unexpectedly worsened. I began to panic and seeing the look on my face as I clutched my stomach, the school receptionist called for an ambulance. When it arrived, I manfully refused the stretcher and walked down the stairs.

Once in the hospital, I was subjected to an X-ray and a few other cursory tests. While I lay there, I attracted quite a crowd. It wasn't every day that a foreigner would turn up for them to prod and experiment on, so they had a field day. As I was lying there on my back, after a while I noticed about six of seven young physicians hovering around me. Just as I was contemplating how pretty some of the female nurses were one broke away from the X-ray that the others were all standing around and grinning at and asked an unusual question.

"Have you been to the toilet today? I mean a poo."

Taken aback, I replied that I hadn't. I was puzzled as to why she would ask such a bizarre question. Before long I was told that I was absolutely fine, handed a very expensive bill and a piece of paper filled with writing which I could not read. I walked out £300 worse off and turned up back at the school.

"Did they tell you what was wrong with you?" asked the receptionist.

I handed her the piece of paper and she put her hand over her mouth as she laughed.

"It says you might have had discomfort as you're blocked up with poo."

My mind flashed back to the huddle of nurses all grinning at the X-ray and I felt mortified. As it turned out, I subsequently discovered that my poo wasn't the cause of the pain. They'd misdiagnosed it completely, but at the time I felt hugely embarrassed.

**

It would be hard to accurately paint a picture of urban Japan without paying heed to a mainstay of its landscape, convenience stores. Peppered throughout cities and towns amongst the haphazard jumble of old and new buildings, sandwiched between coin laundries, office buildings and train station entrances, these 24-hour beacons of light are an essential part of life. I was less surprised by the sheer number of them in urban areas as I was to discover that they were seemingly everywhere in the suburbs, between car repair shops and golf driving ranges, and in the countryside too.

Of course, the deeper you got into the mountains and the forests, away from the cultivated rice paddies, the omnipotent 'konbinis'[51] were fewer and further between, but after years in Japan I never ceased to be amazed when tramping through narrow country lanes and down steep mountain paths to be dazzled by these brightly lit beacons of light which suddenly appeared around a corner, incongruous and out of step with their surroundings.

They are wonderful and somehow different to convenience stores elsewhere, but I can't clearly

---

[51] Japanese for 'convenience store', a mispronounced abbreviation of the word 'convenience'.

explain why. The rice balls are great, often triangular and sometimes circular packages of compacted sticky rice wrapped in a layer of seaweed. The triangular ones are particularly clever. If you're not a fan of seaweed, you can just remove the packaging altogether and enjoy the snack. However, if you belong to the majority of people who enjoy eating the rice balls wrapped in the crisp green sheets, you need only follow the arrows and open as directed, and somehow, in typical Japanese fashion, like some complicated origami, once you pull the red tab this way and that, the rice ball comes out magically and neatly wrapped in the green stuff.

The trouble for me in the early months was, not being able to read Japanese, it was always a gamble what I'd get inside. My favourite was always cooked salmon or the tuna with mayonnaise. But of course, my luck could not always hold. On some days I sat at my classroom desk during my lunchbreak and grimaced and shivered when my first tentative bite revealed not some delicious fleshy fish but overly salted cod roe or pickled plum.

As well as the food and drink on offer, the cheap packaged underpants, t-shirts and socks for no more than 500 yen a piece, the ubiquitous gaggle of people shamelessly reading for free the many magazines by the window, I love the incredible array of teas and coffees. Year-round you have a section for cold cans and bottles of tea and coffee and then a heated section containing the same products. In the summer months, unsurprisingly, most of the canned and bottled teas and coffees on offer are chilled for your enjoyment and in the depths of winter they are mostly heated to a temperature that was just about holdable after a couple of minutes of playing hot potato between un-gloved hands.

I always derived a strange geek-like pleasure in the transition period, in the months of April and October when I'd see half of the shelves in this section displaying red tags and the other half blue. It was an indication that the seasons were changing and, almost as if by plumping for blue, I was doing my bit to usher in the longer days of summer or by choosing red I was helping to speed up the inexorable countdown to Christmas. Whichever way you take your cuppa the konbinis and the vending machines have got it covered; white coffee with three sugars, extra milky or just straight black; Green tea, barley tea, milk tea and more. I just had to try the 'Royal milk tea' the first time I came across it. It comes in plastic bottles, tin bottles and cans. On the front is a picture of a china tea set and a crown. It tastes very sweet and only vaguely like a real British cuppa. The hot version is bearable, the cold one less so, but I'll give credit where it's due, they've got the colour spot on.

There was one brand of canned coffee that was my favourite. When I first bought a can, I noticed a vaguely familiar face stencilled on to the side of it, but I just couldn't work out who it was. It was only when I saw Tommy Lee Jones on Japanese TV advertising the product that I made the connection. I don't know if he was hired to fit the face or vice versa but, canned coffee aside, he was hugely popular in Japan in general. I suppose it shouldn't have come as a surprise. Mr Jones appeared to represent much that many Japanese respected; authority, discipline and wisdom, hence the brand name 'Boss'.

If I had been awed by the convenience stores, the vending machines took things to a whole new level. They are often clustered together, and on one little side street I came across in Shibuya I counted fourteen drinks vending machines side by side in a row and almost the same number again on the opposite side of the narrow street. Hot and cold canned coffee in the vending machines made the folks back home laugh but they would scarcely believe the range of products from the bizarre to the ridiculous that you could purchase in a Tokyo vending machine; bananas, umbrellas, hot dogs, fries, octopus balls (whose popularity is easier to understand when I explain this is a spherical snack of battered octopus rather than an octopus' balls), cooked noodles, used women's underpants (with the picture of the woman who'd worn them on the front of the packet) and, I'm reliably told, even a car. There are also 'restaurants' in Tokyo that solely consist of a room of hot food vending machines and chairs and tables- a dining experience I've yet to try.

If popping to your nearest vending machine for a can of hot coffee and a pair of Yoko's unwashed panties is not your cup of royal milk tea, then why not head down to 'The Milk Bar'? I never went there, honest, but I am reliably informed that if you like your milk of the human variety, there is a bar in central Tokyo where lactating ladies will squirt you a glass fresh from source or, for an extra cost, dispense with the glass altogether. Maybe it was an urban myth but the stories I heard were too numerous to make me believe so. Suffice to say, unusual phenomena abounded in a land not unknown for its kinks and perversions.

***

Sometimes bizarre memories and snapshots of odd moments flood back in my mind. Standing on a wide grassy levy beside the Sumida river, I am blindfolded and wielding a huge pole. My target, a watermelon, is somewhere in front of me and I just pray that I feel the satisfying crack of its skin and not someone's skull because that would really ruin the party. How recent a cultural tradition it is in Japan to hit a watermelon with a long stick when blindfolded, I don't know. Perhaps it isn't one at all and this is just some elaborate ruse designed to make the clueless foreigner look stupid. Luckily, I hit it dead centre, everyone cheers and claps, and we sit and gorge on the jagged chunks under the summer sun as the bullet train passes on a bridge before my now uncovered eyes.

In addition to assaulting fruit, Japan has its share of strange festivals and games. There are penis festivals celebrating fertility, where huge phalluses are paraded down the street and young women pose for photos astride giant wooden members. There is log riding up in the Japanese mountains where logs the size of large tree trunks are lashed with ropes and launched down hillsides like out-of-control locomotives with dozens of men teetering on top and desperately hoping that when they do fall off, they don't go under.

Japan is odd but, come to think of it, Britain is pretty weird too. Perhaps I have no right to be surprised at the oddity. I come from a land of Morris Dancing, cheese rolling and shin kicking contests; a place where we burn a terrorist atop a pyre each year with glee and drunkenly watch the sunrise amongst old stones with music and chanted druids and the ubiquitous annoying dickhead playing the only three songs that he knows on his ukulele endlessly through the night. I may have been in a land of weirdos but come to think of it I was from a land of weirdos as well.

***

Japan has a habit of not just putting an ingenious, bizarre or over-the-top twist on the mundane or familiar but of having entities entirely unknown to most of the outside world. Most people outside of Japan have never heard of love hotels, however they are everywhere in Japan. They are where you would expect them, clustered together in whole areas of Tokyo's inner city, but you also find them in the most incongruous of places. I remember once walking past a rice field in the countryside when a solitary building appeared to one side. The giveaways were the panels that sheltered the car number plates and the faces of the drivers from view as they entered the car park, and the tinted windows of the building.

A small minority of love hotels do not allow foreigners, but most do since it's hard to know whether your customers are foreign or not. At the front desk you don't see another human at all, not a whole one anyway, but an anonymous pair of hands through a narrow slit. You hand money to the hands and the hands bid you enjoy your stay. Come to think of it, it must be a funny job. I wonder what questions are asked at the job interview.

Have you got friendly hands? Do you moisturise?

The main difference between love hotels and regular hotels, other than the obvious, is that you don't pay for the night but by the hour. Picture Miami in the 1980s and you will get some idea of the decor of many love hotels. Fake marble pillars, fake gold and shiny chrome doors are the order of the day. The rooms are themed and differently priced. Pictures of the available rooms are often lit up on a panel on both the interior and exterior walls of the lobby. If it wasn't for the nagging thought of who had used the room before you, what they had done, and with whom they had done it, I'd quite like love hotel rooms.

They're over the top and seedy but surprisingly clean and swanky, and you feel a bit like you're in a movie; not a sophisticated movie, nothing romantic like Titanic or Dirty Dancing but something tacky and kitsch and 80's, something involving drug kingpins with poor taste and too much money. That's right, love hotels are pure Scarface. I'm sure Tony Montana would approve of the television mounted into the wall of the bathroom in which I discovered to my delight a huge walk-in jacuzzi. I'm sure he would approve of the mirrors which cover the walls and the ceiling, the abundance of over-the-top bling- fake leather and fake diamonds, but all that sparkles is not gold. I've also no doubt that he would damn the edge of the bed as heartily as I did. The five-inch-wide bed frame may have been fake marble, but it felt just as hard as the real stuff on my poor shins which in the dark kept smashing against it on my trip to the loo. Talk about killing the mood.

There is a selection of costumes that you can hire from the front desk. If you ask the anonymous hands, they will add a small fee to your bill for the nurse outfit or the latex all-in-one or the bunny costume. As with your bog-standard chain hotel back at home, in the basket next to the kettle and mugs there is a small selection of tea bags, sachets of coffee and sugar and those little cartons of milk. Whatever else you might be doing, let's face it, you still need a cup of tea. But next to the teas and coffees in this basket there are a whole plethora of the sorts of disposal and reusable items you'd imagine finding in such an establishment. Most of the dozen or so channels available on the large television all conform to a particular theme and suffice to say it's not Peppa Pig or Wind in the Willows.

Although all love hotels have certain features in common, no two rooms are the same. There are those with shackles, those with huge circular revolving beds, Italianate decor, Disney themed rooms, Mickey Mouse themed rooms, aquatic themed ones and others with a huge range of elaborate obstacles on which you can injure your shins.

Why, you may ask, in a nation seemingly so outwardly prudish, are there so many love hotels? The answer in part is Grandma.

It needs to be remembered, that though, especially in the cities, living habits are changing, it is not unusual for couples, even married ones, to live with their parents. Japanese houses are small, and walls are thin. Love hotels are as much for the married as for those in their twenties and thirties with girlfriends or boyfriends still living at home. They are also of course for the seemingly prevalent extra-marital affairs, hence the huge walls that shield faces and number plates from public view. I've never been to a country that manages to separate the concepts of love and physical intimacy more than Japan. However, I'm thankful because in those moments when I'm sitting in the jacuzzi watching the inbuilt TV and sipping on some over-priced non-alcoholic beverage from the minibar; as I let the hot bubbling water soothe away the pain in my shins, for a brief moment I feel like Tony Montana (cue joke about love hotels and "Say hello to my little friend". Boom boom).

At this point you might start wondering just how many of these establishments I have been inside. In the interest of quashing any scurrilous rumours that I am some seedy pervert, allow me to say this: In my travels around Japan love hotels were often the only option for the night when I found myself alone, late at night in a small town with no lodgings booked. I am a gentleman, don't you know?

***

Away from the sore shin-soothing love hotel jacuzzis, most of the bathing I did was in Japanese bathhouses and hot springs, but I discovered a place to bathe with no water involved whatsoever. Ibusuki is a small town in Kyushu at the extreme southern tip of the Japanese mainland archipelago. It is known for its hot springs and for another rather unusual past time. On discovering that visitors to Ibusuki traditionally bury themselves in the black volcanic sands of its beaches, I just had to do it. I wasn't entirely sure what to expect from being buried alive, but I was assured that it held many health benefits.

In my yukata I traipsed outside to the beach where row upon row of heads stared upwards, unable to move under the weight of the black sand that was being shovelled upon them. I had known it was going to be hot, the temperature outside was well into the late 30's Celsius, but I hadn't quite prepared myself for the oven-like effect my soon to be coffin would produce. The sand was extremely hot to the touch and I began to sweat immediately.

A man began gaily burying me, I went light-headed, and for just one fleeting moment wondered if I'd unsuspectingly been coerced into some form of torture. It would be rather unbecoming to squeal like the coward I was and ask to be un-buried too soon, so I closed my eyes and let myself stew in my own juices. Try as I might, the bizarre thoughts started again. What if a freak wave at this moment raced towards the coast? I'd be trapped. I was fairly sure that the dizziness, pins and needles in my face and loss of sensation in my limbs indicated that time was up on this little venture (or perhaps I was just having a stroke) so I asked the man if he'd kindly hurry up with the obligatory photo of my anxious tomato-red face.

It was several showers and days before I stopped finding grains of black sand in various crevices in my body. I didn't particularly feel refreshed, but I assured myself that I was. If you ever find yourself in Ibusuki, you could try the beach burial. I cannot heartily recommend it as a 'nice' experience, but it certainly was different.

Perhaps I can be forgiven for the one glaring caveat in my slowly improving understanding of Japanese that became apparent on that beach, or should I say *in* it. I had been equipping myself month by month with more and more phrases to cope with everyday life. However, as I tried and failed to move each of my limbs under the crushing weight of black sand in a state of panic, I discovered a glaring hole in my language ability, a phrase I'd never anticipated having to use. How on Earth do you say, "Unbury me" in Japanese?

Chapter 12

Banzai, Biscuits and Bearskins

East meets West

A frog in a well does not know the great sea.
Japanese proverb

Copious books and TV programmes have commented on the cultural gulf between Japan and the West from both a Western and a Japanese perspective so I shall endeavour not to flog a dead horse. Whether or not the horse, part of whose raw liver I sat eating one night, had been flogged, I cannot relate. I only discovered what the meat was as I was chewing my final mouthful. Whether had I known what I was munching on any sooner I would have declined it or not, I don't know. After all, it's not every day you are bought dinner by a middle-aged punk rock band you only met twenty minutes ago.

I've eaten all manner of bizarre things in Japan from bird bones to testicles, hearts and every marine creature known to man. With time I began to realise that in Britain we are squeamish in our food habits, particularly with regards to meat. I understood that I needed to be broad-minded when it came to my diet and much else, but raw chicken is where I drew the line.

"Ah," crowed one chef as he watched me chew on chicken sashimi in one dingy little restaurant. "The British man is scared of raw chicken because in his country they're paranoid about it."

To me this type of statement would fit well beside 'Oh look the swimmer's afraid of sharks' or 'How odd, this guy is anti-cancer,' but nonetheless I chewed and swallowed and played the lottery that would or would not see me slumped on my knees against my loo that night in a sweaty fever. As it turned out, I was fine.

It wouldn't have been good manners to just spit things out. Japan is a country where respect for your fellow man is high on the list of priorities. My second encounter with raw chicken saw me routinely excusing myself to go to the toilet while on a date, as I would disappear with my mouth full and spit it down the squat lavatory. I just about got away with it and explained my frequent lavatory trips as a urinary infection, although perhaps on a date it would actually be less embarrassing to come clean with what I was trying to hide rather than some of the shameful excuses I concocted. Let's face it lads, she may not want to take you home that night because you spat chicken back onto a plate, but she'll be hailing a taxi in five seconds flat after you've informed her that you've got a urinary infection.

The Japanese always managed to present me with delicious meals, which roughly twenty percent of the time they would then ruin at the last possible moment by cracking a raw egg over the top just as I was about to take the first bite. Thus, 'without an egg' is one of the first phrases I learned, possibly before I even knew how to count to ten or say good morning.

***

The gulf between British and Japanese attitudes to food was arguably less pronounced than that which existed between attitudes to personal appearance. While girls in the fashionable Tokyo district of Shibuya routinely tanned their skin in pursuit of that golden tint so beloved of followers of 'Gyaru[52]' fashion, this ran counter to traditional Japanese ideals of beauty. For me, coming from a country where some of the more trend-conscious members of society sprayed themselves until they shone with an orange glow and waved away concerns over cancer as they lolled in sunbeds, this was an interesting counterpoint. Spend five minutes walking through any part of Japan on a summer's day and you'll see women of all ages walking and cycling by with long-sleeved t-shirts on. Those wearing t-shirts of the short-sleeved variety often wear separate sleeves designed solely for sheltering your skin from the sun. Many women wear large, tinted visors over their face and those on foot sport parasols.

If the 'gyaru girls' were an interesting anomaly and counterpoint to the mainstream, the 'gyaru' boys were even more striking. These were the skinny guys who hung around the Shinjuku district of Kabukicho[53] with their long copper or silver dyed

---

[52] A Japanese appropriation of the term 'gal' (girl). This style was particularly in vogue in the early 2000's and is characterised by tanned skin, dyed hair and garish and over the top clothing trends.

[53] An entertainment and red-light district in Tokyo. Kabukicho is often called 'Sleepless Town', a fitting moniker for the loudest, most garish and neon-filled area of Shinjuku, which is itself the busiest, most frenetic and buzzing entertainment district in all of Tokyo. Kabukicho contains many host and hostess clubs, bars, cinemas, restaurants, night clubs and love hotels. Kabukicho is also home to the Robot Restaurant. It is known as a centre of yakuza (organised crime activity), but it is nowhere near as dangerous for tourists as many exaggerated rumours and ill-informed travel guides suggest.

hair, shiny fake-diamond studded belts, skin-tight t-shirts and ripped jeans. They looked oddly effeminate with their high-heeled boots with the pointy toes and large buckles, their necklaces, and flawlessly smooth skin. Some even wore make up.

Kabukicho, more than anywhere else in Tokyo, has for a long time been home to a glut of hostess clubs with subservient women tending to the needs of men. Interestingly, a far more recent phenomenon is the burgeoning popularity of so-called 'host clubs.' During my time in Japan the fashion of the gyaru boys was typified by the workers in male host clubs and the touts who try to encourage women to enter them. Large billboards on the street show the gyaru boys making kissy faces, stroking kittens, pouting, and tilting their heads as they pull the 'v' for peace sign and doing all manner of other things to entice women into these establishments. Maybe this is a new liberated Japan. I am told the clubs contain none of the sleaze you might assume, but a relaxing haven away from the male-dominated world, the sometimes oppressive and overbearing Japanese patriarchy, where women can relax and be attended to, where they are in control and pay for the time and company of men rather than vice versa.

***

I suppose if you want to get a good idea of how a nation views itself collectively there is perhaps no better place to start than by examining how they view the rest of the world. I was always interested to discover which foreigners were well known in Japan. The Beatles, Oasis and David Beckham came as no surprise. Predictably, Brad-o Pitt-o was always a hit but some of the references were obscure. The popularity of the Pirates of the Caribbean movie franchise was at its peak during my time in Japan. It did fairly well in the West, but over there it was absolutely obsessed over. Cinemas sold out, my students talked about it, the Japanese just couldn't get enough. I'll wager that no fancy dress party took place on the Japanese archipelago in the late 2000s that didn't feature at least one Captain Jack Sparrow.

Cameron Diaz was a huge hit, presumably at least in part because she embodied such 'foreign' looks with her blonde hair and blue eyes. Mr Bean was considered the height of humour and little Japanese boys adored Thomas the Tank Engine. As well as the foreign Thomas and even the odd Postman Pat jumpers, the real idol for small children was the Japanese 'Anpanman'. He was a little man with the head of a bread roll stuffed with sweet soybean paste. It might not sound like your average superhero but then again neither does a postman from Yorkshire with a long nose and ginger hair accompanied by his cat - a public sector worker not famous for any feats of strength or an ability to fly or kill baddies but for the jovial way in which he greets old ladies and delivers letters. Anpanman has a series of sidekicks including 'Jam Ojisan', his grandad who naturally is a cheerful grey-haired jam doughnut.

Sometimes little chance encounters opened a small window into how the British were viewed. One day I arrived at the bike park near one of my schools to be greeted by one of the volunteers who worked there, a very chatty old man with long silver hair.

"Hello," he said, "where you from?"

"I'm from England."

"Oh, En-gu-lan-do! Very good. Za queen, za Beatles, Big-u Ben-u."

The following week on the same day I returned to park my bike and he was there once again.

"Where you from?" he asked.

"I'm from England," I replied, surprised that he hadn't remembered me from the previous week.

"Oh, En-gu-lan-do! Za Beatles, za queen, Big-u Ben-u."

I saw him only once more a couple of weeks later and once more he repeated the process. The sad truth is the sweet old man probably had Alzheimer's, but his snapshot image of British life was interesting and the repetitive nature of his brief conversations with me weren't uncommon in all walks of Japanese life.

One event which happened periodically was the school tea party. By late 2009 I was the senior teacher at Suginami school, responsible for increasing student numbers, mentoring staff and in general, coming up with ways to spruce up the English learning experience for all involved. The tea parties were a hit with the old and bold. They were like lessons but more relaxed.

I would make a pot of tea, put out the best china and lay out the tea cakes and cheese and pickle sandwiches for an 'authentic' British experience. We had scones with cream and jam, and whimsical marmite tasting sessions, where I watched the old ladies' wince and shiver. I lathered food stuffs with Worcestershire sauce and HP and the grandmothers nibbled on cheddar with such relish that you'd think I was serving them an exotic caviar. They loved it.

This was high culture at its finest. You couldn't have made it more British if you'd had a marching band of the Grenadier Guards in bear skins, Big Ben outside the window and the Red Arrows screaming through the gaps in Stonehenge to the strains of 'God Save the Queen'. It was trite, it was cliched, but that's what they wanted, and it brought in the crowds.

It was odd to sell yourself on where you were from and it was no accident that our school had a 'no Americans' policy in its recruitment of teachers, even though a few slipped through the cracks, and were in many cases some of the finest teachers in the company. Our school's main selling point was that it taught British English. The schools' interiors and exteriors were festooned with Union Jacks and pictures of the Blues and Royals and the Lifeguards in shiny helmets with red or white plumes on horseback. The U.K. was depicted through poster montages of red phone boxes, Beefeaters, thatched cottages, Big Ben and the Tower of London. Britain it seemed was a currency, and we traded it hard. We wrung every last drop of commercial opportunity out of our Britishness. It was quite a clever angle as it set us aside from the other schools in a saturated and very competitive market, but nonetheless it was slightly odd to see your country through the rose-tinted glasses of others.

***

Returning home was an interesting counterpoint. Was it possible that I'd unwittingly bought in to the stereotype of my own country that I'd helped to cultivate all those years? Did I really expect people to be picnicking on immaculate lawns with tea and scones and the very finest bone china the moment I arrived in the UK? Emerging into the arrivals lounge at Heathrow, maybe I'd lapsed into the same mindset that my students could be forgiven for having. Where were all the smart men in pinstripe suits? Twelve hours ago, I was in Japan with the peaked caps and the pristine white gloves. Where were the Rolls Royces and cucumber sandwiches?

There was one place that the students at our British English school were even more enamoured with than Blighty. France. More specifically, Paris. During a conversation with a colleague, he had casually mentioned *Paris Syndrome*. I asked what he'd meant. Did he not mean *Stockholm Syndrome*? I'd heard of that. No, he meant *Paris Syndrome*. It turns out it has nothing to do with terrorists or their captives but when someone explains what it is to you, as I have to others in the years since first finding out about it, their reaction is invariably the same as mine upon first being told. No, you must be joking.

If the trite images of bowler hats and umbrellas and Wimbledon tennis and gentlemen opening doors for elegant ladies was an over-simplified, cliched and unrepresentative view of modern Britain, then the Japanese views of Paris took things to a whole new level. Paris was perfect, it was romantic and sophisticated and elegant. It was paradise. But of course, Paris though nice in some ways, is not paradise, in much the same way as Tokyo and London and New York and Berlin are not paradise. Sure, there are fascinating and pretty buildings and museums and café culture, but the city is not without its faults. The Japanese just couldn't cope with this.

They'd been led to believe something that just wasn't true. The less than immaculate streets, the run-down areas of the capital, the graffiti and the crime, no worse and no better than in many European cities, did not befit the cliché. Perhaps what sets Paris Syndrome apart is that, unlike any other I've heard of it is suffered by one nationality of tourists visiting one city.

You would expect the Japanese embassy in a foreign country to have a hotline for tourists in dire need. There could be several reasons for such a thing. They might have been the victims of crime in that foreign country, they might fall acutely ill, they might need assistance with a visa or passport. You wouldn't however expect there to be a 24-hour hotline to the Japanese embassy in Paris for tourists suffering extreme culture shock. It is so severe that some of its sufferers require hospital treatment. In December 2006, four months before I moved into Whity Spot, it was reported on BBC News that

'A dozen or so Japanese tourists a year have to be repatriated from the French capital, after falling prey to what's become known as *Paris syndrome*.'

The article goes on to state that the experience can be 'too stressful for some and they suffer a psychiatric breakdown.' (Wyatt, 2006)

It all makes my little meltdown over the tin of corned beef look like a walk in the park.

It was easy to exaggerate in our own minds the paradise of Japan and just as easy to exaggerate to each other how dangerous or dirty or chaotic England was. It was tempting to think that you couldn't walk through the streets at night back at home without being attacked, to falsely imagine that you didn't know a single person who lived in London that hadn't been mugged at least once.

The reverse culture shock was that the staff at Heathrow didn't look immaculate. It was that the baggage handlers and other odd job men loafed about in scruffy high vis vests, leaning on brooms, chatting to each other idly despite the long queues of passengers. It was that we were no longer objects of curiosity to people in the street. Why aren't people staring at me. Don't you know, I'm a gaijin?

The shock at expectations not met was not all one way, however. Like anyone who has ever gone anywhere, I'd turned up in Tokyo full of pre-conceived ideas of the place and its people. Before I went to Japan, I had assumed that the most popular sports were martial arts. They are of course popular, but it turns out that baseball is to Japan what football is to England.

Walk for long enough down suburban streets and you'll find a young boy practising his pitching technique, and if you do find a dad not slaving away in the office, then he's as likely to be in the park with his son sporting a big brown leather glove, as doing anything else. To someone not familiar with modern Japan and its ways the Japanese love of baseball will come as a surprise. There I was back in the late noughties thinking that the USA were the undisputed top dog but watching aghast as Japan beat the Americans at their own game. Indeed, in the World Baseball Classic, an international tournament held since 2006, Japan has won half of the tournaments held to date.

***

In one aspect, our company's staff was diverse. The accents of the teachers were as much Glaswegian and Brisbane, Geordie and Brummie, Toronto and Somerset and the Welsh valleys as the 'Standard English' of the home counties. It was always amusing to watch children who for years had been taught by the same Scottish or Scouse or Cockney teacher speak in those same accents. It's not at all surprising. If that's the only accent in which you've heard English spoken, then of course you would adopt it. It was no different I suppose for me. When I travelled to various parts of Japan locals would remark on my 'Tokyo accent', which I found odd because I had just assumed that I was speaking 'standard Japanese', and in a way I suppose I was. Still, it made me chuckle to see little Taro, all of eight years old, remark "It's a booook," in a shrill Liverpudlian tone like Steven Gerard or to hear little Ryoko say, "I'm fine thank you," in a sing-song lilt because her teacher was from the Rhondda.

Even in my classes, although for the sake of easy comprehension I would always endeavour to keep my accent as close as possible to 'standard English', every now and then the Wiltshire burr would creep in. I noticed this not so much in my own speech but in the way the children I'd taught for years would say back to me, "My favourite fruit is strorbreez," or "He's a six-year-old chai-uld".

Of course, you can be selective with what you show of yourself or your country to the rest of the world. Japan after all was where we ex-pats essentially re-invented ourselves away from the reputations and expectations of home. The references were as expected as they were occasionally surprising. There was a kindergarten near my house in Tokyo, on the high metal gates of which stood the plastic figures of five squat Guardsman playing trumpets, drums and symbols. I doubt the toddlers behind those gates knew they were soldiers, let alone British. The scarlet tunics and bearskins were, I suppose, just the sort of over-the-top costumes the Japanese loved. Countless handbags and t-shirts and rucksacks sported Union Jack logos and there were nods to mod and rocker and punk fashion in odd and unexpected places. The icons were mostly archaic. They were butlers and lords and princesses; Britpop and football hooligans to those with their fingers slightly more on the pulse but even these were at best a decade out of date.

It is by no means only the Japanese who latch on to odd celebrities. I've no doubt that 'Shaky Hand Man[54]' from the noughties British show 'Banzai[55]' has never been heard of in Japan and I was just as surprised to discover that Peter Rabbit was everywhere in Japan (on a mountaintop on the edge of Kobe I once stumbled across a shop that sold nothing but Peter Rabbit merchandise) as I was to discover many years earlier when I briefly lived in Canada that Coronation Street was aired on their television sets.

---

[54] A Japanese character on the TV show 'Banzai' who would greet celebrities and shake their hands relentlessly.
[55] A spoof Japanese game show first aired in 2001 mocking the over the top and bizarre nature of Japanese game shows.

While I was in Japan, Barrack Obama was elected as president of the U.S. His election to office was welcomed across the country, but in one place it was celebrated more than others. On the Sea of Japan coast lies one of the nation's lesser-known prefectures, Fukui, which is small and largely rural. It is a region of deep valleys and heavy snows and sits at the crux of the 'Back of Japan[56]'. In a small fishing town in Fukui celebrations for Barrack's election hit fever pitch and were broadcast on national TV. NHK[57] showed cheering mothers holding up their babies, banners, cakes and photo opportunities galore, because they lived in the small town of 'Obama'.

Every year at the schools in mid-December, I would invariably dress up as Father Christmas for the children's Christmas party. Terrified three-year-olds clung to their mothers' legs as the parent prodded them towards the strange man dressed in red with a white beard. The child, on the verge of tears, would stand in fear as if abandoned by their guardian while mum happily captured their abject terror on her digital camera for posterity. Whether the children were aware that the sack was for carrying presents and not abducting them, I have no idea. As a child, it is of course wise council to shy away from strange men approaching you while clutching a sack large enough to hold you, and given the Japanese absence

---

[56] 'Ura Nihon' or 'The Back of Japan' is a term sometimes used for the Sea of Japan coast in the west facing Russia and the Korean peninsula, as opposed to the more developed and highly populated Pacific coast of Japan. It is a somewhat derogatory term implying backwardness due to its out of the way remote location and how undeveloped it is.

[57] Nippon Hoso Kyokai (Japan Broadcasting Corporation), Japan's national broadcaster, equivalent to the BBC of the U.K. Like the BBC, NHK is funded by viewers' licence fees.

of Christmas traditions, the children could certainly be forgiven for having misgivings about this odd man in fancy dress.

It is however not strictly true to say Japan has no Christmas traditions. Ever since a TV campaign a few decades ago by KFC, 'Kentucky for Christmas', it has become customary for Japanese people to eat KFC on Christmas Day. On 25th December every year, KFC staff all dress as Santa and enormous queues form down the street outside these fast-food outlets. People order their bucket of fried chicken in advance and really feel that they are having an authentic Western Christmas experience. Many of my students were crestfallen when I told them we didn't eat KFC on Christmas Day in Britain, and positively blown away when I explained that we didn't eat chicken at all but in fact turkey or occasionally goose.

"You don't eat KFC on Christmas Day?"

The Hoya school Christmas party was strictly for adults only, which I suppose is a good thing given the proclivities of the school owner. She was a cheerful lady in her late sixties. Respectable and well mannered, she was kind to her teachers and threw lavish Christmas parties at local restaurants each year for staff and students. The trouble was she'd get very drunk and come on to the male teachers. I'll never forget the first year I went. As I made my excuses to leave, she followed me into a quiet corner of the restaurant and said, "Please stay a little longer Tom," then grabbed my hand and put it on her breasts. "You can touch these if you want." But I didn't want. Dumbstruck, I smiled and left. The following year, thinking that what had happened twelve months before was an anomaly, an aberration, I went to the party again. But I hadn't been dreaming. I watched as she cornered my friend Nigel coming out of the restaurant toilets and stuck her hand down the front of his trousers. Judging by the pained look of disgust on his face, he definitely didn't want but she most certainly did.

***

The unusual views the Japanese often hold of the outside world appeared less surprising when I took into consideration the interesting perspectives they seemed to have on their own nation. It's no secret that the Japanese education authorities are as selective with the fragments of history they choose to include in school textbooks as they are creative with the interpretation of events they do see fit to include. The narrative of the Japanese attack on Pearl Harbour to many Western scholars is considered an unprovoked act of war. To a sizeable number of Japanese academics however, it is viewed as an unavoidable retaliatory strike on a superpower that was slowly suffocating Japan to death with trade embargos.

Certain events in world history become fixed in the collective consciousness, their very mention uniting all in quiet contemplation. Regardless of the moral and military rights and wrongs surrounding the decisions to drop enormous atomic bombs on cities full of civilians, and of the consequences of and alternatives to not doing so, everyone with even a scintilla of compassion recognises that the atomic bombings of Hiroshima and Nagasaki are tragedies of incomprehensible scale and misery. They were a previously unknown horror, a Pandora's box that once opened could surely never be firmly shut.

Around the world every year, memorials are held to commemorate these, the first and, mercifully only lives to succumb to the new horror - weapons of the nuclear age. However, there are no candlelit memorials in the West for the more than 100,000 Tokyo residents who died in one night of American firebombing alone, far more than in either atomic bomb strike. The carnage caused by the incendiary bombs that turned the largely wooden-built capital city into a raging inferno in February 1945 exacerbated by the closely packed buildings, while no less a tragedy, is little known outside of Japan.

It is hard to visit Hiroshima or Nagasaki without being deeply moved. Standing by the peace dome in the centre of Hiroshima, one of very few buildings for miles to survive on that fateful day, saved by its being directly below the bomb's detonation, I found the horror hard to imagine. Given the nearby proximity of the vibrant heart of the city with its trams, cafes, nightclubs and shopping malls, just a stone's throw from the memorial park and peace dome, if you turned your back you could be forgiven for thinking you were in any modern Asian metropolis. The suffering of that August day and many thereafter became far easier to imagine after I strolled through the large memorial park, past the river that boiled that fateful day in the intense heat, and I entered the museum.

It is of course not only the Japanese who are selective in their memories of the past. Every nation on Earth is guilty of a reimagining of their nation's glorious or inglorious history, but it was the magnitude of Japan's omissions that staggered me. It wasn't that I found the emphasis given to the devastation of Japan in the war surprising. What did take me by surprise however was the lack of knowledge of what happened outside of Japan.

I remember once when talking to Yuka about the bombing of British cities during World War 2.

"Who was bombing Britain?" she asked me.

"Who do you think?" I replied.

"Was it the Russians?"

"No, the Russians were on our side."

"Oh, it was the Americans?"

"No, they were on our side too."

"Who was it then?"

"It was the Germans, of course."

"The Germans. Why would they bomb Britain?"

It is all too easy to scoff at others so perhaps at this juncture I should turn the mirror towards myself. Sometimes I marvelled at just how much of an ignorant idiot I could be. There was a little shrine a short walk from Nogata station on the corner of a road. It was a small wooden affair with long sweeping red fabric draped from its sides on which were imprinted two large swastikas. How dare they?! I had thought at the time, angry at the fact that they were still celebrating their wartime alliance with Germany. But I was wrong. Yuka pointed out that the swastika was the ancient symbol of peace connected with the traditional Japanese religion of Shinto and of course, to anybody who isn't as pea brained as me, it obviously had nothing at all to do with the war. Absolute idiot!

***

Japan's complicated relationship with 'the West' is perhaps displayed nowhere more starkly than in Japan's use of foreign words, particularly English. The Japanese have borrowed words in much the same way as other nations do, indeed in much the same way that Latin and French terms have been absorbed into English. They have appropriated the German word for job 'arbeit' and use it to refer specifically to part time jobs as 'arubaito'. 'Tarento' (talent) is used for TV personalities and there is no Japanese word for bread, so they simply use the French 'pan'. Romantic couples are referred to as 'abekku' a mispronunciation of the French 'avec'. Some of the references however were more obscure. If you wore a smart suit it would be said you had a nice 'sebiro'. This derived from Savile Row, the famous street of tailors in London. The list of foreign words the Japanese have borrowed is endless. They are occasionally tricky to decode with their altered pronunciation and unusual origins. At the more bizarre end of the spectrum there are such phrases as 'datchi waifu' (Dutch wife), the Japanese phrase for a sex doll.

The borrowing of words between English and Japanese was just as prevalent however in the opposite direction. Most people in the West, even amongst the older generation, know what sushi, karaoke, karate, ninjas, samurai, geisha, kimono, origami and tsunamis are. A significant number of younger Americans and Europeans would be familiar with a whole plethora of Japanese terms from sashimi, katana[58], kawaii[59], manga, anime, emoji, shiatsu, wasabi. In many cases people use these terms not knowing from where they originate. In much the same way, Japanese friends of mine would appear shocked when I informed them that many of the words they used and believed to be 'Japanese' originated from my native land. The cultural exchange is far from one-way and by no means simply from West to East.

***

How's this for irony? Perhaps no single Japanese-English loan word has permeated world culture as much as 'karaoke'. The word literally means empty (kara) orchestra (oke). What's ironic is that, though the word karaoke has been appropriated into English and many other languages from Japanese, the ending 'oke' is itself a loan from English. The Japanese pronounce orchestra 'o-ke-su-to-ra'. Karaoke is therefore a half Japanese half bastardised English Japanese word which has been appropriated by the rest of the world. So Japanese.

Say karaoke to a British person and they think of a drunk bloke with curry stains on his shirt in the Kings Arms on a Friday night murdering Bohemian Rhapsody, but karaoke in Japan is a whole different affair. It is huge, almost to the point of an obsession. Whole tower blocks in Japanese cities are given over to it. Some of them are ten floors high and have twenty rooms on each floor ranging in size from those designed for a single person to rooms that cater for

---

[58] A traditional Japanese curved sword used by samurai in feudal Japan.
[59] The Japanese word for 'cute'. Overused and ubiquitous throughout Japanese society.

groups of up to thirty. The people who do it alone practise for when they have to do it for real in front of their colleagues. You can even find karaoke parlours in the middle of nowhere amongst rice fields at the foot of mountains.

Of course, in typical Japanese fashion, it is taken to the nth degree. There are themed rooms and racks of costumes in the lobby you can wear. Most karaoke places are open very late, if not twenty-four hours. They serve drinks and hot and cold food straight to the room. It's very easy to lose hours in the karaoke buildings constantly ringing up reception from the phone in your room for more octopus balls or fried chicken and fries and more beer or orange juice or tea or a new ashtray because yours is full as you've got through a whole pack of Mild Sevens somewhere between 'Wonderwall' and 'Hey Jude'.

It is a timeless warp, as you wander off intermittently to the drinks bar, or more naughtily to other rooms, which you gate crash. Even the scuffles with the room full of twenty-year-old firefighters was fun, because what happens at karaoke stays at karaoke. It is where the Japanese let loose after long workdays and journeys to and from the office on silent and packed trains in the stifling heat. It is where neckties are loosened and too much alcohol is drunk, and all the hits are sung too loudly and increasingly off-key with every beverage consumed.

Nigel told me that on his first night in Japan he'd ended up at karaoke in Osaka with a group of drunk Japanese businessmen he'd only met a couple of hours previously. One got over-excited during a rendition of his favourite song and as his singing reached a crescendo, he jumped on a sofa and dashed his beer glass onto the floor. And of course, people are drunk because it's one-hour, or two-hour, or all night 'all you can drink'. The 'all you can drink' policy of many restaurants, bars and karaoke places was something that I imagined just wouldn't work back at home. Were we expats exaggerating when we imagined the carnage that would ensue back at home, or was it really true that it would be a recipe for disaster back in Plymouth and Nottingham and Cardiff? Were we yet again just mythologizing about how drunk and out of control we Brits were?

The first year I travelled home for Christmas I had the bright idea of not going to sleep at all the night before. Instead, I'd spend the night merrily singing away at karaoke with Yuka and then head to the airport. My logic was that I'd be so tired after a sleepless night that I'd be able to do the one thing I was otherwise always incapable of doing, sleeping on a plane. At first glance my theory was fairly watertight. When flying direct the journey took twelve hours, and you felt tired enough if you failed to nod off with the resulting jetlag. I however couldn't afford a direct flight so instead had booked an indirect flight via Bangkok - six hours from Tokyo to Bangkok and twelve hours from Bangkok to London. If I'd thought about my plan of not sleeping, I'd have realised that it was as likely to be a disaster if I failed to sleep on the plane as it was to be a stroke of genius if I did. It wasn't just the eighteen hours of flying I needed to take into consideration. With the wait in Bangkok between flights and the distances to and from airports at either end, door to door this would be a thirty-one-hour slog.

I sang the night away with my huge suitcase crammed into the small karaoke room. As dawn broke, red eyed and with a hoarse voice, I rolled my suitcase to the nearby station and headed to the airport ready to flop. Can you imagine how it felt, the relief of six hours and then twelve hours of wonderful, peaceful, soothing deep sleep on both my flights after over thirty hours of being awake? I can't because I didn't sleep a wink.

Home for the first time in nearly a year, I can only imagine what I looked like after nearly sixty hours with no sleep as I wheeled my suitcase and dragged myself through the sliding doors from baggage collection to the arrival lounge at Heathrow. What on Earth must my family have thought as this pale, zombie-like creature appeared?

So, this is what Japan does to people!

***

In the years to come, I would travel home every year for two weeks at Christmas and occasionally in the summer for the odd wedding or other special occasion. Central Tokyo was familiar and rural Wiltshire was home. There shouldn't have been any surprises or feelings of disjointedness when arriving in two places I knew so well. However, the transit between the two was poleaxing for the emotions. It was almost as if it just wouldn't translate, my mind just couldn't compute the abrupt shift because the difference was too vast. The jet lag, the disoriented feeling and the disruption to your body clock are due to covering huge distances at an unnatural speed. I think in many ways culture shock works in a similar way. If you were to travel overland to the Far East, you would witness and experience gradually the slowly changing landscape and people. The cultures would shift in increments and the evolution would be natural, giving you time to assimilate and process it in your mind.

Flying from Europe to Tokyo is like arriving suddenly at extreme altitude and the tiredness and jet lag that go with it only exacerbates this feeling of cultural disjointedness. I'd find myself sitting in my flat crying after returning to Tokyo and not knowing why. I wasn't sad, it was sometimes just all too much. One minute you're sitting around the dinner table with your family having Christmas dinner in a familiar setting, the next you are back in the madness that is Tokyo.

The moments of nostalgic impact were more intense than I could ever have imagined. It was all about the long drive south west out of Heathrow and away from London and then the rolling fields of barley and the little metal pig houses and then finally and unmistakably from miles in the distance, the first stone-grey hint of that majestic lofty spire, its top poking through the trees. With my face pressed sleepily against the window as the tight bends in the road and the high hedgerows gave way to open stretches, it wasn't neon signs and skyscrapers flashing by but a lush green summer vista with animals grazing in the fields or a quaint snow-blanketed chocolate-box picture of cottages and chimney smoke.

A world away from the frenetic pace of the Eastern metropolis, I felt a lump in my throat as I stared at the deep green of the grass and heard the familiar caw of the birds in the trees. It was roast potatoes and BBC news. It was the scrape of the wooden chairs on a stone kitchen floor. It was the dulcet Wiltshire tones and the owl in the tree beside my house that hissed like a snake the moment you opened the car door in the driveway. It was a sense of permanence, of things strongly built and long-lasting.

Like the pathetic Western weakling that I am there were times I would cling to all things that reminded me of home. In Nogata there is a foreign food store called 'Jupiter' where I would greedily stock up on cornflakes, Twinings tea and Cadbury's chocolate in a spree of gastronomic nostalgia. It was expensive but brought me an amount of joy disproportionate to its monetary value. Perhaps for all my snobbish looking down the nose at the fat, red expats on the Benidorm beaches, I wasn't so different from them after all.

I would long, when back in Japan, a land of impermanence, of newbuilds, of ever-changing cityscapes, for Digestive biscuits and Jaffa Cakes, builder's tea in chunky mugs, Match of the Day and proper beds. I never stayed in England long enough to grow irritable with it, although if I did, I surely would, and Japan would no doubt beckon as a land of intrigue and ease and excitement. I couldn't have had two homes more different, and neither would I have wanted to. Sometimes though it was just a little too overwhelming. There was too much to take in. I was overstimulated and couldn't even identify quite what was going on in my head, let alone articulate it in any meaningful way.

Chapter 13

'Get Out of the Pool!'

Breaking rules and the sleep deprived nation

When you enter the village, obey the village.
Japanese proverb

It's fairly hard to conform when you are patently, visibly different to everyone else. I've no doubt at some point or other every foreigner living in Japan has wished to just fit in. Of course, being different has its benefits but you have no choice and couldn't blend in with the crowd if you wanted to. At Japanese baseball games there are designated chant leaders and the crowd sing in time and in unison to set songs during certain parts of the game. It's a world away from West Ham vs Millwall. That nobody swears or tells the ref he's a wanker and needs glasses is obviously a good thing. That nobody comes up with imaginative and witty chants on the spot that they'll then daringly lead the goal-end in, I believe is less so. I find it hard to reconcile the organised support with passion and pride, but then again nobody gets glassed at the Yakult Swallows[60] vs Seibu Lions[61] game and the fans are more likely to hang about to clean up than to take on the away firm.

I once stumbled across a punk rock concert in a Tokyo park. Surely punk rock, the most anarchistic of

---

[60] Japanese professional baseball team based in central Tokyo.
[61] Japanese professional baseball team based just outside of Tokyo in the neighbouring prefecture of Saitama.

all music types, would encourage unruly behaviour and a divergence from the rules? What I saw when the band began their most popular number was the crowd swaying in time, all of the several thousand pairs of arms swaying in perfect unison from left to right, everyone standing in neat rows and nearly every one of them wearing exactly the same T-shirt with the band's name printed in neon pink across the back of it.

It was inevitable that before long I would break the rules, unwittingly but in spectacular fashion, and when I did it happened in a swimming pool. After much befuddlement, a charming member of staff had helped me with the ticket vending machine at the entrance, for which I was very grateful. I didn't know what any of the buttons were for, there were at least twenty of them and all I wanted to do was swim. I had my brand-new swimming trunks and my goggles. I hadn't forgotten my 100-yen coin for the locker, and I knew what time the swimming pool closed. I had my locker key on its rubber band around my wrist and I'd showered before I got in. What more could you possibly need?

I dived in at the deep end and then it started. I heard the whistle while I was still underwater. It sounded as shrill and as loud as any noise I'd heard in my life. It was almost as if the very pitch of it conveyed the anger of the pool attendant. Muffled though it was to my submerged ears, I didn't want to come up. I wondered how long I could stay below the surface. How long could I hold my breath? long enough that by the time I surfaced the stout little woman with the whistle would have forgotten about me? Alas, no. And as I slowly rose, my cheeks already flushed with embarrassment, I knew it was me. I knew *I* had been the idiot. I knew *I* had done something wrong. In those brief seconds I wondered what on Earth my transgression could be? I had concluded that there must be a 'no diving' rule. I'd apologise and vouch never to do it again.

As my head emerged from the water everyone had stopped and was looking my way. I had felt self-conscious enough walking to the edge of the pool with my hairy chest and hairy feet like some bizarre furry foreign hobbit, but my by-now bright red face was a glowing beacon to all. Look at the foreign prat. The eyes of the splashing families were laser beams but that was nothing. The squat little pool attendant removed the whistle from her mouth and pointed straight at me.

"Where is your swimming cap?"

My swimming cap? And then it dawned on me. As I looked around, with my stupid pasty hairy legs treading water frantically beneath me, I noticed something that had at first completely passed me by. Everyone, absolutely everyone was wearing a swimming cap including the cheerless pool attendant. She pointed with an angry finger back in the direction of the changing room.

Well, if people hadn't been staring at my strange semi-naked figure until this point, they certainly were now. I bowed and waved and grinned feebly as I apologised to the angry woman and headed back out to the changing room. I was so flustered I didn't even have the wherewithal to dry myself off and get changed. Instead, I traipsed dripping wet to the reception desk and the kind man who'd helped me obtain my ticket from the vending machine. The mouths of the children and their young father who were standing at the desk were agape. Who was this beast that had just crawled out of a swamp? Daddy, help!

I pointed at my head like a bad mime artist and shivered and said, "Swimming cap please." The man laughed with his female colleague and produced a tray from under the desk. It contained swimming caps, swimming caps for people who had been foolish enough to arrive without one. They were rented for 50 yen and looked like they had been sewn by a charitable grandmother. They were like a swimming-based dunce hat which not only highlights the misdemeanours of the person forced to wear it but makes them look like a clown at the same time.

"That'll be fifty yen please," said the man.

"Oh," I said as I dripped all over his pristine ledger.

He stared at me in disdain as he wiped off the drips. I flapped around in apology for my dripping, my apologetically flailing limbs only serving to spray water further across the desk and the astonished children. I should have been glad by this point that I looked like Mr Bean, the Japanese loved him. But Mr Bean is perhaps only funny to watch from afar, to cringe at his buffoonish mistakes from the detached distance of your sofa. But when Rowan Atkinson's idiot character turned up at your workplace it was perhaps harder to see the funny side.

I plodded back into the locker room and discovered I hadn't a clue where my locker was. After five minutes of being viewed suspiciously by everyone in the changing room as I put my key into one locker after another, I found it. I trudged back out to the reception desk, fifty yen in hand, and waited still sopping wet behind a queue of newly arrived swimmers. After enduring the round of astonished looks and comments of the fresh arrivals, I handed over my money and was given a swimming cap that looked like one of granny's tea cosies.

By this time, I almost didn't want to swim. I almost wanted to just give up and go home. I certainly didn't want to head back out to the pool and the queueing masses waiting for Bozo the clown to perform an encore, and I certainly didn't want to clap eyes on Mrs Trunchbull the pool attendant again. But I'd come this far so I bloody well would. I re-emerged and, just in case it turned out that diving also was a transgression, I decided to use the metal steps. I tried to be light footed, I tried to be inconspicuous but the hairy chest and legs and hobbit feet and tea cosy on my head made this impossible. Worst of all, the only set of steps was next to Trunchbull. I smiled and bowed and to my enormous relief she grinned and nodded and laughed and she didn't seem so fierce after all. She almost seemed nice. And I've no doubt I'd provided her with an anecdote to tell at home and at parties for years to come. *First, he walks out looking like a pale gorilla, then he dives in without a swimming cap. Urgggh! So, we put a tea cosy on his head.*

The entire incident had left me so abashed that I didn't even have the energy to be giddy over the swimming trunks drying machine in the changing rooms which was like a cross between a hand dryer and a washing machine. And, in my new state of high alert, desperate to not make any more slip ups, I paid heed to the notice that warned you not to leave the swimming trunks in for more than ten seconds or they might catch fire. That would simply be too much. I had done enough for today. The dripping journeys to and from the reception desk, the hairy body, the strange feet, the tea cosy on my head and the vending machine incompetence were all enough without burning down the building.

***

Refreshingly, every now and then I'd get a glimpse of those who weren't bothered about blending in, those who refused to conform, the rebels who bucked the trend and didn't give a damn for convention. One such person was Mrs Okuma. I met her within the first week of moving to Tokyo and she brought a ray of sunshine into my life. Nearly all convenience stores in Japan are chains although occasionally you stumble across a privately run business. Okuma's convenience store, a two-minute walk from my flat, was a family run business. 'Okuma' means 'bear' in Japanese. The shop sign sported a picture of a massive teddy bear and I suppose in some ways Mrs Okuma was like a friendly old bear. When I say Mrs Okuma, I'm referring to the white-haired grandmother, because technically I've no doubt several of the ladies who worked there were called 'Mrs Okuma'. Okuma's was the shop where I'd bought that small tin of corned beef on my first day in Japan. It was open twenty-four hours a day and was a beacon of light. Mrs Okuma looked like Joe Pesci's mother in Goodfellas with her curly white hair, glasses and a big warm-hearted smile.

Most strikingly of all, Mrs Okuma treated me with more kindness than any other single person (bar Yuka) that I met. The very first time I bumped into her she cornered me with a grin and was delighted to find out I had moved into the area. From then on, she'd greet my appearance with winks and grins and regale me with tales of her family, stories from her youth, questions about my friends, my girlfriend and my job. She'd ask after my mother and what the weather was like in England. Whenever Yuka would enter the shop with me, Mrs Okuma would clutch her by the forearm in a most un-Japanese way, more like an old Italian lady, and cluck and coo, and tell us what a lovely couple we were and say how beautiful Yuka was and what a nice young man she'd found.

One day Mrs Okuma showed me a black and white photograph of a man in immaculate navy whites leaning on the railings of a ship.

"This was my father," she said. "He was in the Navy. He sailed to England. London. Glasgow. Portsmouth."

She once gave me two large expensive looking calendars that she'd fetched from upstairs, huge scroll-like wall hangings with beautiful calligraphy. But my most vivid memories of Mrs Okuma were of her marvellous theft. From the very first week Mrs Okuma would sidle up to me after I'd paid and was heading for the shop door, wink at me and whisper in my ear then grin and usher me to one side and surreptitiously stuff a loaf of bread into my carrier bag. Sometimes it was a yoghurt or a bar of chocolate or a bunch of bananas. It happened most of the times I bumped into her in the shop, and more often than not it was bread. We'd go through the same hilarious ritual every time. I'd grin and protest and say that "I couldn't, but thank you," and she'd insist and grin and stuff it in, nonetheless. It was only food from the reduced shelf, but I'm sure it still got the tacit disapproval of the younger members of the family.

The cheekiness and the friendliness and the naughtiness and the easy familiarity, the lack of distancing from me because I was other, I loved it because it was all so brilliantly unconventional. She couldn't have given a toss for convention, and why should this ninety-year-old woman who'd no doubt lived through the war and goodness knows what else? It was heart-warming and in those tough early days it lifted my spirits immeasurably to know that I had my own little Japanese grandmother living just fifty metres away.

When I first returned to Japan four years after I'd left, I went to Okuma's to find her. I spoke to a younger lady behind the checkout and asked after her. I was sad to discover she was senile and confined to an upstairs room. The younger woman explained that she didn't recognise anybody anymore. I left the shop almost in tears because that place was so familiar, the aisles, the red sign with the picture of a cartoon bear on it, the smells. But the old lady, the gregarious, generous, wonderful old lady was now confined to her room where she didn't stuff bread naughtily into the carrier bags of young foreign men and she didn't give out hugs to their girlfriends and ask after their mothers.

The shop floor was quiet without her and minus her presence the few staff I saw that day had the usual impersonal air about them. The shop almost seemed to have died in spirit. It is sad but I cherish the fond memories. I haven't been back in some time. I would love to know if Mrs Okuma is still in this world but if she is, I'd rather not think of her sitting up in her room alone but somewhere in a corner of the shop looking around cheekily as she stuffs a loaf of bread into someone's carrier bag.

***

To overcome the homesickness, I threw myself into fitness in a big way. It provided routine and was a welcome outlet for the pent-up stresses and strains of living in such a bewildering place. I'd lift weights three nights a week and use the cycling machines on alternating three nights, giving myself one day's rest. The gym rules were: No soap in the showers - an issue over which I repeatedly got in trouble (apparently this had to do with soap getting into the water system - heaven forbid!); no shoes to be worn in the changing room; no shoes on the gym mats; thorough wiping of all gym equipment after use, and absolutely no unnecessarily loud noises. Oddest of all were the unfathomable days when the gym would be closed. Try as I might, I couldn't work it out and still turned up after four years to find the gym closed every so often. It was something like, 'Every fourth Thursday when the moon is waxing' or 'Every Wednesday that falls on an odd number when the North Star is visible.'

The staff at Kami Igusa gym were developing quite a hobby. It went something like this: Let's all gather round the gaijin on the bike machine and watch him sweat and then one of us will fetch a mop and while the others stand around and gasp and laugh and point, I'll soak up the results of this barbarian's exertions and wonder aloud if all foreigners sweat this much.

**

The nightclubs were fun without the raucous behaviour of home. Even the dancing seemed organised. Neat rows of young men at Ageha nightclub down on Tokyo bay with wispy goatee beards in baggy jeans and even baggier white t-shirts performed the latest hip hop moves in formation. They would dance in rows like an urban incarnation of a Texan line dance by the swimming pool with the five am sun slowly rising behind the DJ hut. How no one fell or was pushed into the pool was amazing, and surely the wisdom of having a deep pool in a dance area of an establishment where most people are drunk has to be called into question. Japan is 'safety' country.

Outside the nightclubs in central Tokyo, as the early morning revellers headed home, members of staff would stand ten metres apart strung out down the streets in long lines. They'd put their fingers to their lips to remind the punters as they staggered off into the dawn light to please refrain from making any noise, in case they disturbed local residents. Everyone obeyed, no one told them to piss off, no one was fighting in the street or telling the staff they should mind their own business. Even amongst the hedonistic and reckless abandon of a drunken night out, the rules were followed.

***

As well as the explicit rules and customs, every culture has a set of implicit norms that are followed almost subconsciously. This is a minefield for the newly arrived as these habits are nuanced and subtle. You won't find them listed in the dog-eared copy of Lonely Planet you chucked into your suitcase between your y-fronts and wart cream. One of these oddities was the Japanese sleeping habits. What a psychiatrist in the West would make of the standard end of workday expression that Japanese people say to one another, I'd be fascinated to know. In most parts of the world, it would be 'See you later' or 'Well done today' but in Japan 'Ot-suka-ra-sa-ma-deshii-ta' roughly translates as 'Thank you for exhausting yourself today'.

Exhausting yourself in Japan it turns out is a virtue. One need only ride the trains of urban Japan to see how tired everyone is, children included, and you must be pretty tired to be able to fall asleep on a rattling train. Teachers in schools forgive children who fall asleep at their desks as this clearly shows they've been working hard. But is quantity of work really as important as quality? The old adage in Japan of working 9-9-6 speaks volumes, and the knock-on effects of fathers who work from nine 'til nine, six days a week on their families, not to mention their own physical and mental health, must be immense.

From TV commercials encouraging people to keep going to the profusion of energy drinks in many vending machines, you can see that Japan is a nation in which working until exhaustion equals a job well done. It's a well-known cliché for anyone who's lived in Japan, and probably by now also for many who haven't, that the junior employees often don't leave the office until the manager does. Perhaps being seen to work is more important than working itself. Children would come to my lessons exhausted. They'd been to school all day and when I'd see them off at the end of our evening lesson, usually they would not head home but to their cram school where they'd stay until eight or nine pm before heading home to do their homework.

It wasn't just the lack of sleep that was apparent but the odd places where people did it. To nod off on a train or bus was one thing but visiting the local internet café I was astonished to discover that people slept there. In fact, people lived there. For the people that fell between the cracks, lost their jobs or had just generally fallen on hard times, with the monthly rent on an apartment beyond their means, a small compartment in an internet cafe was home. What more did they need? There were toilets, sometimes showers, hot food and drink vending machines, unlimited access to the internet and a soft sofa-cum-bed on which to sleep in a modicum of privacy. They lived in a black, windowless, subterranean world. The walls in the internet cafes were black, the computers were black, the four foot by seven-foot wooden cubicles themselves were black and so were the leather sofa beds within them.

You needn't spend much time in Japan before you hear the phrases 'fight', 'gaman' (endure) and 'gambatte' (good luck/keep striving) being used routinely by all and sundry. To strive, to endure, to persist can often seem almost more important than to succeed, to prevail and to achieve. This manifests itself in many ways. I've noticed Japanese people love taking the hottest possible baths, emerging as red as lobsters. They will stay in saunas until they can't bear it anymore and relish drinking liquids that are almost too hot to bear. "Nekojita[62]!" (Cat tongue!) they would say and laugh at me when I blew on ramen broth to cool it down.

There is evidence everywhere in Japan that taking things to the maximum is deemed desirable. Was I living among sadists? Every week I taught a young couple in their twenties called Hiroyuki and Miyuki. Hiroyuki apologised once for having missed three previous lessons with me. In what I initially took to be a joke, he explained to me that he had been unable to come as he hadn't left the office for a month. Taking this to be a deliberate exaggeration, much in the same way as a British person might complain about walking 'miles' or that the weather was 'boiling' hot, I let out a little laugh.

It became apparent however as I read the deadly serious expression on his face, that he was speaking literally. I proceeded to ask the questions that are no doubt on your mind as you read this. How did he eat? where did he sleep? And where did he wash? He informed me with no fanfare, as if it was a perfectly normal set of circumstances, that he slept at his chair,

---

[62] A slang term meaning 'cat tongue' to describe people with a sensitive tongue who are incapable of drinking or eating anything hot. Usually used in speech and in jest.

ate from the office vending machine and that there was a staff shower in the office. The one question I never asked was how he changed his clothes, and I can only hope that somehow, he did.

***

Of course, I am generalising. There were people who did break the rules and when I saw it happen it was sometimes in the strangest of places. I had never expected to witness one clear example of rule-breaking on a tiny little island nine miles offshore from Nagasaki. Then again, I hadn't expected to be thinking of Daniel Craig either. On a clear day one August, I boarded a boat with about fifty Japanese people and headed for Gunkanjima, ('Battleship Island') so called because of its shape and silhouette. We passed huge shipyards full of cranes and warehouses and beautiful little inlets covered in jungle-like thick green foliage over small subtropical islands. The man on the loudspeaker pointed out a church high on a mountaintop and explained that it was where a small group of Christians had held out several hundred years ago before eventually being brutally murdered for their faith.

However, I wasn't here to learn about murdered Christians or to view shipyards. I was here to see battleship island. Gunkanjima would be familiar to anyone who has seen the Bond movie Skyfall. It is the dilapidated and deserted island on which the villain forces James to shoot a glass of whisky off a young woman's head, although I'm reliably informed that the island in the film is a studio mock-up of the real island.

The island's real name is Hashima. Coal mines were opened there in 1887 and in 1959 the tiny island's population peaked at over five thousand people. The mines closed in 1974 and soon after the island was abandoned. As well as the mining site, bleak concrete housing blocks, which are crammed on to every inch of available space, tower over the tiny streets below. It certainly would have been a hard and cramped experience back in the day. As the hulking form of the island appeared on the horizon our guide informed us that at the time of its use it was the most densely populated piece of real estate on Earth.

With the island looming ever nearer, our guide tells us that we will try today to stop at the island and get off the boat and have a look around, however this is usually only possible on about one in every three trips as the sea is often too rough. He emphasises repeatedly that this piece of Japanese real estate is strictly off limits to everyone except organised and licensed boat tours. Perhaps my barometer for the state of the sea that day should have been the elderly woman bent double from the moment we stepped on the boat with her head between her knees vomiting and groaning and having her back rubbed by her worried daughter. The fifty or so Japanese and one gaijin on board (minus the puking granny) snapped away, recording for posterity this interesting place from all angles as the boat did a full circumnavigation of the island.

It turns out that the seasick old woman is a poor indicator of sea conditions because all of a sudden, and to our immense surprise, the coxswain announces it's fine to dock and I've no doubt the poor old lady would welcome a little time on dry land. As the sun beat down on us at midday and the temperature soared to 38, our tour guide showed us round the quarter of the island we were allowed to see. It's a truly fascinating yet haunting place and I wouldn't spend the night there if you paid me. Every inch is concreted over on this dystopian industrial rock. We were barred entry to three quarters of the island because it is deemed unsafe and culturally sensitive, so thank god for zoom lenses. Even at this distance we could see the relics of abandoned lives, chairs and tables in apartments whose walls had crumbled, an upturned pram or handcart rusting in the courtyard below.

Amongst the fascinating tour and eerie sights, the old woman, who was by now leaning over a railing and looking green, couldn't give a damn because right then I'm sure she'd spend a whole week on this island alone just to get rid of the feeling that her spleen was doing cartwheels around her large intestine. But she couldn't because the guide through his megaphone instructed us that we needed to head back to the boat. We were each handed a frozen hand towel and the back rubbing started again in earnest.

"Here you go Michiko. Maybe a frozen hand towel will make you feel better."

"Shove off."

Curiously, as we set off, I noticed two or three men with long fishing rods standing in the shadows up on the high walls of battleship island deep within the area we were forbidden from entering, the three quarters of the island supposedly 'off-limits' to visitors. When I quizzed the guide on this, he got rather flustered and, in a state of embarrassment, reluctantly gave a vague explanation that they shouldn't have been there but that they came on little boats and it was hard to stop them.

We were each handed a small packet containing a tiny lump of Hashima's coal and arrived happily back in Nagasaki. The old lady was now positively turquoise, but I was beaming. However, a niggling question remained in my mind. Those ghostly figures upon the sea wall that surrounded Gunkanjima, they weren't following the rules. That wasn't very Japanese. But I suppose, all things considered, if you are going to break the rules perhaps the best place to do it is in a place we associate with that greatest of renegades, the maverick British secret agent, Bond, James Bond. No licence to fish.

Chapter 14

You Can't Sit There, That's Takako's Seat

Knowing your place: Sumo wrestlers and bossy old ladies

The nail that sticks out gets hammered down.
Japanese proverb

The first lesson of the day for most teachers in my company was an hour-long 'old ladies lesson'. Of course, it wasn't marketed as such but 1pm-2pm tended to consist of classes of between four and six old ladies and was very much conversational in nature. We covered no great swathes of grammar and in truth probably made little or no progress, but they loved it. They loved the ritual, and they loved the drama, and I know that many felt this was high culture at its most cosmopolitan and chic. In truth it was a one-hour chat about trivial rubbish in a dingy windowless room with a group of ladies who, more often than not, were secretly vying for top dog position in the class.

I didn't realise this at first. At first, I believed that the women were best friends, but it tended to be a veneer. They all wanted to be teacher's pet and sit closest to me and it was enough to sit staring at the British man and to 'be there' without really needing to go to the hassle of actually learning English. One such class I had was positively a war zone. The outward appearance of smiles and false courtesy between the students was a wafer-thin veil.

Whenever a new student joined the group, they were scrutinised like an outsider to the tribe.

"No, you can't sit there," said Michiko to one terrified woman on her first day as she entered the room. "That's Takako's seat."

The woman smiled and chose another chair.

"No, you can't sit there. That's Tamako's chair."

The poor woman appeared on the verge of tears and looked to me for help. It was my job to mediate, it was my job to intervene and solve the petty squabbles of these seventy-three-year-olds going on three.

"Actually," I piped up full of righteousness, "anyone can sit wherever they like. No student has an assigned seat."

The room fell silent and the women all nodded in unison in reverence to my comment. I sat back imperiously. Move over UN secretary general. The pecking order not only applied to where people sat but to who got to speak first and for longest. The length of time you'd been in the class seemed to carry with it a prestige. The new students bowed deeply, nodded and made noises of wonderment at everything their seniors said, a good example of just how hierarchical Japanese society can be.

Where real conflict occurred was when you had a student come into a group who was better at English than the remainder of their 'seniors'. If this was discovered, they would be treated with disdain as upstart imposters who should know their place. I saw more than one instance of a new student joining who refrained from using their true level of English just to fit in. If they arrived first for class, they'd chat away quite fluently to me but then upon the arrival of their judgemental and jealous classmates they'd retreat into themselves and become quiet. Then there were the gobshites, the ones that never shut up. In a children's class it's quite easy to turn to one 7-year-old boy and tell him that it is someone else's turn to speak but how do you do that when he's sixty-seven and a high-flying businessman?

***

In the West we are taught to respect elders. I can't imagine there's any part of the world where this isn't a basic tenet of society, however in Japan hierarchies are taken to a whole different level. Relationships between two colleagues, schoolmates or club members are often defined by an informal interpersonal hierarchy known as 'senpai' and 'kohai'. The seniority of the relationship may be due to hierarchy, age, status, level or experience or, more often than not, a combination of those. While the senpai are responsible for guiding and counselling the kohai, the kohai in turn should show respect, gratitude and a willingness to learn. Senpai-kohai relationships in Japan are a crucial bind, a glue that holds so much of society together. They alleviate ambiguity and help people to know where they stand, and the roles expected of them.

I shall never forget meeting up with my friend Mike in Yoyogi park. When we introduced our Japanese girlfriends to each other they both bore frantic expressions and after saying, "Nice to meet you," in unison they immediately asked how old the other was. When they both replied 28, they became even more frantic, the ambiguity of hierarchy having made them anxious. My girlfriend resolved this by saying, "In what month were you born?" Mike's girlfriend it turned out was born in April 1981 whilst Yuka was born in March. To Mike's and my astonishment, on establishing that she was the older of the two (by a month), Yuka adopted a subtle but noticeable authority over the other girl for the rest of the day.

***

Japanese society's strict adherence to hierarchy is nowhere better illustrated than in its most iconic sport. As I sat in the nation's grandest sumo stadium watching the huge men hurl each other out of ring and perilously close to the laps of the audience in the front row I felt relieved that I was sitting in one of the higher tiers.

Sumo tournaments last virtually all day so inevitably you don't watch every fight with full-on focus but save your keenest attention for the big-ticket acts, the great Yokozuna[63] who wear the famed white rope belts, appear on TV and enjoy a celebrity status. The lower division matches begin at eight-thirty in the morning. As the day progresses so do the divisions and as the quality of the wrestlers increases throughout the day so the crowds grow until the highest ranked wrestlers fight just before six pm to a full crowd. The list of competitors and scheduled fights is displayed both in the fold-out paper programmes and on the huge wooden tablets that

---

[63] The highest rank in sumo. The word Yokozuna relates to the thick white rope belt they wear around the waist that symbolises their rank.

hang from the front of the stadium in Ryogoku[64]. You can immediately tell who the big boys are because their names are writ large at the top of the bill and the Yokozuna are biggest of all (both metaphorically and sometimes literally).

Much to the ire of the fans, for years and years including my time in Japan all the Yokozuna were foreign - more specifically, all of them at that time were Mongolian. The big guy at the top of the tree when I was there was the hulking Mongolian 'Asashoryu', one of sumo's modern icons. The trouble was that Asashoryu was badly behaved and refused to follow some of the rules and the sport's code of conduct both in and out of the ring. And that was just not on because sumo is not just a sport, it is intricately tied to religion, part of an ancient Shinto tradition whose origins stretch back around two thousand years.

Sumo wrestlers, like geisha and maiko (trainee geisha), are required to wear a kimono or yukata at all times when out in public and they must also wear their hair in a topknot. As a result, in addition to their huge size, this makes them easy to spot when out shopping or riding the train. I would see them every now and then on the streets of Tokyo quite incongruously going about ordinary, mundane tasks like shopping for groceries, quite divorced from the romance of their sport.

Sumo referees, who make a commitment to the sumo association for their entire career, are as much priests as adjudicators of the sport. Between each

---

[64] A district in the Sumida ward of East Tokyo where sumo tournaments are held and where many sumo training stables are located.

bout they pour sake as an offering into the sand before raking it with incredible precision. The wrestlers themselves fling a handful of salt into the ring before they begin in order to purify it. From the entrance ceremonies when the wrestlers come out and stand facing the crowd in a large circle on the edge of the ring to the blessing and chanting and bowing of the wrestlers to the audience, every aspect of the ancient contest is holy, stylised and ritualised. This is the Japan of old that lives on, cherished as a national and cultural treasure.

To the enormous delight of many Japanese fans, a few short years ago I hear the Japanese had their first homegrown champion in decades. I can only imagine the elation.

The sumo tournament was great. It was a tick on the must-do list while living in Japan as much for the ritual and the stadium and the aesthetics as the wrestling, but when I had the rare opportunity to attend a training session at a sumo stable in Tokyo I jumped at the chance. The sumo training stables are dotted around the east of Tokyo in the Ryogoku area where the nation's grand stadium the 'Ryogoku Kokugikan[65]' is located. The violence was all there, there was just as much sweat and grunting as at the tournament but with none of the fanfare. This was pure unadulterated aggression, rhinos smacking into each other with solid thwacks, the noise of palms on sweaty chests, of shoulders in cheeks and the occasional skull on skull. It was brutal yet exhilarating to watch.

---

[65] Tokyo's sumo stadium located in Ryogoku.

The stable master sat unmoved throughout in a t-shirt and jogging bottoms scratching his back with a long shoehorn and shouting encouragement and tips and occasionally berating the younger wrestlers, some of whom were still teenagers. Others were wise old heads, grizzled veterans who put the fresh blood through their paces and pushed their faces to the ground.

In one corner of the room was a thick wooden post which the waiting wrestlers took it in turns to slap and ram. As pairs of wrestlers continued to battle it out in the centre of the stable, the dull thwack of sweaty palms smacked against the timber. The system it seemed was winner-stays-on and the three or four strongest men out of the ten or twelve there would mockingly toss their weaker opponents into the dust to despatch of them. They were so exhausted they almost couldn't breathe as they struggled back to their feet time and again and were repeatedly tossed back into the dusty ring and then out of it, pushed face-first into the ground and slammed bodily into the wood-panelled walls.

Even here in this tiny sumo stable, once the exhausted wrestlers had finished their relentless three-hour long marathon session, they swept the sand with care and built a perfectly formed conical pyramid which they shaped with precision with brooms and planks. They then poured a bottle of sake into a cavity at the top and blessed the ground, clapped, chanted, and a priest was summoned from somewhere to perform the ritualised purification ceremony and its chanted blessings. I hope these traditions never die. Sitting in the stable and watching these men who totally ignored the handful of people watching them hurl themselves around was humbling. Then off they trudged for litres of water as they stood outside almost naked in the midday sun and obligingly had their photos taken with me and smiled and laughed. Suddenly they seemed human and many impossibly young and, despite being twice my size, not so scary after all.

***

Despite the respect for age, status and position, the Japanese tendency to not get involved in other people's business can have negative consequences. One night after leaving the gym as I rushed to catch a train, I dashed across when the lights on the level crossing began to flash. As the yellow barriers came down a bus driver ill-advisedly made the dash and just about made it. The far barrier however came down on top of the roof of the bus and as the vehicle passed through, the barrier went with it, stretching back like an elastic band. Once it reached the end of the bus roof it twanged back and, to my horror, smashed an old lady in the face. She was utterly poleaxed and lay on the tracks in shock and considerable danger. Without thinking, I rushed over, picked her up and helped her off the railway line. She was, as it turned out, relatively ok, slightly bruised but mainly just shaken up. I think she escaped a potentially far worse injury because the barrier had caught her at near the very end of its trajectory, but I shudder to think how it could have turned out.

As I headed home on the train, I wondered why no one else had come over to help. I was by no means the nearest person at the time. There were at least a dozen others who observed the accident and did absolutely nothing to help. Although this and similar incidents I saw of people not intervening to help shocked me, I came to view them as the darker side of the 'minding your own business' coin - a coin whose other side made living in Japan a pleasant experience but no less shocking for that fact.

Well-known clichés of Japanese society proved mostly true and sometimes refreshingly false. There are the workers who stay in the office until late in the evening, even if they aren't actually working just waiting for the boss to leave before they do; there is the junior female colleague going around the izakaya table on her knees pouring the drinks starting with the boss and then proceeding by order of seniority; there are groups of workers limbering up each morning with company aerobics to 'Radio Taiso[66]', a station which plays a melodic jingle solely for this very purpose. There are heavy drinking salarymen, straight-faced and serious by day, falling out of bars paralytic by night. The male/female divide in roles and responsibilities in the workplace, the school, the home and in public is clear to see. This is the Japan that the outside world glimpses and likes to caricature. But change, though slow, is in the air.

Whilst Japan's breath-taking economic ascent in the post war decades was fuelled by 'economic samurai', men who worked such long hours at their offices that they'd seem to rarely be at home, a worrying number of Japanese youths today are

---

[66] Radio calisthenics broadcast early each morning by Japan's national broadcaster, NHK, with music and exercise instruction.

reluctant to leave theirs at all. The 'hikikomori[67]' (shut-ins) are shunning the corporate life in favour of holing up in their rooms and isolating themselves from society.

Men and women are not pairing up, getting married or having babies as much as they used to, and in 21st century Japan women seem more empowered than ever to shun and speak out in opposition to traditional roles and expectations. Despite this, I found the culture of duty, honour and shame persisted. I discovered early on that to do wrong perhaps wasn't as severe a transgression as to be seen to do wrong. The much-written-about Japanese phenomenon of shame in standing out and being different is perfectly encapsulated in the old Japanese proverb, 'The nail that sticks out gets hammered down.' Was it true to a lesser degree in the late 2000's than it had been in the preceding decades? I don't know, I wasn't there, but I could see the hammers were still banging those nails. Some yielded easily, others not so.

***

I hadn't needed any reminders of how different my country of origin was from my newly adopted home. I felt and saw the differences in attitude and behaviour. It shouldn't therefore have hit me so viscerally when I returned to the U.K. and began training as a schoolteacher just how different were the ways in which the two countries raised their children. The onus, the driving message behind so much of the

---

[67] Reclusive Japanese adolescents and adults who shut themselves away from society in their bedrooms and refuse any interaction at all with society at large. The phenomenon is alarmingly widespread.

training in my one-year fast track PGCE course was the celebration of all that made us different from one another, the beauty of diversity and in being unique.

The message was, we are all different and that is our inherent strength. Don't fit in, don't be cowed, don't be a sheep. Stand out, follow your own path, and work to your strengths. It was unity of sorts, but unity forged through diversity. The education system in Japan seemed to be producing young adults to whom that mantra had never been taught. It was a totally alien way of looking at the world for them. To not rock the boat, to fit in and to conform was to do one's duty. Strive and succeed, by all means, but do so for the greater good of the group, the school, the company, and for the honour of your family.

It is facile and pointless to ponder which system, which mode of raising your nation's children is better. Perhaps there is no 'better', and it is entirely subjective. What is right for countries in the West may well never work in an entirely different cultural context. Indeed, the most suitable methods are likely to differ between neighbouring countries or even in one country itself over time and as culture and society evolves. While many Western countries study with awe the latest Maths technique that children in Singapore use to do addition problems or the method used in Seoul for learning times tables, students from the Far East pour into the universities of Western Europe and North America in ever-increasing numbers. You can't necessarily take an engine from one car and expect it to work in another. Some of the time it will work but other times it won't, and the reasons behind whether certain methods and practices translate to another culture are often nuanced and complicated.

***

In Japan even the landscape is subject to hierarchy. For centuries it has been common to rank various natural wonders or popular views in terms of the 'best three'. There are the three most sacred mountains, top of the list (both literally in terms of the mountain's height, but also in how sacred it is) is Mt. Fuji; there are the three most beautiful parks and there are Japan's 'top three most scenic places.' The lists of best threes or top threes or 'three most...' are endless. And so, I was pleased but not at all surprised to be told while visiting Nagasaki, that the city had one of the three most beautiful 'night views' in all of Japan.

Nagasaki is undoubtedly beautiful at night and belonging to the 'best three night-views' club was unsurprising given the city's layout. The city is located between and up the sides of steep beautifully forested mountains which provide an excellent vantage point from which the sparkling lights and port can be viewed. It was this same quirk of geography which in August 1945 spared Nagasaki an even worse fate than the horrific one it endured during the atomic bombing.

The high mountain ridges, which switch back tightly on one another, hide whole portions of the city from the view of other parts of it in the same way that they shielded parts of the city from the immediate effects of the nuclear blast that fateful day. Indeed, although 'Fat Man[68]' was significantly more powerful[69] than 'Little Boy' which had been dropped over Hiroshima just three days earlier and caused easily the largest loss of life in a single bomb strike in history, the eventual death toll in Nagasaki is generally considered to be approximately half of Hiroshima's.

Nagasaki wasn't in fact the intended target of the second atomic bomb at all, that was the city of 'Kokura' (now subsumed within and simply known as Kita-Kyushu) further north on the island of Kyushu. Heavy cloud cover or smoke had obscured the city from view, so the bomber carrying 'Fat Man' turned and headed back to base. Nagasaki was on the flight path of the bomber's return route but as the American plane flew over the city, Nagasaki too was obscured by cloud. It seemed that all opportunities had been lost until, as the plane began leaving Nagasaki's airspace, the clouds began to part and the snap opportunity to release the bomb was seized.

To take full advantage of the city's top three-night view status, I boarded a coach and headed off with a gaggle of domestic tourists on a long and winding journey up the city's steep hills to its highest point. The summit of the mountain also happens to be the

<hr>

[68] 'Fat Man' was the codename for the atomic bomb dropped on Nagasaki. 'Little Boy' was the codename for the bomb dropped on Hiroshima. Estimates vary, but it is thought that between 90,000 and 146,000 people died in the atomic bombing of Hiroshima and that between 39,000 and 80,000 died in Nagasaki. It is estimated that in the cases of both attacks, roughly half of the deaths occurred on the first day. The remainder of deaths occurred later after victims succumbed to their wounds and radiation poisoning.

[69] Estimates vary as to exactly how much more powerful 'Fat Man' was than 'Little Boy'. A lot depends on how you classify the bombs' 'power'.

site of a tall communications tower and mast raised on a large platform. It was hard that evening to reconcile the casual 'night view bus tour' jaunt with what I'd seen that day - the harrowing photos and charred artefacts in the museum and the statues, the fountains and the wind chimes in the peace park. The horror Nagasaki endured in 1945 seemed so strangely distant when we all debussed and climbed on to the windy platform. The city looked gorgeous, twinkling below us between the forested folds in the land, serene and luxurious with its brightly lit thoroughfares, bustling evening activity and huge cruise ships at harbour.

All the way up and all the way back down again the tour guide, a lady of about sixty with the hoarse voice of a chain smoker, educated us over the bus intercom on all she knew. The only problem was that the majority of what she told us had no relevance to our trip whatsoever. I was hoping for fascinating insights into the city's history, to find out about its famous buildings and to be filled in on the local culture and the exploits of its key historical figures. What we got instead was a long diatribe on her favourite TV shows and the actors she fancied. It was more Loose Women than The History Channel.

"That house over there is where the actor Ryusuke Takamori lives and he's just my favourite, and do you know he is in that new drama that has just come out? Oh, what's the name of that drama? It's so good, he's such a good actor. Isn't he handsome? Oh my gosh."

By the end of the trip, I'd been as awed by the beauty of Nagasaki at night as I had been irritated by her cheese-grater voice which warbled on about her favourite song and her favourite drama as she pointed out the houses in which those she idolised lived. If you're ever in Nagasaki and fancy a guided bus tour I do not recommend her. I don't know how many gravel-voiced ladies in their sixties run tours to Nagasaki's highest points. I'm sure she's a lovely lady but even though I have only experienced that particular one I can categorically say that if I were to experience only three more, 'Old Smoky' would definitely not be in my top three.

Chapter 15

The Good, the Bald and the Ugly

My colleagues

Better than a thousand days of diligent study is one day with a great teacher.
Japanese proverb

My fellow teachers came from all corners of the UK and the commonwealth and a few from elsewhere. Roughly 70% of them were British. Of the remaining 30%, there were Irish, Canadians, South Africans, Australians and Kiwis. There were the odd one or two from the Caribbean and even a couple of token Americans even though, strictly speaking, the company 'don't employ Americans'.

There were teachers for whom this was the first ever experience of teaching, fresh-faced and straight out of university, some as young as twenty-one with degrees in everything from the Classics at Oxford to Sports and Leisure at Bournemouth. There were those that had taught in Egypt, Korea, Italy, China, Poland, Taiwan, Thailand and Brazil. They'd been around the block and knew the score, knew the shortcuts and were aware of what the company could and couldn't ask them to do. They were in many cases older and more experienced than their managers and had them bang to rights. Then there was a curious group of teachers who were back in Japan for their second, third, sixth time; teachers who, for whatever reason, over the years and decades would yo-yo back and forth between their country of origin and Japan. There were teachers with masters and PhDs. One of my colleagues was a fully trained chef with a Masters in 'Chemical Engineering'. There was a man who used to work on oil rigs in the North Sea and another was a former nurse at St Thomas' hospital in London. There were ex-military, ex-financiers and ex-journalists.

One of the first things a fellow foreigner will ask, upon meeting you, is, "Why did you come to Japan?" My story tended to be treated with incredulity, disbelief and occasionally disdain. I can see why as many of my colleagues were Japanophiles or had deep-rooted reasons for coming to Japan that related to an ambition, a hobby or a childhood dream. Jake was into aikido, a martial art he'd taken up back home in Manchester, and he had come to Japan to pursue it. Dean was fluent in Japanese before he'd come to Japan, having gained a degree in it from SOAS[70] in London. He'd been obsessed with Japan since getting into manga and anime as a child.

Perhaps the old and the bold were reminded by the new teachers that joined of the enthusiasm they themselves once had and the magic of coming to Japan for the first time. Perhaps they saw their former selves in the enthusiasm, the nervousness or the naivety. Some teachers jealously regarded the new blood while others took them under their wing. Sadly, for the younger, more nervous and more homesick of the constant round of incoming teachers, the company had no specific recruitment season and, as a result, teachers would just turn up throughout

---

[70] The 'School of Oriental and African Studies' University of London.

the year in little groups. Therefore, there was very little effort put in by the company in helping teachers to get to know each other. If you had the misfortune to only work in three different schools, you may have no more than three colleagues all week, and if they happened to be non-communicative, grouchy or jaded, as invariably quite a few of the longer-serving teachers were, it could give a rather negative impression of the company.

Plonked in the middle of Tokyo in an apartment block with virtually no other foreigners, let alone colleagues, in your neighbourhood, very much as I was, it was easy to feel isolated and alone, and many did. It was easy to feel homesick and in at the deep end with nobody to talk to and it was easy to jack it in at the one or two or five-month stage and just go home, and quite a few did. Hence the need for a year-round influx of new teachers. There were the stories that did the rounds, like old passed-down lore, no doubt exaggerated and with details altered depending on the teller and the audience. There were tales of teachers who had literally given the company no notice at all, teachers who had quite literally just got on a plane and gone back home to Coventry or Calgary or Canberra. Maybe the teachers had known for weeks that's what they'd intended to do and had kept it a secret from the management because we were all on year-long contracts that you weren't supposed to break as they were 'binding'.

Maybe they hadn't known they wanted to leave themselves, and simply snapped and woken up one morning and, instead of picking up their briefcase and heading off to work, had hastily packed a suitcase instead, turned up at Narita[71] and asked for a ticket on the next flight for their country of origin leaving that day. The first our managers would know about it would be the receptionist of the school contacting the head office and saying that "Ben is half an hour late." Even as they uttered those words and the management put the phone down to angrily phone up the presumably over-sleeping teacher to remonstrate with him, Ben may well be musing over the air hostess' offer of 'Beef or chicken' and starting to watch his second movie of the flight.

Of course, those colleagues that linger in my memory are the inept and the ridiculous, the creepy and the hilarious. The truth is less remarkable. The reality is that there were many skilled teachers who were dedicated to their craft. There were competent and diligent educators who were in it for the right reasons, who taught with a passion and knew their stuff. That the clowns and the wideboys were a minority, is true. There were those who didn't prepare at all, who would lazily wander out five minutes late after they'd finished their coffee into the reception area to escort their next student in, grabbing the textbook from the shelf of the resources room as they waltzed by and then spending precious paid-for minutes of the student's time cueing up the CD or the tape and trying to work out how far they'd got in the textbook the previous week. It was lax and sloppy and unprofessional. Please bear in mind that the example individuals I illustrate below are the more

---

[71] Narita is the busiest international airport in Japan. It serves the Greater Tokyo region and is located 37 east of central Tokyo.

colourful and memorable amongst them and were not by any means the norm.

***

Gareth from Romford at five foot three and nearly as wide, was a cheeky chap with the wheezing laugh of an East End barrow boy and a mick-taking sense of humour to match. One notable fact about Gareth was that he lived in by far the largest apartment of any of my friends. It was nice too and in a good, central location. As a result, he always had people over for the evening and in fact often had friends over from London to stay. Some of his friends, both expats living in Japan and friends from back home on three-month tourist visa holidays, would stay for days or weeks at a time. One Canadian bloke actually stayed in Gareth's spare room for months. This is notable not only for Gareth's kindness but as a rare case of a Japanese apartment having a spare room. Gareth's heart wasn't in teaching, but he couldn't get a visa to do anything else. He was running a side business from his apartment in computer games and toys. He'd trawl the shops of Tokyo for rare or collectible items and sell them internationally online. The trouble was his business occupied all his thoughts and all his time. He'd sit in his classroom between lessons tapping away on his laptop and he did zero lesson preparation.

One of Gareth's weekly students was a nine-year-old boy called Kenta. Every time I walked by Gareth's classroom when teaching Kenta, the boy, half excited, half terrified, would be standing on the small circular desk as Gareth span it round like some cheap fairground ride. And just like the scruffy bloke with an earring and B.O. eagerly twirling your cup on the Waltz ride, the more you'd make desperate eye-contact with him and urge him to stop, the more it would egg him on. Let me hear you scream! But the boy would walk out wide-eyed and grinning from ear to ear at the end of each lesson, so mum was always delighted with the 'wonderful teaching' her son was receiving.

Gareth was a nightmare when he was drunk. He became aggressive and obnoxious and an embarrassment to be around. One night while travelling on the train back from some bar or other to Central Tokyo, one of our group made the suggestion that we all go to Nakano to carry on the evening in a different bar. I was hoping Gareth would call it a night as he'd clearly had far too much and was being a nuisance and rude to everyone around. His station was midway on the journey we were now taking so I held out a hope that he might get off there. However, he enthusiastically decided to come along with everyone else. The trouble was it was midnight, and he was swaying around the train like a fat little weeble, bumping into people and annoying them and then getting surly and aggressive when they grunted or looked at him in disapproval. There was one middle-aged businessman nearby who was getting particularly annoyed with Gareth's loud voice. The otherwise silent carriage was filled with the Londoner's loud, drunken rambling. I told him to be quiet as people were getting annoyed with him. He must have sensed the gentleman I was referring to and began to rant even more loudly in the man's direction.

"I don't care what he thinks, he can fuck off!"

I'd had enough. He'd pushed it too far. I didn't want to spend the rest of the evening with him and I'd no doubt the rest of our group felt the same. The remainder of the carriage had clearly had enough of him too. Gareth's home station arrived, and I suddenly decided what to do. He was standing with his back to the automatic doors. I timed it perfectly and just before the doors slid closed again, I pushed him hard, and he staggered back off balance onto the platform. As the doors closed and as Gareth stared at me through the windows in disbelief while the train pulled away, the annoyed businessman looked up at me.

"Thank you."

***

Ray was an interesting character. He was about thirty, Australian and gay, very masculine, broad-shouldered with close cropped hair and a small goatee beard. Every Friday for two years at Naka-Itabashi school he would tell me loudly in front of the old ladies waiting for the first lesson of the day about his recent sexual exploits. He'd go into extremely graphic detail about which Japanese guy he'd picked up on a dating app and taken back to his flat the night before and the exact things that he'd done to him. All the while I smiled and nodded and the old ladies chatted away in the lobby and threw glances our way, no doubt imagining their teachers were nattering about English grammar and that the graphic hand gestures were teaching techniques.

***

Liam, the eccentric cravat-wearer I met on my first day, was marmite. The students either loved or hated him. One afternoon, he was sitting in his classroom having his breakfast when the school receptionist knocked on the door. She explained that she'd forgotten to write down a lesson he had at the beginning of his day's teachings schedule.

"I'm sorry Liam," she said meekly, "I'm afraid you have a lesson in ten minutes that I forgot to tell you about."

Liam exploded and insisted that the student wait while he sat a bare three feet away loudly eating an enormous bowl of muesli on the other side of the frosted glass. He seemed to have two modes, 'off' and 'on full' but nothing in between. He either rubbed students completely up the wrong way or fawned all over them. There was one businessman he taught weekly that Liam absolutely adored. Gareth and I would stifle our laughter as we hid below the windows outside his classroom tittering. For two straight years Liam did the same pronunciation activity with the middle-aged student. Every time the student did well Liam would scream in his incredibly posh voice, "Yes Sachio, that's amazing!!"

The trouble for Liam was that the mundane pettiness of everyday Japanese life got to him. The one thing he really hated were the old ladies who blocked the pavements and got in the way of him cycling along them. To solve this problem, he fitted an enormous air horn to the front of his bike. I hadn't believed how serious he was until he gave me a demonstration one night outside a bar. It was deafening. I'd imagined that perhaps he would eventually realise just how over the top his solution was to oblivious old ladies. But alas, a friend showed me a video posted on YouTube a few months after Liam left Japan. It shows him commuting to work one day in Tokyo. As an old lady steps into the road ten metres ahead of him without looking, he squeezes the horn, and she nearly dies in fright.

Liam wanted to do his own thing. He found no pleasure in following the curriculum or the textbook. He was his own man and wanted to leave his own mark. He wasn't lazy, he was passionate about what he loved but his energies were misdirected. Instead of properly preparing for lessons, he'd sit for hours designing elaborate games. He spent ages building a huge wooden labyrinth game with marbles for the children he taught. He also constructed a homemade game of Kerplunk with a cutlery drainer he'd bought and wooden kebab skewers.

Liam was a keen cyclist and would head off to the mountains at weekends on his custom-made bicycle worth thousands of pounds that he'd had imported. He'd film and post online his epic downhill exploits. One night as I sat in a bar with Liam, he leaned over and said casually, "I'm going to cycle home." Of course, I'd assumed, as you would, that he was about to get on his bike and cycle back to his apartment. But no, what he meant as I later discovered, was that he was going to cycle home from Tokyo to England.

I don't think he made it the whole way on the epic journey. I think he got halted somewhere in Vietnam, but the videos of his exploits through China were entertaining; shaky handy-cam footage of him arriving in dusty little backwater towns, familiarising himself with the locals in his eccentric and over-ebullient way. By the fanfare to which he often arrived and the manic crowding round of the locals I guessed he might have been the first foreigner they'd seen. Perhaps there are whole regions of rural China where the locals now hold it to be true that all Englishmen wear cravats.

***

Jack Rowe comes to mind as another of the more eccentric colleagues I taught alongside. In his forties, gay, posh and privately educated, he had a booming 'Brian Blessed' voice that you could hear resonating around the building even behind closed doors. Passing his classroom one day I noticed he'd drawn a cartoon character of a woman on the whiteboard in high heels and skimpy clothing. As the old ladies sat around smiling at Sensei, he boomed at them.

"And what type of woman is this?! She's a slut! She's a cheap whore!"

The grandmothers all nodded and repeated this in unison. Five minutes later another colleague walked past the classroom. Jack could still be heard.

"Repeat after me: Easy, loose, a woman of poor morals."

Jack was unstoppable. He revelled in his sexual conquests and made no apologies for his appetite for Japanese men. I bumped into him in a bar one night in the early hours. He was wearing mustard-coloured corduroys and a tweed jacket.

"Ah, Tom, my boy! How the devil, are you? Gosh, you should have seen me last night. I took this Japanese lad to a love hotel. I tell you what my boy, the Union Jack was flying over Shinjuku last night!"

He then slapped me on the back and disappeared amongst the crowd.

***

Jordan Chivers is one of my closest friends. I first met him in the spring of 2010. He was sitting on a park bench in a white vest and shorts, smoking a cigarette. His bicycle was parked up beside him and the park was deserted except for the two of us. I'd seen this man before. He was one of only a few visible foreigners I'd seen passing through Nogata. I'd glimpsed him a handful of times whizzing through the narrow streets on his bike and had vaguely nodded to him once as I passed him in the entrance of one of the local convenience stores. I sat beside him and greeted him with a nod and a hello.

"You alright mate? Where are you from?" I enquired.

"England," he said. "You?"

"Oh, me too. Whereabouts?"

"I'm from Gloucestershire, what about you?"

"Oh, no way!" I replied, "I'm from Wiltshire."

Jordan became a good friend. We would hang out and go out clubbing together. We got into countless scrapes and I always seemed to be getting him out of ill-advised confrontations, including with the police. One evening as we cycled through Nakano together the police yet again stopped me due to my broken bike light. I was used to this by now and did what I always did, apologised profusely, and promised to get it fixed. The two policemen were about to wave me on when Jordan thought he'd add his tuppence-worth in protest at what he (wrongly) perceived to be an unjust stop.

Two policemen quickly became three and then four as they radioed for backup and before we knew it seven policemen encircled us as I desperately tried to calm Jordan down. I didn't fancy getting locked up and I became increasingly irate with Jordan. The assembled policemen looked on in amazement as I began to berate him, eventually squaring up to him and telling him if he didn't apologise to the police, I'd knock him out there and then. I have never knocked out as much as a fly, but he must have sensed how serious I was because he grudgingly apologised to them before I led him off down the street like a teacher berating a naughty child.

***

Tim Dean was an American from Maine. He always seemed to walk around in a filthy mustard-coloured trench coat and matching hat with a bottle of whiskey in his pocket and a packet of Golden Bat[72] cigarettes. He looked like a cross between Columbo and Tom Waits. What can I say about Tim that doesn't sound like fiction? One story about him sums the man up to a tee. In the immediate aftermath of the Fukushima nuclear reactor meltdown, he decided to leave Tokyo on a series of trains and buses, sneak through the exclusion zone cordon with a long lens camera and embark on a photo mission merely days after the second biggest radioactive leak in world history. When on his return I asked him what the hell he was up to, he replied, "I had to, the plum blossoms had just come out and they were stunning."

***

---

[72] A Japanese brand of incredibly strong filter-less cigarettes.

My friend Wayne was a relic of a different age and possibly the most incongruous person to find teaching in a land as foreign as Japan. Hailing from Hertfordshire, he was a mad Arsenal fan and seemingly spent his entire time in Tokyo in a Gunners shirt and shorts. Wayne had been in Japan for several years when I first arrived but didn't speak any of the lingo.

"I can't be bothered mate. Do you know what I mean?"

Perhaps Wayne's most incredible attribute was that he never ate Japanese food, and I mean never. He seemed to subsist on poor quality sandwiches and McDonalds. Every weekend he'd head down to the 'What the Dickens' pub in Ebisu, order a pie and mash, and wolf it down in a heartbeat before ordering exactly the same again. When I once asked him about this he replied, "Well, I've hardly eaten all week. I don't like any of that Japanese crap. I like real food, British food."

To get through the long days of teaching, Wayne found myriad ways of amusing himself. Once a week he taught in the biggest and busiest of our schools. The classroom in which Wayne taught had a window looking onto a wide main road which was spanned by a footbridge perpendicular to and just below the classroom. This quirk of the city's layout was too good an opportunity for the Arsenal fan to miss, so every Saturday morning he'd coerce one poor nine-year-old lad he taught to lean out of the window and shout "Oi, you!" in English to each of the no doubt bewildered businessmen walking from the station to their office. Given that the school was located on the edge of Shinjuku's thriving business district, there was no shortage of targets and little Sota's half hour lesson would whizz by with no need for any planning or preparation and a much-needed bit of light relief for Wayne.

***

Most of the teachers in the company were in their twenties or thirties. There were a few teachers however who didn't fit this demographic. Colin was one of them. He was a tall, skinny, grey-haired man in his fifties who chain smoked and wore a permanent scowl. I first met him when I'd been called in to cover a sick teacher. As I walked into the seemingly deserted school, I became aware of a faint hum coming from the rear classroom. I poked my head round the door and said a cheery hello. Colin was slouched in a chair facing away from me, his feet up on the table. He was watching a grainy old video tape of Sunderland F.C. on a ropey old VHS player propped up on a bookshelf. "Hi," I said expecting the man to at least turn and nod his recognition of my presence. Nothing.

"I've come to cover here today," I said.

He slowly turned and shrugged. Colin had been in Japan for the best part of thirty years. He was married with adult children and any spark of enthusiasm that he may have once had had long been extinguished. He scowled during lessons and he scowled at the young and energetic new teachers who joined and then left the company at a turnover rate of roughly eighteen months on average. He scowled and complained during meetings and training sessions, leaning back in his chair and staring at the ceiling with folded arms. He always seemed to be trying to take out a lawsuit against the company for something or other. If it wasn't working conditions, it was the hours we worked or the distance we had to travel to our schools.

***

There were some teachers who seemed to have almost sleepwalked into living in Japan. My friend Will went out to Japan in 2010 because his girlfriend was going, and she was going because her brother was already out there. But the tag-along boyfriend who initially had no impulse to head to the Orient, quite content with his hitherto small-town life in the West Country, became the permanent resident. He is married to a Japanese lady now with several children and after the death of his new wife's father, he has become the owner of a farm and an English school business of his own in the Japanese countryside. Meanwhile, the girlfriend returned to the UK after several months to marry a local English boy.

Bob, a shaven-headed Australian in his forties seemed perfectly normal until one evening after a day of training, Nigel, Bob and I plus a few others stood drinking outside a convenience store somewhere in Saitama. Slightly drunk and red-faced, he looked around and suddenly burst out, "They're all monkeys, just look at them, they're like apes." None of us ever saw Bob again after that night. Two weeks later I received a phone call out of the blue in the middle of the night. It was Bob talking in hushed tones. He was asking me if I could help him evade the authorities by pretending to be him. I don't know what he'd done to incur the wrath of the Japanese authorities, but I put down the phone and never heard about him thereafter. I've no doubt he's on the run somewhere in Asia being racist down to his bald bones.

***

End of year parties were always a sight to behold. The teachers got drunk, the students got drunk, and, free from inhibitions, what could possibly go wrong? Asagaya school's Christmas meal was a roaring success. I was dressed as Father Christmas and cheerily went along handing out presents from my sack to the assembled thirty or so adult students who sat strategically between the seven or eight teachers who were there. I had planned a quiz and a selection of games that would have put Bruce's 'Price is Right' to shame. The food was good, the teachers were all on their best behaviour and I'd just come to the end of my wrapping up speech to a round of applause. Just as the applause was coming to an end, I saw and heard a commotion at the far end of the room. Amy McIntyre, a contrarian, outspoken lesbian from New Zealand with no obvious redeemable features was yelling at the top of her voice to a middle-aged Japanese female student sitting beside her.

"Just fuck off, will you?!"

The party stopped, I dropped my sack and stared in horror through my white beard as Amy proceeded to shove the woman around.

"You fuckin' bitch, fuck off!"

The school manager looked on in horror and rushed over to calm the situation down. Amy stormed off to the bar and was later joined by the school manager who, once she'd finished apologising profusely to the upset student, spent the next ten minutes begging Amy to apologise to the student concerned.

"I won't apologise to that fucking bitch!" screamed Amy, and eventually stormed off.

Apparently, the cause of the outburst was the student repeatedly putting her hand on Amy's arm to get her attention, most un-Japanese but understandable given the noise and the levels of inebriation. It just goes to show that as the old saying goes, 'You can take a horse to water, but you can't make a drunk Kiwi lesbian apologise to an annoying Japanese woman'.

Surely the following year's Christmas party couldn't be such a disaster as that? As the senior teacher, I was jointly responsible with the school manager for organising it. We chose a lovely venue that served good food and drink. A colleague and I decided to lay on some live entertainment. In a departure from the regular quiz that I would do for the adult students, Alan, a cheerful New Zealander in his forties, and I performed a few pop and rock numbers with me on vocals and him playing the guitar. We set it up properly with an amplifier and I had the lyrics in front of me. Our music probably sounded dreadful, but we received a polite round of applause and everyone was in high spirits. Alas, I knew it was doomed for disaster when I saw a drunk Colin starting to grope one of the school receptionists. This was the same grumpy Colin of Sunderland VHS tape lore. He then began shoving around Jake, an American colleague and friend of mine. I nearly dropped the microphone mid-song in frustration. It was almost as if there were a curse. Something had to happen towards the end of the night that left a sour taste in the mouth.

Colin was married with children, but this didn't seem to hold him back. The receptionist, being meek, had tried but failed to put an end to his slap and tickle. The argy-bargy came when Jake, the young American teacher, stepped in to stop Colin's wandering fingers. Looking for another outlet for his energy, Colin started pulling on Jake's tie who was none too impressed and pushed him back hard. Colin then responded by chucking his glass of red wine over Jake's shirt and things went rapidly downhill from there. The last thing I remembered before setting up for our next musical number, was seeing out of the corner of my eye Colin's throat in Jake's very firm grip, with the Englishman bent backwards over the bar. Once again, the students had got more than they bargained for, although in truth perhaps it wasn't such a bad thing. If all the tea and cake British events were a trite and unrealistic depiction of British life, this surely was a more down to Earth representation; a dishevelled, drunk middle-aged football fan brawling at Christmas. Ah, so British!

***

A running joke amongst a few of the male teachers was the fact that you could do better with the ladies than back at home. It no doubt had a certain element of truth to it. You would sometimes see bald middle-aged men accompanied by stunning ladies. That said, Tokyo was no Bangkok and Japan quite rightly doesn't have the sleazy reputation of some Southeast Asian countries for old foreign men with money attracting young women. I suppose it was a levelling of the playing field. The good-looking jock types with the muscles and chiselled features were going to get attention from the fairer sex wherever they went in the world. But for the losers, the geeks and the socially maladjusted (anyway, enough about me), their awkward foibles could go unnoticed, and they would for a change stand a chance. One of my co-workers, Glynn, called it the 'exchange rate' and joked that just as the real exchange rate of pounds to yen was at an all-time high when I arrived in country, it was favourable for foreign men in Japan.

Capturing this cultural phenomenon, one ex-pat cartoonist had even started a comic book series entitled 'Charisma Man'. In the spoof magazines a tall, square-jawed, muscular foreigner with blonde hair and blue eyes woos Japanese ladies and impresses the local men with his suaveness, dancing ability and general charisma. His arch nemesis is the character 'Western Woman'. The cartoon depicts the man shrivelling before on-lookers' eyes to his true self when Western Woman approaches him, thus becoming the snivelling, spotty, skinny loser he really is and bursting the bubble of the mythical persona he had developed whilst in Japan. Glynn coined the term 'LBH' to describe the Losers Back Home who enjoyed some sort of perceived suaveness, unlike back in Blighty where they were just plain, spotty tossers. It was he with whom I shared a building on the fateful day, March 11th, 2011, during the great Tohoku earthquake, by the end of which we felt lucky that we'd ever be able to go 'back home', losers or otherwise.

It is often said that newcomers to Japan go through stages of feelings towards the country. The first stage which lasts for the initial few months is referred to as the 'Honeymoon Period'. During this time everything is golden, in my case quite literally as I arrived just before the commencement of the Golden Week[73] national holiday. In this period Japan is a fairyland of wonder and excitement. You're bowled over by the politeness and efficiency and cleanliness of the country and it is a paradise in which to live. Next comes the normalisation stage. In this stage the things that once amazed you and intrigued you become every day and mundane and ordinary. The next stage is irritation. It is quite possible that certain foreigners in Japan never reach this stage, but many do. Gaijin whining is an age-old tradition. As vociferously as you marvelled over the gadgets and the trains and the manners, you now moan at the inflexibilities and the rigidness and the lack of spontaneity.

Whining gaijin are annoying. They're annoying because surely if you dislike a place, you should just leave it. They drag people down. They are the proverbial rotten apples in the barrel. In every school there's one. He or she saps energy and picks faults and positively hates the enthusiasm and get up and go of the newly arrived teachers. At this point you have a choice. The obvious one would be to leave but many stay and whinge and become bitter, almost ironically unable to return to the West because they

[73] A week of national holiday across Japan which stretches from 29th of April into the first week of May.

have lost all touch with that world. Colin the Sunderland fan was one such case.

"You just get to your limit with Japan," said one female teacher to me at the company's head office one day.

I didn't quite know what she meant. She continued.

"You're new, right? How long have you been here? A year? Oh well, trust me. It's when you've been here for about five years, you just reach this kind of limit with Japan and you feel you can't stay here any longer."

True to her word, she did indeed leave and even today is somewhere in the Middle East presumably building up to the five-year mark where she'll no doubt bounce off to pastures new once more. She was by no means unique in this outlook. Teachers would hit a sort of invisible ceiling, that stage three where they would have had enough. Of course, for those with children and wives or those with nothing to return to it was different. The irony never escaped me that the pillorying of the West that so often characterised the Honeymoon Stage, "Oh, this is so much better, cleaner, faster than back at home," is almost flipped on its head in the final stage when the country of origin can do no wrong. I suppose this is inevitable and that both are ridiculous. Neither Japan nor our home country had perfected any aspect of living. The truth undoubtedly lay somewhere subtle in the middle amid nuance, dependent on context and perspective, away from the cliched and conveniently packaged stereotypes.

There were the stories of ex-teachers, mythical, legendary half-truths that were passed on down the years. The guy that used to write swear words on the whiteboard and take photos of the kids standing next to them, the guy that would write 'I like giving blowjobs' on the whiteboard with big arrows in marker pen pointing to the young woman who he'd position in just the right place before taking a photo. There were tales of teachers who refused to not wear trainers, teachers who dated students, teachers who moonlighted by getting their students to take private lessons with them and sometimes then leaving the company altogether with the students. One of the most bizarre stories of all, and I know for a fact that this one was true, was of a middle-aged male teacher who actually lived in a cupboard at one of the schools. Suffice to say, it wasn't always the brightest and the best that found their way out to Japan, sometimes it was the weirdest.

Perhaps it's a triumph of the English teaching industry that such a wide spectrum of British and Canadian and Australian society ended up there at all. For all the eccentrics and the creeps, the pranksters and the wide boys, the majority of my colleagues were just regular, nice, ordinary people. For every one of them worth writing about, there are at least five or six who are not. The single invariably settled down, had children and in roughly equal measure, either made homes for their new families in Japan or back at home, wherever that might be. A minority still work for the same English school while many have gone on to teach at universities and high schools.

If you are a native English speaker and wish to work in Japan then teaching English is your ticket, although of course there are foreigners working in journalism and finance and other industries. To teach English in Japan you need a degree to get a visa and often are required to have a rudimentary TEFL[74] qualification. I suppose where I differed most to many of my colleagues was that I had wanted to teach abroad, and Japan was where I ended up doing it. For them, they'd wanted to live in Japan and teaching English was a means by which they could do it. So perhaps it wasn't surprising that amongst the charming, the enthusiastic and the diligent, there were the bizarre, the socially awkward, the apathetic and the incompetent.

---

[74] Teaching English as a Foreign Language, sometimes also known as TESL (Teaching English as a Second Language) or TESOL (Teaching English to Speakers of Other Languages).

Chapter 16

Japan has Four Seasons

'Japan is unique'

Autumn is a second spring when every leaf is a flower.
Japanese proverb

Japan is unique, we have four seasons.
Anyone who spends any period of time in Japan will hear this sentence many times. It is spoken as a lesson, an instruction to you who, from whichever country you may hail, clearly don't know that a country can experience seasonal change. You are supposed to appear surprised. I feigned shock that one place could experience snow fall in Winter, blossom in Spring, heat in Summer and falling leaves in Autumn. I'm not quite sure what Japanese people imagine the rest of the world to be like, but they were insistent. I am of course being flippant. Japanese cherry blossom is beautiful; the scarlets and bright yellows of the autumn leaves in Japan's mountains are as vibrant as anywhere, and the prefectures of The Sea of Japan[75] coast receive some of the heaviest snowfalls of anywhere in the world. But the insistence was that such marked seasonal change, as with so much else, only existed in Japan.

It is deemed to be the case that Japanese people appreciate and notice the natural beauty of their

---

[75] The sea between the Russian mainland, Japan and the Korean peninsula. The 'Sea of Japan coast' usually refers to the western coast of Honshu, as opposed to the Pacific coast.

surroundings more than others. Although this may have not adequately produced enough protestation to halt the systematic post-war desecration of the Japanese landscape on an industrial scale, I can see some evidence for this claim. My girlfriend loved the autumn leaves in particular. One day in October we were walking down the road when she bent over to pick up a leaf.

"Look, it's so beautiful," she said.

Bringing it closer to her face, she realised in horror that it wasn't in fact a leaf but a toad that had been squashed flat by a vehicle and baked hard and crispy in the sun.

The miraculous ability of the Japanese to find beauty in the most unlikely of places, often amidst ugliness, and to filter out anything around that could sully it is as true for photographs of autumn leaves and mountains that ignore the concreted rivers and messy electricity pylons that surround them as it is for views of an otherwise beautiful and serene park full of cherry blossom trees spoiled by the swarms of people viewing them en masse.

Amidst the seasonal festivals it's easy to get confused. I'll give you an example. 'Hanami' takes place in April and sees tens of thousands of people gathering in one place to go "oooh!" and "aaah!" while sitting on blue tarpaulins and observing an explosion of colour. 'Hanabi' on the other hand takes place in late July or early August and sees tens of thousands of people gathering in one place to go "ooh!" and "ah!" while sitting on blue tarpaulins and observing an explosion of colour. At both there are food stalls selling street food favourites such as fried noodles and chocolate covered bananas on sticks, not to mention copious amounts of beer. At both events camera SIM cards are filled with hundreds of almost identical images. Women and men often wear a yukata at both events and there is generally a bit of a party atmosphere. 'Hanami' means cherry blossom viewing party. 'Hanabi' means fireworks.

***

Although it obviously isn't true that Japan is the only country to have four seasons, they perhaps win first prize for marking the arrival of each new one. Fresh produce and seafood are highly prized when in season and high streets and shopping malls are adorned with decorations to mark each new season's arrival. Plastic cherry blossom petals hang from the rafters in April and scarlet maple leaves in Autumn. Japan has no history of a 'structured' religion such as Christianity with which to frame 'God's hand in bestowing upon Earth the fleeting bounty of the harvest, no scripture-based periods of preparation and anticipation such as lent and advent. As a result, Japan's all-consuming focus on the yearly cycles of the weather, of growth, bloom and decay is afforded an even more critical reverence, not the gifts of a benevolent ever watchful higher power but of the Earth itself and the spirits which inhabit it.

No time of year is as long and eagerly anticipated as the coming of the cherry blossom and, once it has arrived, none is celebrated with such vigour in every park that has so much as a whiff of a single cherry tree. Due to Japan's elongated shape, its nearly 2,000-mile-long archipelago, the cherry blossom season does not arrive in one instant but like an ever-moving wave of shades of pinks and whites sweeping the country from South to North and monitored by every Japanese news and media outlet with such attention to minute detail and such breathless enthusiasm that it's a wonder to observe. The first blossom arrives in Okinawa at its 24 degrees of latitude, just one degree shy of the Tropic of Cancer and level with the Bahamas, as early as January, and in Hokkaido with its offshore icebergs and ice sculpting festivals in Japan's far north at 45 degrees of latitude, level with Canada's Great Lakes, in May. For the bulk of the Japanese population, including the residents of Tokyo, the brief yearly delight of 'Hanami', and its mere one week of full bloom, straddles the final days of March and the first few days of April, the anticipation and appreciation of its coming so greatly enhanced by, and largely predicated upon, its fleetingly brief, beautiful life and sudden inevitable loss.

I viewed the cherry blossom approaching their prime on cherry-tree flanked roads from my classrooms and on my walks through the city streets and along its tree-lined pink-petal carpeted rivers at the point of its demise. However, by some cruel twist of fate, or perhaps more likely some strange quirk of my weather-sensitive immune system, having missed the cherry blossom in Tokyo by a mere three weeks the year I arrived, for the climax of the brief Hanami season of three of the next four years, I lay in bed with swollen tonsils in a sweaty fever imagining the parties in the parks but unable to attend. I missed my only other chance in the Spring of 2008, flying off to Europe and then Africa immunised against God-knows what and, with all the lack of sleep and jetlag, feeling almost as exhausted and washed out as in those other sore throat years.

***

Japan's festivals are intimately tied to the changing of the seasons. My body which so frequently let me down at the height of Spring, was forgivingly robust throughout the summer, autumn and winter months. The Awa Odori dance of late August in Koenji, Tokyo was incredible, but I had an itch to see the dance performed in its traditional homeland. When I did see it, it was purely by chance. One August, I found myself in the town of Ikeda in the ancient province of 'Awa' itself, now subsumed into the modern prefecture of Tokushima. It is here in August that the dance is performed to mark the harvest as it has been for many hundreds of years, long before 'Edo', later 'Tokyo', grew out of the fishing village it had always been. It wasn't actually what I'd come for. I'd come for a nearby misty remote valley of lore and legend, but it was a welcome and opportune surprise, nonetheless. The locals in the little coffee shop I stopped at informed me with glee of the coming evening's festivities. After finishing my coffee, I wandered through the town's covered mall which was completely empty, and I went and had a hot bath in the town's sento.

When I emerged an hour later, the mall was a hive of activity. There were trestle tables being set up, chairs being laid out and children running around generally being a pain in the arse and getting in everybody's way. Below the setting sun preparations were under way for the dance. I hadn't expected

much, I knew this was not the main Awa Odori dance
of the region because that took place in Tokushima
city itself, but this was its true home. I was in for a
pleasant surprise. The mall filled up and before long
the trestle tables were covered with plates of
skewered chicken and huge kegs of beer and every
man and his dog had turned out to see the dance.

It turned out not to be as big or as grand as it's
Tokyo cousin, but the raw energy was electric. The
male drummers looked about as rough a group of
men as I should ever want to meet, all crew cuts and
scars and that quiet toughness that people in this part
of Japan seem to exude. One troupe in particular
seemed to outdo all the others, not with their finesse
or their style but with their sheer 'throw the kitchen
sink at it' performance. They were a troupe of about
thirty. There was a section of about eight female
dancers and behind them the male dancers.
Following on were the men with symbols and then at
the back, the drummers. They moved past in a
deafening cacophony which reverberated around the
mountains. A huge bear of a man, who seemed to
ooze the confidence of 'Chief Drummer', turned
around to offer me one of the fans hanging from his
waistband. I nervously plucked one out. It was a
tacky affair, black and glossy with a golden symbol
written across it, which denoted the name of their
group.

The women in this troupe wore huge-hooped
earrings and one looked positively high on drugs, her
eyes rolled back in her head as if she were about to
pass out, while the men mostly looked as if they'd all
done a bit of jail time, but for energy I couldn't fault

them. One of the dancers bounded over and grasping me by the hands tried to encourage me to dance. Noticing this, nearby members of the crowd nodded and grinned for me to oblige but my bottom remained firmly on my seat. I smiled and blushed and not knowing what else to do since I'd brazenly refused the kind offer, I gave a feeble little half wave and a stupid gap-toothed smile. I couldn't have been more awkward if I'd fallen flat on my face.

The performers followed the crowds down to the station and did an impromptu encore just outside its entrance. Sweat poured from the drummers' foreheads as they pounded the enormous drums. As I watched them lean back to obtain the leverage with which to pound the drum skins ever harder, it stuck me that this was the dance's true home, not in Tokyo as incredible though that was, not in Tokushima city but here at the mouth of the valley in the ancient land of Awa, signalling the coming harvest in a tough and rugged land.

Years later I went to the famous big Awa Odori event in Tokushima city, and, for all the build-up and expectation, I have seldom been so disappointed in my life. The announcer, the tiered seats, the strictly organised printed programmes and the over-the-top presence of police and wardens and sub-wardens over-sanitised and spoilt the whole thing. Somehow, they'd lost the spontaneous carefree spirit of the festival. The many-centuries-old dance was destroyed by the petty nonsense and red tape and the officious and stuffy bureaucracy of the modern era.

***

And what of the misty valley of lore and legend I'd come to visit? There are parts of Japan that have a mythical and magical feel and the Iya valley is one of them. The dance in the mall was in a town near the valley's entrance. Iya is a remote and, until the early twentieth century, virtually inaccessible part of Shikoku, the smallest of Japan's home islands. Within Iya is the deepest gorge in all of Japan. It feels like a forgotten kingdom, an ancient, enchanted land lost in the mists of time. The bright green forested mountainsides rise up high amongst the clouds and a beautiful sparkling turquoise river runs along the valley floor, its bright colour coming from the mineral deposits unique to this region. Houses are perched high on the mountainsides amid little terraced fields, and midway up the valley a vine bridge spans the gorge at Kazurabashi, a remnant of the many vine bridges that crossed the valley in ancient times and speaks of a history of fleeing warriors.

In the twelfth century the 'Taira[76]' or 'Heike[77]' clan finally lost the years' long Genpei War[78] to the Minamoto[79] clan. It is widely believed they fled to this island and then to these remote mountains to escape their pursuing enemy and they'd cut the vine bridges

---

[76] One of the four most important samurai clans that dominated Japanese politics, founded in 825 AD. Also referred to as 'The Heike clan' (see 'The Heike clan').

[77] The Taira clan are commonly referred to as the 'Heike' because of the alternative reading of the Chinese characters (see 'The Taira clan').

[78] A five-year-long national civil war between the Taira (or Heike) and Minamoto clans in the twelfth century which resulted in a defeat for the Taira and their resulting demise. As a result of the Minamoto victory, the Kamakura Shogunate was established.

[79] One of the four great samurai clans who fought and beat the 'Taira' clan in the Genpei War.

to halt the pursuit of their foe. Today the vine bridge at Kazurabashi is not rushed over by retreating warriors but stepped over cautiously by weekend visitors from Osaka and tourists from China who snap excitedly away with their cameras while keeping half an eye on their footing as they negotiate the widely spaced wooden slats.

After queueing amongst the sweating families and paying for the pleasure, it was just my luck that when I crossed the famed bridge a middle-aged man, in the way that dads so often do, decided to show off to his children by bouncing on the bridge. As he rocked it the whole thing swayed and I clung to the sides for dear life, cursing under my breath and trying to breathe slowly and ignore my heart palpitations. I tried hard to conjure romantic images of how fleeing sword-wielding warriors would have crossed this same vine bridge over this same river in the exact same spot of this remote, misty valley eight hundred years before.

However, it's hard for your senses to capture this iconic scene, because even while in my head I played the strains of some ancient Japanese flute or stringed instrument for added atmosphere, inescapably just metres away some dickhead in tracksuit bottoms and a pair of purple crocs was acting the clown, and the only sound was the annoying pop music ringtone coming from the smartphone in his pocket, which is hardly conducive to conjuring a mysterious atmosphere. How I wished as I watched the grinning idiot, that I was one of the Minamoto armed with a sword, because all I wanted at that moment was for him to flee to the other side and get lost in the mountains forever like the Heike.

If the swarms of tourists at the vine bridge had detracted from that spot's beauty and history, the beautiful ryokan I stayed in, with the little cable car up the mountain to a private hot springs complex, was glorious. The hot springs were rented by the hour and you had them all to yourself. Best of all, as you bathed at the top of this mountain, you could enjoy the unbroken view of the valley below you and the mountains on the other side.

The people of the Iya valley are markedly different to the traditional stereotypes of the Japanese. They are ruggedly independent, and they do not come across as bound to the conformity of modern Japan. They are down to Earth and plain speaking with ribald humour. As a general rule, they do not grow rice as they do on Japan's flat plains but buckwheat and potatoes instead. It's a haunting and beguiling place and although this last bastion of a secluded paradise is opening up rapidly to the bus loads of snapping tourists, you still feel something of the magic when you visit.

As with all of Japan, the valley is finally succumbing to the irresistible forces of public works. The forests are logged, and concrete is poured to cover exposed mountainsides and riverbanks, while mountain roads are built to allow for the heavy machinery that chugs up them. To this scourge is added the region's rapid depopulation like much of rural Japan as the young head to the cities to find work, leaving old wooden houses abandoned and fields lying fallow. That Iya is a remote and beguiling wonder is unmistakably true but it's one on the brink of irreversible change. I can only hope it's a few more years yet before the fragile intrigue of this region, so long cut off from the rest of Japan, its haunting magic and its bewitching beauty finally disappear forever.

***

'Japan is safety country' is another phrase that you'll hear many times when living in Japan. I suppose the grammatical error reflects badly on me. After all, it was usually my students who said it. Many of my Japanese students displayed an almost irrational fear for their safety when abroad. Their depictions of other countries tended to focus on the dangerous and the lawless, especially the United States with all its drugs, guns and gangs. Aside from this, it is unarguably true, Japan is safety country. In the summer in the centre of the largest city on the planet I'd keep my patio doors open at night to alleviate the stifling heat with no fear of burglary or assault. On numerous occasions I saw drunk businessmen asleep in an alley after a night out on the beer, their wallet, phone and money having fallen out of their pocket and remaining wonderfully untouched. I never heard of assaults or muggings or burglaries.

While it is undeniably true that the yakuza ostensibly ran huge underground crime rackets, petty street crime seemed so rare as to be almost non-existent. Bizarrely, I did once see a man stealing a single can of tuna in a supermarket. He looked around suspiciously before stuffing the tin into his jacket pocket. I immediately reported this to a member of staff, but they waved me away. My report of the crime it seemed was more troublesome than the crime itself.

***

Though Japan sees itself as unique for its four seasons and its safety, foreigners are more likely to set the country apart for its range of innovative or wacky inventions. In fact, given that the phrase 'wacky inventions' is often synonymous with Japan, perhaps it is facetious for me to mock the Japanese for their belief in being unique altogether. Famed the world over as high-tech and sometimes strange, they seem to provide solutions to every problem or difficulty you've ever had in life and even more solutions to problems and difficulties you have never had and never will. Yuka had a strange device that she used to stroke her face. It was like a stethoscope but had little rollers on each end. When I asked her what it was for, she answered as if it was perfectly normal.

"It's for making your face smaller."

Of course, I should have known. It solved the age-old problem of having too big a face.

My local bike parks in Tokyo were jazzy enough with extendable racks that allowed you to roll your bike up on to them, so they sat in rows one above the other. One of the bike parks I used even had two little travelators, one on either side of the steps that led to the next floor. Both were just a few inches wide and allowed you to place your bike tyres upon them for ease of transport. How nice? But there was one bike park that was like Blade Runner. At street level there was a little kiosk with automatic doors. When you placed your bike in front of the doors they would open, and your bike would be whisked away and stored in a subterranean warehouse with thousands of other bikes. To retrieve your bike all you need do was enter your code and in a flash a huge metal arm would extend down into the bowels of this bike repository and spit it back out. It was amazing. In fact, it was almost as revolutionary as the face roller.

***

Despite the remote mountainside communities such as Iya, with their own cultures and customs, seemingly divorced from 'mainstream' Japanese life, a significant number of Japanese people appeared eager to emphasise how they thought, felt and acted as one with one heart and one brain moulded in the national conscience. Thus, Japanese notions of their uniquely safe country which experienced unique seasonal change need to be looked at in a broader context. There were many other, often but not exclusively Japanese held, theories of the specific differences of Japan. 'Nihonjinron' is a term which loosely translates as 'theories of Japanese uniqueness' and these studies focus on the social and cultural identity of the country. 'Nihonjinron' as a mode of thought and as a genre of texts covering a huge wealth of books published on the topic became popular after World War 2 and reached its height during the 1980's when Japan seemed unstoppable and on the verge of overtaking the U.S.A to become the world's largest economy.

The phrase 'Japan as Number 1' so often spoken with great enthusiasm and an iron-clad conviction during the decade of my birth was understandably no longer uttered in my time there, other than perhaps in irony by embittered businessmen who'd lost it all in the huge recession at the beginning of the 90's. The bursting of the famed economic 'bubble[80]' gradually put paid to the notion held by many Japanese and foreigners alike that Japan was indestructible and that the nation's fortunes could only continue to rise.

At the more extreme end of 'nihonjinron' papers and studies abound of how the Japanese use entirely different parts of their brains to solve problems than all non-Japanese. The appreciation of nature, of art is all deemed at the more extreme end of 'Japanese studies' to derive from the unique wiring of the Japanese mind. I'm pretty sure this all contributes to feelings of racial uniqueness which can only be dangerous and, in any case, are palpably and provably untrue since the DNA of the modern Japanese can largely be traced back to China and the Korean peninsula. More to the point the so called 'Yamato' race were not the original inhabitants of these islands anyway.

The original inhabitants were the native Ainu whom the modern 'Japanese' shunned and mistreated for millennia and whom they pushed further and further north. The Ainu were eventually 'conquered' in the 9th century. Though today, the discrimination the Ainu receive is less obvious, they exist in small communities almost entirely on the northernmost Japanese island of Hokkaido, are rarely mentioned in the media and have just a few token

---

[80] The 'Bubble' was an economic bubble in Japan in the late 1980's which saw a huge inflation in the prices of property and in the stock market. When the bubble finally 'burst' in 1992 the Japanese economy immediately plunged into a deep recession from which many argue it has never recovered.

museums and cultural centres for their woes. As a result of intermarriage with the 'Japanese' populace very few people of solely Ainu heritage exist in Japan today. Suffice to say, the current treatment of these people, their language and culture, though less markedly appalling than in the past, leaves a lot to be desired.

Seeing your nation as unique can galvanise the populace. Who doesn't want to belong to a special club, the chosen few? No doubt, notions of Japan's uniqueness helped the nation sell itself during the latter half of the twentieth century, 'Japanese made' becoming a stamp of credibility and quality to set the country aside from the rest of Asia. However, there's perhaps a darker side to being preoccupied with your country's uniqueness. As a result of its more than two hundred years of self-imposed isolation from the rest of the world, by the mid 1800's, Japan had become woefully out of touch with foreign trends and technologies not to mention the prevailing morals of the time.

Japan had come to the game of colonisation late in the day, but that fact didn't hold them back. Japan may have been late to the party, but for leaders who often saw their nation as a 'European state outside of Europe' surely a little empire of their own was rightfully theirs and who were the likes of Britain and the other major powers of Western Europe to insist that such repression of and cruelty towards other peoples was now out of vogue? Such retrospective shunning by Europeans of what had benefitted themselves for centuries, now that they had moved on to a self-professed higher moral ground was just hypocritical surely? And what of America? Well, pot, kettle, black.

Sitting in my house in England and planning and preparing to move to Japan, I had imagined a land as foreign and removed from everything I had ever known as was possible. It may seem overstated for Western visitors to Japan to emphasise how 'different' Japan is. I mean, it's not as if remote jungle villages in Sub-Saharan Africa or the nomadic Bedouin cultures of Arabia are a carbon copy of English or Italian life. Perhaps the oft-vaunted emphasis on Japan's 'difference' to the West is because Japan is itself a developed, industrialised, first world, and in many senses of the word, 'Western' country.

If you travelled to the Congo or Nepal, you would expect extreme culture shock because, without meaning to offend, in no possible sense of the phrase could either be considered a 'first world' country. Even China, though its meteoric economic ascent seems to know no bounds, is still today regarded as a second world nation. It has a huge economy, yes (the second largest on Earth), and an increasingly powerful military, but it is still considered by major international organisations and report after report in 2020, to be 'developing'.

Japan then was an anomaly. Perhaps only South Korea, very much playing catch up to Japan's meteoric cultural, economic and political rise in the second half of the twentieth century, could come close to comparing. The shock therefore was that visitors from other 'first world nations' were often lulled into not expecting such differences from a 'wealthy' and

'Westernised' nation but find them they did, in abundance.

Despite this, while in many everyday ways it was true that Japan was very 'different', for me many of the biggest surprises came not from the differences but the similarities. With time I came to see that living in a reserved island nation on the edge of a continent with which it had a complicated relationship was a situation closer to home than I might have at first thought; a nation with a 'royal family', a former empire, a nation whose collective conscience was shaped by its wartime experiences. Perhaps more than I was comfortable to admit I recognised in the mirror a nation who believed itself to be somehow different with a self-deprecating, and yet sometimes strangely superior attitude, a setting aside of oneself as a land of knights and chivalry ready to defend itself against foreign invaders. Was it possible that I had initially been blind to the realities of just how alike my two homes were? The pride, the defensiveness, the often painfully evident attempts to highlight how we aren't like that lot across the water. We're different.

Was it possible that this strange little white man from five thousand miles away, who had never so much as set foot in Asia before moving there had in fact unknowingly known Japan all along?

Chapter 17

All is not as it Seems

A land of contradictions

Even a sheet of paper has two sides.
Japanese proverb

Japan is an enigma. It has the uncanny ability to seem something and at once not be that thing. Japan's attitudes towards and adoption of new technologies is a good example of this. I am no aficionado on technology, in fact I am almost a Luddite in my inability and reluctance to move with the times. In 2008 I was still using my big, clunky CD Walkman which elicited stifled smirks as I clumsily changed discs mid- journey on train rides through the city before I finally relented to the inexorable pull of the, by then, ubiquitous i-pod.

I would imagine that most of the Western world views Japan as technologically very advanced, and in many ways this is true. After all, wasn't this the land of the bullet train, the all-singing all-dancing toilet, karaoke machines, robots, flashing neon and all manner of other ingenious gadgetry? Indeed, one need only tour their own household appliances or cars for evidence. Names such as Sony, Hitachi, Toshiba, Nintendo and the endless vehicle companies such as Toyota, Honda and Mitsubishi are ubiquitous around the world.

However, there is a lot about Japan that remains strangely low-tech. The schools I taught in were a good example of this. Each school I worked in was equipped with a fax machine to receive messages from Head Office and our schedule for the following day. When I left in 2011, I had assumed that before long the schools would be decked out with computers, at least at the reception desk, but I am reliably informed that head office still communicates with each school by fax. All student records are kept in writing in big ledgers and there are no computers or interactive whiteboards in the classrooms. When I worked for the company most of the listening exercises were on CD but a significant minority of them were on tape. Cumulatively, over my time teaching there I probably spent a day or two re-winding tapes to just the right place to listen for the fifth, sixth, ninth time to exactly why Mary doesn't like going fishing with Brian.

When I found myself in a Japanese police station, I sat at the detective's desk looking around in barely concealed amazement at the mountains of paper sprawled messily on desks and not a single computer in sight. Bear in mind that I was not in a rural backwater but in the centre of Tokyo. I've been in Japanese hospitals where the same is true and some that are positively dirty and dilapidated with peeling paint and dusty corridors.

Toilets perhaps sum up the Japanese high-tech/low-tech dichotomy best of all, either uber high tech with perfume sprays, heated seats, musical tunes to hide any embarrassing sounds, vibrations, water jets, dryers and a whole range of wonders, (I once in fact counted forty-three buttons on one toilet's control panel); or they are a hole in the ground over which you must squat. It became a lottery when out in public. I'd open the door with trepidation, my heart sinking at once should I be greeted by the latter. I refused to use the squat toilet at Naka-Itabashi school for a number two, so I held it in and would pray for a gap between lessons big enough to allow me to dash over to McDonalds and use their 'Western toilet'.

***

It wasn't just in the toilet department that matters of hygiene left me perplexed. It came as a surprise to me that sitting on the train snuffling and snorting away like a water buffalo with sleep apnea wasn't frowned at. It was considered better etiquette than simply blowing your nose into a tissue or handkerchief, and on more than one occasion I got a dirty look for producing the red chequered affair that I kept in my front pocket. A decade before face masks became commonplace outside of East and South-East Asia amidst the Covid-19 pandemic, I was living amongst people who routinely wore them. They wore masks if they were sick with the flu, a cold or a whole range of other illnesses; they wore them when they were perfectly well during the cold and flu season to prevent them from catching illnesses from others; and they wore them during hay-fever and pollen seasons to mitigate against allergies; so, all things considered, quite a lot of the time.

I suppose the mask-wearing East Asians are probably revelling in how silly we look. How many Westerners have mocked Japanese tourists for arriving fresh from the airport into the centre of

European or American cities looking ridiculous in a face mask? Little did either the mockers or the mocked realise how in 2020 people worldwide would be compelled to don masks by law in many public spaces. Well, if it weren't for the fact that we can't see people's masked mouths at all, it may well be clear that we're laughing on the other side of our faces now.

What confused me were the inconsistencies. I'd look around in the winter months to see half the carriage wearing a face mask despite seemingly not feeling ill, while amongst the non-masked other half many coughed and sneezed without bothering to cover their nose or mouth with a hand. It just didn't make sense to me. In this nation so enamoured with cleanliness I found many public toilets had no soap dispensers by the sinks and no method to dry your hands. People would instead wash their hands with water alone and then dry them with the ubiquitous hand towel they kept in their pocket- the same hand towel they would then use to mop sweat from their faces.

I was certainly not a fan of the gents' portion of the public toilets in parks, the urinal section of which was semi-exposed to the public. It struck me as odd in such a reserved nation and I really felt uncomfortable knowing that the postman or Mrs Suzuki from number 18 could watch me urinate without my knowing while walking the dog or popping out for a loaf of bread and the paper.

***

The contradictions were everywhere - the 'uniquely safe' nation whose preoccupation with safety comes across as bordering on paranoia. I never cease to be amazed by the security measures taken in people's homes. In no country outside of Japan have I seen front doors that look as if they belong in a bank vault. Many of them are huge steel shields bristling with locks. Every night, like all the people in the neighbourhood, Yuka's mum would press a button and huge metal shutters would automatically come down and cover all the windows of the house and click as they locked at the bottom. I don't suppose the police have much cause in suburban Japan for kicking down people's front doors and maybe that's a good thing because they simply wouldn't be able to.

Yet amongst this paranoia of safety and security Japan's record on safe disposal of toxic waste is appalling and companies routinely close ranks and choose the tight-lipped 'sweep it under the carpet' approach in the face of glaring health and safety breaches. Whether the fact that Tokyo parents often let their seven-year-olds ride the train to school alone is indicative of this contradiction or whether, on the contrary, it is testament to the nation's safety, I'm not quite sure.

Perhaps oddest of all for a nation famed for being so technologically advanced, and whether testament to Japan's mistrust of credit cards, paranoia over fraud or, more likely the incredibly low interest rates put in place by the Bank of Japan since the late 90's, the Japanese mostly pay for things in cash. While the rest of the developed world and Japan's closest Asian neighbours pay by card for most transactions, even today the Japanese seldom do and, as a result, they carry large quantities of cash on their person.

***

I suppose it's ironic that this famously thin nation's most iconic sport is performed solely by the obese. In a country well-known for its cuisine the stereotype that Japanese diets are immaculate, largely holds true. However, with surprising regularity, popular fast-food chains in Japan release over-the-top limited time only items like ten-patty burgers and it seems almost a monthly occurrence that global fizzy drink brands release Japan-only sickly concoctions with even more sugar in them than their usual amply sugar-filled, tooth-rotting recipes.

A large number of TV channels feature eating contests for a surprisingly large amount of airtime. There seems no end to the Japanese public's appetite for viewing stick thin, heavily made-up young women tottering up to the contest table in high heels and skimpy clothing before devouring two dozen bowls of ramen or an ungodly number of hotdogs at a pace that would give even a Rennie heartburn just to watch.

I was surprised by how much the Japanese drank and smoked, particularly the men, before tottering red-faced from the bars to the train station at midnight to get four hours sleep before doing it all again. Intense work and stress, copious amounts of alcohol, tobacco and a deficit of sleep, but still the Japanese live to great ages so they must be doing something right. I guess it must be the hedgehog cafes and the used underwear vending machines.

It's a good thing the Japanese are by and large in good health, because while I was impressed with the police cars whose flashing red lights actually raised up on a platform above the car, if I ever find myself in the back of a Japanese ambulance again, and, un-like 'poo-gate', in need of genuine emergency treatment, I may have to use my last remaining breath to tell them to hurry up. Why Japanese emergency vehicles with flashing lights and sirens blaring crawl so slowly through the streets I do not know. As I watch firemen, paramedics and police address the public through the loud hailer, "Would you please mind moving? We're rushing to an emergency. Mind out. Thank you ever so much." I am impressed by the manners, but I feel for those to whom they are rushing and wonder if the emergency services will even be needed by the time they arrive.

***

Japan's attitudes to gambling speaks volumes of the nation's contradictory approach to so many issues. Officially, gambling is illegal in Japan. Not knowing this, one day I sat merrily in a game centre in Nakano, racking up a bucket load (literally a whole bucket load) of metal tokens at this strange whirly-gig machine with bright flashing lights and loud ringing noises, only to discover when I sidled up to the information counter with my booty that I couldn't in fact exchange the tokens for money at all.

"What's the point of the game then?" I asked. The man behind the glass screen looked at me blankly as if I was missing the point and said with no hint of irony, "The satisfaction of winning." The tokens were worthless and at the end of the game you'd simply put them all back.

It was with this thought in mind that I went one evening with Yuka and her mother to their local pachinko parlour with a quite lack lustre sense of interest. Pachinko is one of the many oddities of Japan. It is incredibly popular, almost to the point of a national obsession and yet very few people who neither have been to Japan or who have a specific interest in the country have ever heard of it.

Pachinko to the uninitiated is a huge, bizarre fanfare of lights, noise and surprisingly little action, situated in huge garishly coloured halls that often have the outward appearance of a warehouse that has been designed by someone on LSD. The names emblazoned above their entrances are tacky and ridiculous. 'Oriental Passage', 'Win it big', 'Winning Streak', and they serve as a beacon to all around.

Rows and rows of vertical pinball machines are crammed into these buildings. The first thing you notice is the noise which assaults you the moment you enter. In fact, it assaults you before you even enter. With all the doors closed you can hear it, muffled, as if some bizarre, annoying rave is taking place inside. All of a sudden, the doors automatically open to let a customer in or out and you get this aggressive flood of noise before the doors close behind them. If standing on the outside is an assault on the ears, then going inside is like being bludgeoned with a blunt instrument. When I stand in pachinko parlours I wonder if all who spend a significant period of time there are partially deaf. And there are many who do spend significant periods of time there. Walk through any Japanese town or city just before nine am when pachinko parlours open, and you will see long snaking lines of customers queuing up, usually with a can of coffee, a cigarette and a three-inch thick manga comic in hand.

The object of the game is to use the metal crank to shoot the balls up and around the pins and hopefully down into the frantically glowing but narrow open jaws at the bottom of the machine.

If you succeed, the already impossibly loud noises and incredibly bright flashing lights somehow become much louder and much brighter. More shiny silver ball bearings then spew out into the tray below the machine. In fact, it is a challenge when walking through one of these Alice in Wonderland-esque establishments not to kick over the trays of excess ball bearings that are stacked up beside the feet of the more avid players. Literally thousands upon thousands of balls can be won by the players who sit utterly mute and expressionless in a zombielike trance, cigarette clamped between their teeth with long trails of ash teetering from their cigarette tips (one interesting point being that smoking is still allowed in nearly all public buildings in Japan despite the ban in most of the developed world).

I am told by ardent players that the release comes in the very monotony and the repetition, the very brain-freezing sensory wall of noise that makes me shudder every time I pass by these places. You don't have to think, you *can't* think with all that colour and sound. Perhaps your very capacity for dwelling on thoughts is eroded when your receptors are so inundated.

The staff, who are dressed like waiters in a Victorian restaurant, dash in their waistcoats and bow ties between the punters, ferrying extra trays and reserving machines for those that need to nip to the loo. I can only imagine that the Japanese find some form of pleasure in this, some release in the satisfying repetition, but to me it's an incessant assault on the senses. And no winnings?! So, this leaves me wondering, is there something unique within the Japanese psyche that finds this particularly appealing? I can't think of a single other country on Earth where this would be a popular pastime. And this from the country of Zen! Give me a raked stone garden and a trickling mountain stream any time. But as with so much else in Japan, all is not what it seems.

I watched in amazement when Yuka's mother strode to the counter with her trays of balls that she had won, and the lady swept her hand behind her showing the shelves of gifts for which she could exchange her ball bearings. If the cuddly toy rabbits and bottles of champagne on display don't take your fancy, fear not. All you need do is ask the nice lady for a token with the value of your winnings printed on it and walk ten metres down the street to a small window, most of which is obscured by tinted glass. All you can see is a pair of hands at the bottom. If you hand this pair of hands your token, they will exchange it for cash. But you didn't win any money, you just swapped a token for cash, and swapping is not illegal and it's definitely not gambling, right?

***

The incongruity of Tokyo life is abundant. Somehow Tokyo, despite its size, is orderly and organised. The very numbers that live there should produce chaos. The calm is sometimes attributed to the repressed emotions which can eventually bubble to the surface in both harmless and harmful ways. The hard-drinking salarymen letting off steam by night are harmless enough. The cosplay and manga reading and cartoon figure collecting adults are all harmless enough, I suppose. After all, if you hadn't the time to indulge these interests as a child - which would hardly be surprising since you had school and then English school and then cram school, not to mention mountains of homework to do- then they might as well emerge years later in adulthood. But not all vents are harmless.

Just like Mt. Fuji, which can be seen from the centre of the city on very clear days, there are rumblings beneath the surface. It is undoubtedly true that the drinking and the gaming and the pachinko act like miniature fissures in the side of the volcano allowing pressure to escape slowly. That said, the big once in several centuries' eruption is always a possibility. You could read the Monday morning announcements that pop up on the screens in the train carriage blithely; you could ignore the true significance of the subtle shift in semantics all too easily. But, unlike 'derailment', 'signal failure' or 'mechanical fault', when I read the words 'human accident', I knew immediately and with alarming regularity that someone somewhere in Tokyo had had enough and had leapt in front of the rapid commuter express on the Chuo line.

It's harrowing because you want to believe it is avoidable in a nation as developed as Japan; you want to believe that no mother or wife or child would get the news they dreaded that day. It's harrowing because you know that someone had given up all hope. It isn't always the depressed businessman; it is often the student who has failed their exams and sometimes it is the woman who's lost her job. It is real people, and it happens far, far too often. The blue tarpaulins by the tracks were a grizzly reminder that when the volcano did erupt, it often did so with fatal consequences.

***

The weather threw up as many surprises as the people and the machines. October is a time of typhoons. The word 'typhoon' conjures images of horrendous damage and destruction. Surely out here on the Ring of Fire in a land of volcanoes and earthquakes and tsunamis these typhoons would bring more carnage than the moderate hurricanes we had back at home? No doubt some of the more clueless amongst the ex-pat community didn't know the difference between a tornado and a typhoon, a typhoon and a monsoon or between a hurricane and a storm. Anyway, isn't typhoon a brand of tea?

The reality was somewhat of a let-down. The much talked about typhoons appeared little more than a mildly windy and rainy day. Perhaps we shouldn't have been so blasé, we shouldn't have scoffed at the timidity of natural events. In a country like Japan that can really come back to bite you. Trains were cancelled, routes closed, and events rescheduled and there was always the odd fisherman swept out to sea. But the great storm that was predicted just never seemed to materialise. Maybe the Japanese weathercasters were just clever. Maybe they'd realised that by announcing a typhoon Mother

Nature wouldn't oblige to prove them right. They were calling her bluff. If we wanted to see a typhoon, we needed to refuse to believe one was coming. What we needed was Michael Fish[81].

Well, one autumn day after scoffing derisively at a forecasted typhoon, I certainly ate my words. I must have looked rather silly to my Japanese friends with my mocking and sarcastic bravado that day as we got caught on the concourse outside a train station in Tokyo's suburbs. The winds whipped up from seemingly nowhere turning a mildly wet scene into something dreadful. Mothers clutched their children to stop them blowing away and an old man was plastered painfully against a nearby pillar. The metal spokes of the umbrella I was holding snapped and, jagged metal edges and all, it was ripped powerfully from my feeble grasp and sent hurtling off over the roof tops, narrowly missing the head of a nearby teenage girl. Anoraks and hats and all manner of objects were swept away.

The crowds ducked and shrieks could be heard as the twisted metal of my umbrella innards and airborne shop signage threatened to decapitate anyone foolish enough to raise their head. As if it had proven its point, within minutes it had died down. I was a fool. After all the careful double-bluffing of all the Japanese news networks, after successfully

---

[81] Michael Fish was a popular and long-standing British weather forecaster. He is infamous for one monumental weather forecasting error. When he was live on air in October 1987, he said with a wry smile to the camera, "Earlier on today, apparently, a woman rang the BBC and said she heard there was a hurricane on the way. Well, if you're watching, don't worry, there isn't!" ("Michael Fish revisits 1987's Great Storm", BBC News, 2017) Just a few hours later Britain was battered by one of the most powerful storms in its recorded history.

keeping the natural phenomenon at bay by asserting that it would happen, one silly hapless gaijin had ruined the party for everyone. As if in subconscious tribute to the unfortunate forecaster of my childhood days, I'd only gone and Michael Fished it.

Chapter 18

'Read the Sign, Damn it!'

Making a nuisance of myself in the provinces

We must never forget the explorer's spirit.
Japanese proverb

If Japan appears almost bi-polar in its attitudes, its
night and day faces, its honne and tatemae, then what
of its geography? Osaka is Japan's second city, not its
second *largest* city, that is Yokohama. Though its
proud residents would bridle at me saying so,
Yokohama is in many ways culturally and
geographically indistinct from the capital. Osaka on
the other hand, 250 miles to the west, and Tokyo are
poles apart.

Perhaps for Brits a useful comparison would be the
English 'North/South divide' in terms of differences
in dialect, language, food and attitudes. The famed
'Kansai Ben[82]' or 'Osaka Ben', the dialect spoken in
those parts, is as immediately distinct from the
'standard Japanese' of Tokyo as a Sheffield or
Geordie accent is noticeably different to someone
from Devon or London. Like in many countries across
the globe, the capital can seem at best stuffy and
impersonal and at worst stuck up and self-important.
Far from being an attribute unique to Japan, the more
friendly atmosphere and easy-going nature of 'the
provinces' is a global tale to which many who have

---

[82] 'Ben' is Japanese for regional dialect.

escaped Paris for Lille or London for Manchester can attest.

There has always been a fierce rivalry between Tokyo and Osaka and it's easy to see why. The two main hubs of Japanese population, commerce, industry and culture are the Kanto[83] region in the east of Honshu (Greater Tokyo, Yokohama and environs) and the Kansai[84] region in the west of Honshu (an area which encompasses the four large cities of Osaka, Kobe, Kyoto and Nara). Though in ancient times the journey between the two regions would have taken weeks on the famous ancient trade route, the 'Tokaido[85]', today on the bullet train the journey takes a mere two and a half hours.

It is in the Kansai region that many of Japan's early centres of power developed around the historic cities of Nara and later Kyoto. It was also here that the well-known arts and cultural tenets and sensibilities of much of what the world now associates with ancient Japan first developed. It wasn't until 1868 that Tokyo became the capital of the nation and power firmly moved irrevocably to the east.

History aside, Tokyo and Osaka's rivalry continues unabated. Osaka has always been seen as Japan's great centre of commerce, a city of merchants. It has well-known signature dishes such as okonomiyaki (a savoury pancake, usually cooked at

[83] The Kanto region is home to the Greater Tokyo urban area. It encompasses seven prefectures (counties) on the island of Honshu. Approximately one-third of the entire Japanese population live in the Kanto region.

[84] The 'Kansai' region is in the west of Honshu and is Japan's secondary centre of population and major conurbations.

[85] The most important historic trade route of the Edo era, the Tokaido linked the old capital Kyoto to Edo (modern-day Tokyo).

the table and often by the diners themselves on a hot plate) and takoyaki (fried, battered balls of octopus). Osaka is also well known across Japan as the centre of comedy. It has a long history of producing many of the nation's greatest comedians, and it is in fact seen as a rite of passage for any would-be stand up to cut their teeth on the Osaka scene. Many tourists to the country prefer Osaka. They like it because it's more relaxed than Tokyo, because it has a more laidback, casual vibe. They like that it doesn't take itself as seriously. They like the off the wall accents and the slang and the brusque manners, the warm easiness of the people and their propensity for fun.

I don't. Osaka is not my cup of tea. Unlike most people who visit both cities, I prefer Tokyo with its regulations and manners. I recognise that the city and its people may come across as cold and impersonal to some, but to me it is a home. The capsule hotel from Hell had been in Osaka and I think that left an indelible mark on me. Like many 'second cities', Osaka has a complex. So perhaps I should forgive the angry man in the ticket booth at the underground station, who when I asked for directions to Osaka castle, just wafted his hand vaguely without looking up. When I asked him to repeat what he had said, he flew into a rage.

"Read the sign, damn it!"

Maybe it was my Tokyo accent that had enraged him so, but I sense it was more likely that he was tired of pointing idiots like me to the signpost that was in all honesty fairly obvious. I am sure that if I were to give the city a chance, I would learn to love it and find in it many redeemable features. As is so often the case, one or two negative experiences can leave a lasting and often unfair impression.

***

Intense as the Osaka/Tokyo rivalry may be, Kyoto's testy relationship with the modern capital is a much older and more fundamental chapter in Japan's history. Just thirty miles from Osaka, Kyoto has one of the world's largest collections of UNESCO World Heritage Sites and is unanimously regarded as Japan's cultural capital for its collection of temples, shrines, historic buildings and artisan crafts. Parts of Kyoto appear unrivalled in their beauty.

Indeed, it is Kyoto's beauty and historic significance that spared it from the catastrophic bombing of nearly all of Japan's major cities in World War 2. Kyoto had initially been on the list of targets for America's atomic bombs in place of Nagasaki. In fact, at one point, it was at the very top of the list. At that time, a man named Henry Stimson was secretary of war under the Roosevelt and Truman administrations. Stimpson had visited Kyoto twice before, first in 1926. He'd been so touched by the city's beauty that he persuaded Truman not to bomb Kyoto. It was only on the 24th July 1945, just two weeks before the atomic bomb destroyed Nagasaki, that Kyoto was finally removed from the list altogether.

It is even more startling then, given that Kyoto was spared total annihilation merely seventy-five years ago, how local government and city planners chose to chip away at the city's beauty in the decades after the war. Undoubtedly, Kyoto is still special. However, in the erecting of a gaudy new station and the ugly

Kyoto tower in the centre of the city's skyline and the systematic removal of old buildings starting in the 1960's, the Japanese administrators and planners began to destroy what the Americans chose not to.

Desperate for their city not to be viewed as a relic, in the post-war years they insisted on transforming the city centre with new buildings of concrete and plate glass, to refashion the city as a forward-looking metropolis, not some antiquated has-been. Can you imagine the justified outcry were this to happen in Bath or Cordoba or Rome? In recent years, hopeful signs have sprung up that this desecration, which luckily is far from total, is being opposed by locals and foreigners alike.

Although the Kyoto of 1950 was by all accounts a far more majestic and romantic place than the Kyoto of 2020, its jewels in the crown remain - the temples and shrines which ring the edge of the city, dotted as they are on the forested high ground, protected from the ugly development they overlook happening in the city centre below. If the developers' touches don't take the edge of Kyoto's charms for you, then the sheer volume of tourists, huge parties of cackling schoolchildren and busloads of pensioners that cram and jostle at every temple and shrine may. Great expectations and disappointment are common bedfellows, and it is both Kyoto's blessing and curse that the city benefits in such abundance from the former.

I recommend Kanazawa, it seems to strike a good balance, about a third of Kyoto's size and despite being a tourist hotspot, the crowds don't seem so overwhelming as to detract from the pleasure of visiting. Kanazawa is famous for being a historic samurai city and in appearance it is in many ways a little Kyoto. It has the temples and the cobbled old streets flanked by ornately decorated wooden buildings, the beautiful little vermillion bridges over sparkling streams in the shade of cherry blossom trees but, refreshingly, less of the fanfare. Besides, Kanazawa must be a good place to visit, because much like Mt. Fuji or the Nagasaki night view and old gravel-voice, it is home to another of Japan's 'top threes'.

Kenrokuen park in the centre of the city is officially one of Japan's top three must-visit gardens, and believe you me, from the moment you enter the city or even open a guidebook to Kanazawa, you are told this in no uncertain terms. I ambled past the newlyweds in kimonos having endless photographs taken on all the park's many little stone bridges from every conceivable angle. At each couple I came to, the same ritual played out. I paused for each photo and then the next and the next and they waved me past apologetically. I bowed and grinned and apologised with little waves of the hand and ducked below camera height, and by the time I'd reached the central lake I had bowed and ducked and darted and apologised and grinned so much I felt I'd had a rather good workout.

If I were more agile, less pasty or not in possession of so sweet a tooth (or ideally all three) the ridiculous scene that soon followed may not have occurred at all. With the rising heat of the summer's day and after my photo-ducking aerobics I'd built up quite a sweat.

Having applied more factor 60 (yes, pharmacies do stock it, before you ask) than my skin could possibly absorb in a lifetime, I was reminded as I headed towards the park's exit that the downsides of my SPF-over indulgence were not limited to simply looking like a French mime artist or Queen Elizabeth 1st.

I like to think of myself as a man of culture, but I simply am not. I'm the sort of bloke who congratulates himself a little when he leaves a museum or an art gallery on having lingered at each artefact longer than I'd ever want because it was the 'right' thing to do. The ponds full of carp were lovely, the stone lanterns, the statues, the pagoda and the tea house by the lake all added a very sophisticated and very 'Japanese' ambience to the park. However, I was most thrilled of all when through streaming red eyes that felt like they were on fire I spotted a little ice cream shop by the park's gate that sold gold ice cream with flecks of real gold in it. Don't get me wrong, the park was lovely, but one stone bridge and one carp-filled pond and pagoda and newlywed couple look very much like another, and, as delightful as they undoubtedly are, the park's other sugar-less charms could never do as much to win my heart as this surprisingly regal take on the good old Mr Whippy. My eyes were in agony, I was hot, tired, hungry and my white face was dripping all over my clothes but strike me down, that ice cream was delicious.

Do spare a thought for the newly wed Mr and Mrs Tanaka. In the weeks to come while their families and friends no doubt swooned and gasped in delight at the pictures and commented on the beautiful bride in her kimono there may have been a few whispered comments about one or two of the final snaps. Was the romance of their special day at all diminished by the strange character looming in the background? Were the memories at all tarnished by this scruffy foreigner? It may rain on your wedding day, you may lose the ring, your fiancee may even jilt you at the altar, but be thankful. Be thankful that your wedding photos are not ruined by a red-eyed crying snowman whose face is melting off, licking ice cream from his soiled clothes, clutching at his eyes and moaning through dripping gold lips.

***

Dogo Onsen is the most famous hot springs in all of Japan. It is also the oldest with a history dating back well over a thousand years and said to have been the inspiration behind the bathhouse in the famous anime 'Spirited Away[86]' and suffice to say, as a result, it is now a major tourist attraction. It sits deep within Ehime prefecture on the island of Shikoku, a good several hours by bullet train and then a series of local train rides away from Tokyo. But still the crowds come and photograph the ornate decorative wooden building with its beautifully tiled roof and its serene mountainside setting.

Whenever I catch a glimpse of myself in traditional yukata like I did that day in Dogo Onsen, I wrongly assume there is something of the air of James Bond about me. 'You only Live Twice' was filmed in Japan and released in 1967 at a time when the nation's post-war economic and cultural resurgence was at its zenith, just three years after Japan had signalled its

---

[86] An internationally popular 2001 Japanese animated fantasy film set in and around a bathhouse.

arrival on (or 'return to' if you like) the world stage in an emphatic manner with the hosting of the 1964 Tokyo Olympics. In the film it is the macho Sean Connery and not the smooth-tongued Roger Moore who strides around looking stylish in a yukata and is fawned over by adoring Japanese ladies in a traditional bathhouse. He's suave and sophisticated in a way that I can only dream of ever being. In my yukata, with my chunky legs, ruddy features and gap-toothed grin, I look like I should be sitting astride a stile somewhere with a stalk of wheat clamped between my lips, not serving Britain's interests overseas and defeating global terrorism by bedding beauties and battling bad guys.

When I wear a yukata, I always feel I have the appearance of a child who's dressed up in his dad's clothes or a madman who's gone out in public in his dressing gown but humour me if you will by entertaining the illusion that I appeared refined, cultured and mysterious. As I sat post-bath on that warm summer's evening with the refreshing breeze fluttering through the open walls under the building's sweeping awnings, unlike Connery, I wasn't surrounded by fawning women, but it didn't matter because the green tea tasted good and somehow in a rare moment of dexterity, I'd managed to sit down in my yukata without my balls showing. Victory.

***

Ancient bathhouses were one thing, but for real history and for a mysterious and enchanting atmosphere, I would head to some of the more remote temples and shrines dotted across Japan. Not far from

Ehime's Dogo Onsen bathhouse, in neighbouring Kagawa prefecture, there is a famous temple at the top of a misty mountain called Konpira-san. One summer evening I trudged up the ancient moss-covered stone steps in the rain until I felt giddy. Every flight of steps presented at its top a false horizon until I convinced myself that the steps would never end and maybe the burning sensation in my thighs and the chill of the rain just wasn't worth it.

When I finally crested the true summit, I realised instantly that it was. It's hard to describe the beauty of a single temple in a land where you are truly spoilt for them, but there is something magical and haunting about Konpira-san. It feels like the ideal setting for a samurai movie, shrouded in cloud, inaccessible and remote. The rain fell steadily from the darkening sky and as afternoon turned to evening, with the fading light casting eerie shadows, the scene felt incredibly atmospheric.

I forgot the rain, I forgot that the rubbish anorak I had bought for 500 yen was made of a material that seemed to absorb water like a sponge. I walked around in a childish trance and looked at the carvings and the ancient woodblock pictures. I liked Konpira-san because it felt more real than the gilts and golds and bright scarlets of each of the many temples in Kyoto. I liked the fact that because of the rain and the time of day and the number of steps I had it to myself. It was haunting and marvellous.

By the time I got back to the station I was soaked right through, and during the hour-long train journey back to Takamatsu city the air conditioner blew cold air down my neck and I shivered, and my teeth chattered. I had no change of clothes and my frigid t-shirt clung to my goose-pimpled skin. I was convinced I'd get ill, sure that I'd wake up the next day with a fever and the chills and a sore head and hear the whine of my subconscious asking me what the hell did I expect if I climbed to the top of a mountain in the pouring rain? But I didn't, I woke the next day with a spring in my step feeling rejuvenated and full of life. Maybe the spirits of Konpira-san had watched over me, maybe the mountain had granted me fair passage, but more likely it was just the enormous steaming hot bowl of ramen noodles that I devoured when I got to Takamatsu city that staved off the illness. They came in a thick broth with doorstop thick chunks of pork and went well with the delicious steaming pork and herb dumplings I had as a side. Lovely!

***

No trip to any region of Japan would be complete without visiting its castles. Though markedly different in both style and building materials to European ones, they are nonetheless beautiful and true feats of engineering. They tend to be wooden, painted bright white and sit atop high large drystone walls of boulders. Sadly, as a result, as with so many of Japan's traditional buildings, temples and shrines, they are at great risk of succumbing to fires and of course the ever-present hazard of earthquakes.

Himeji castle is widely considered to be the most beautiful in all of Japan. It is said to resemble a graceful white heron about to take flight. Aside from its beauty, it has a bit of a St. Paul's cathedral vibe to it too. Not in its appearance of course, since Himeji in true Japanese castle style is wooden with a tiled roof, but in that while the city around it was relentlessly bombed during World War 2, the castle remained intact. And just like St. Paul's, though a bomb did hit it, it failed to explode, a fact that only adds to the place's mystique.

The castle must have been an impressive prospect because it alone was the reason why I had stopped on the bullet train between Osaka and Hiroshima. I walked along the wide main street that leads from the station to the castle while contemplating the beautiful structure looming in the distance. As I was strolling along the near empty street pondering how the castle almost seemed to float majestically above the city, all of a sudden, a figure appeared right beside me. I turned around and standing just two feet away was a tall African man.

"Hey, my friend," he said to me in English. "Please tell me, where is the nearest discotheque?"

I was immediately aware that we were the only two people in the entire vicinity. As if the situation wasn't strange enough, I had to remind myself that it was still only 11am. I apologised that I had no idea and continued plodding toward the castle. Turning around twenty metres down the road to check that the entire encounter hadn't been some strange apparition caused by my dehydration or an odd mirage or trick of my mind in heat of the day, he was gone. He'd completely vanished, and the road once again was completely empty. I couldn't see any side streets that he could have ducked into and there were no shops on this stretch of the thoroughfare into which he could have popped. How strange, I thought.

The castle is impressive, and I recommend a visit. Of course, the odds, if you go, of a lone African man approaching you before noon and asking you where the nearest discotheque is are almost non-existent. Or are they?

Years later when I was talking to a Japanese friend, somehow Himeji came up in conversation. I kid you not, with no prompting or prior knowledge that I'd even been to the city, she said, "Yeah, I've only been to Himeji once. It was very strange. As I approached the castle, an African man came up to me and asked where the nearest discotheque was."

Who knows, if you ever go to Himeji, you may meet him too. He was very friendly and polite, but 11 o'clock in the morning seems a bit early for dancing.

***

For many people, although three quarters of a century have passed, when they think of Japan, World War Two comes to mind more readily than cute cartoon characters, high-tech machinery or factory workers performing synchronised group aerobics each morning. When I walked out of my interview in London, having crossed out the word 'China' and replaced it with the word 'Japan' on my application form, I thought of the war. Having a keen interest in military history and none whatsoever in Japanese food, fashion or pop-culture such as anime, I had little else to occupy my mind on the train journey back to the South West. Most of what I knew about my soon-to-be new home was what I'd read of the nation's aggressive militarism in the early twentieth century and its wartime atrocities.

It was with great interest therefore that deep within the mountains of the southernmost peninsula of the southernmost of Japan's home islands, I found a museum. It is in the ancient province of Satsuma. Say the word 'satsuma' to people in the West and they picture little sweet oranges, and aptly so, since it was through this southern province in the Meiji[87] era that the fruit which grew in the area was exported to the West. In Japan the region is better known for being one of the main areas that rose up against the Tokugawa shogunate[88] in the mid-19th century.

I found the museum in a place called Chiran and no-one I knew had ever heard of the place let alone its museum. Given the long, winding bus journey that wended its way up narrow switchback mountain roads for a seeming eternity, I could fully understand why. I was staying at a hotel overlooking a tranquil bay, which was notable for the great active volcano of Sakurajima which was visible at its other side. A city lies close to the volcano which routinely cloaks its buildings and people in its ash, and primary children wear hard hats to school to protect them from falling debris.

It was with the volcano as a backdrop that across this same bay nearly eighty years ago Japanese warplanes rehearsed for the attack on Pearl Harbour. They were the same beaches in which I was soon to

[87] A period of huge change in Japanese politics, the economy and society at large. The Meiji era lasted from 1868 to 1912. During the Meiji era Japan transformed from an isolated feudal country to a modern, industrial nation state. Under the previous Tokugawa Shogunate Japan had been a closed country for over 200 years.

[88] The military government of feudal Japan during the Edo period of 1603 to 1868.

find myself buried and sweltering and wondering if any of my orifices had escaped volcanic intrusion. Sitting on the bus that wound its way to Chiran was quite a relief after being buried alive but arriving in the tiny settlement there were no jolly holiday makers, for Chiran is the home of the kamikaze museum. In addition to Kagoshima bay being the location of the practice runs for the attack on Pearl Harbour, nearby Chiran at the bottom tip of Kyushu was also the principal (and southernmost) base for kamikaze pilots heading to attack allied shipping off Okinawa.

I've never been in a museum as deathly silent. Even in the museums in Hiroshima and Nagasaki there's a quiet but audible hum of whispers and shuffling bodies. But here there were almost no sounds at all. The first thing that greets you as you enter is a painting of a kamikaze pilot on fire being carried from the burning wreckage of his crashed plane to heaven by two white-robed angels. This is the only exhibit you are allowed to capture on film as photography is prohibited beyond that point. A salvaged zero fighter plane stands in the centre of the museum surrounded by other relics. The letters the pilots wrote before their fateful missions are mounted on the walls around the entire circumference of the museum next to photographs of pilots themselves.

What strikes you as you read those letters and look at the photos is how young and handsome the men were. Most seemed to be about nineteen or twenty and full of life. They had girlfriends and babies and hobbies; they were happy, loving and loyal. They are photographed drinking and smoking, stroking a dog tenderly or playing sports with friends. The men had parties the night before they flew. They danced and sang and fought and cried and some worked themselves up into a such a frenzy that they smashed up their accommodation knowing that the following day they would be flying to their certain death. I didn't expect to be so moved by the museum, but I was.

The rows of wooden huts where the men slept are a visible reminder that it was here that hundreds of them set off knowing they'd never return. A single bronze statue stands outside the museum of a pilot in his leather headgear. But the museum itself is not well signposted and almost entirely hidden by thick stands of trees that cover its entrance from view. As you step away through the car park you are lost in a little cluster of restaurants and houses. To stand fifty metres away you wouldn't know the museum was there at all, so no wonder even most Japanese people had never heard of it.

A pleasant surprise in the small town of Chiran proper was the discovery of a historic samurai village with row upon row of beautiful thatched little cottages each enclosed by high green hedges. They have beautiful stone gardens with pristine ponds of carp. The houses stand on stilts with beautiful wooden floors and immaculate verandas and back on to thick forests of bamboo which sweep up the mountainsides. It was strange to find such beauty and horror on the same non-descript mountain top, tucked away, not trumpeted or advertised. It is quiet and calm and almost hauntingly peaceful.

Here in the middle of nowhere, at the very bottom of Japan, I had found a hidden place that symbolised the idolised warrior Japan of ancient history and the more complex recent history of the nation's modern warfare. On this sweltering day, my head filled with images of noble sword-wielding warriors in armour on horseback. I also thought of young men and terrified teens full of life deliberately flying to their deaths over the Pacific in airborne bombs. As I descended from the mountain and headed back to the black volcanic beaches of Kagoshima bay my mind was awash with snapshots of vibrant life and its sudden, brutal loss. The faces of the car drivers I saw as I trudged bore great surprise because as each one passed, they registered this blubbering wreck of an Englishman wandering off into the sunset struggling and failing to hold back the tears.

Chapter 19

Bad Things Come in Threes

Earthquake, tsunami and nuclear disaster

After the rain, earth hardens.
Japanese proverb

At 2:46 pm on Friday eleventh March 2011, I was sitting at my desk in a school on the sixth floor of a seven-story building in a western suburb of Tokyo. I had just finished my class of four old ladies sixteen minutes before and was waiting for another two old ladies to arrive for their lesson at 3 o'clock. They never did. I imagine they were on their way, walking along the pavement or on the bus en route, but that lesson never took place. There were no more lessons that day or the next day. In fact, my school closed for the next ten days. What I experienced that day was a mega-quake, 9.0 - 9.1 on the Richter scale[89]. It was the fourth or fifth most powerful earthquake ever recorded on planet Earth and the most powerful ever recorded in Japan.

I felt it at first as a gentle rattling. I knew it was an earthquake but wasn't unduly worried. I'd been living in Japan for four years by that point and had experienced my fair share of tremors, some bigger than others. They didn't particularly scare me, not as they once had. In a briefing in my training week in 2007 during my first week in Japan, our trainer had

---

[89] The internationally recognised scale used to measure the strength of earthquakes.

casually informed the new arrivals that Tokyo was expecting 'the big one' and I'd gone to bed that night with apocalyptical visions of high-rise buildings toppling over, the pavement cracking and molten lava spewing up through the Earth's broken crust.

Over the coming years I was to experience earthquakes while I slept (some woke me, but the smaller ones didn't); earthquakes while I taught; earthquakes while I was on the toilet and earthquakes while I travelled about the city. If you were sitting on an over ground train when an earthquake struck, it'd come to a halt and you'd sit nervously looking around you as it rocked noisily back and forth on its springs. When on an underground train you'd feel even more nervous, the train stopping in a darkened tunnel as thoughts flashed through your mind of blocked escape routes. I am told that being in an underground train or tunnel is not as dangerous as you might think. Apparently, like a wave on the sea, though the movement originates from below, most of the damage is on the surface and therefore, in a strange way, you are better off underground than over it. Still, the idea of the exits to the underground collapsing and being buried with no oxygen preyed on the mind just perceptibly whenever I took Tokyo's tube.

When earthquakes struck at night it was particularly unnerving. It took quite a while before you realised in your sleepy state that the shaking beneath you wasn't part of your dream. On other nights you'd relate your dream of an earthquake to a colleague at work the following day and they'd inform you that it was no dream. Sometimes you'd sleep right through. The windows and walls would shake a bit, the train you were on might stop momentarily and then you'd all play a guessing game as to the magnitude.

"I reckon that might have even be a 5."

"No, I reckon a 4.5 max."

As with so much in life, familiarity dispels fear and I realised that by and large, earthquakes in a modern city like Japan were more of a curiosity, more of a talking point than a genuine terror. Living in arguably the most earthquake-prone nation on Earth was a mixed blessing. On the one hand you had more earthquakes and more powerful ones than possibly any other country. On the other hand, Japan as a result is more prepared than any country on Earth to prevent the serious damage that earthquakes cause to property and life, and deal with the effects of such quakes. The design of modern Japanese buildings, especially in large cities, though often utilitarian and ugly, is a wonder of science. The Japanese are leagues ahead in their earthquake-proof building technology. Huge buildings of steel and concrete flex and sway when tremors hit, thus absorbing the waves and moving with them.

I remember watching from the sixth floor of the building I was teaching in that day and seeing the buildings jiggle around. In the days that followed I saw the skyscrapers in Shinjuku wobble. It was all very surreal and my respect for the intelligence and ingenuity of structural engineers increased enormously. By unlucky happenstance, Christchurch in New Zealand also suffered a large earthquake less than three weeks before the big quake in Japan. The buildings of the New Zealand capital crumbled under the effects of the magnitude 6.3, whereas Japan's cities withstood the ravages of a magnitude 9.

It is worth bearing in mind the science behind the earthquake measuring system. With each number higher on the Richter scale the earthquake's power increases by a factor of ten. Thus, a magnitude 5 earthquake shakes ten times more violently than a magnitude 4, which in turn shakes ten times more violently than a magnitude 3. The quake that hit Japan on that fateful day, though its epicentre was out to sea, was therefore many times more powerful than the one which razed much of Christchurch city centre to the ground, and yet nearly all buildings in Japanese cities stood.

As on so many other occasions, the shaking began gently. This time as I sat writing up lesson notes it struck me that the shaking differed from usual in two ways. Firstly, it wasn't stopping and secondly, it was getting stronger all the time. There was that intangible point at which you mentally say, right, this isn't a joke anymore and you instinctively kick into a different gear. For me that point came when I heard the windows rattle and flex like they were about to shatter. It felt as if a giant had picked up the building and was gyrating the entire thing. What you *should* do in an earthquake is get under a table or something similarly sturdy. What you *should* do is make sure you are not beneath anything that could fall on top of you like a lampshade or a heavy bookcase. And what you definitely *shouldn't* do is leave the building under any circumstances.

I ran out of the building without a second thought. I got down the six flights of stairs faster than Usain Bolt and found myself standing on the pavement. The buildings all around rattled and whined and creaked. The noises of metal and stone under stress were unnerving as I now found myself beneath buildings and hanging signs. This is why you're told to stay inside. My colleague that day, Glynn had stayed inside, he had done the right thing. I'd seen him race under the table with his students as I fled past his classroom. I'll never know what he thought as I disappeared out of the door. It was probably something along the lines of 'that idiot's going to get himself killed'.

Obviously, I didn't die, but I did stand holding on to the railings that separated the pavement from the road and stare at a middle-aged office worker in shirt and tie who was standing right next to me. He, like me was an idiot who didn't crawl under his table. We looked at each other and burst into uncontrollable laughter. I don't know why, I guess it was just a release of tension. When we'd both finished giggling, we looked up in unison at the swaying buildings and then over to the vehicles on the road which had all come to a sudden, panicked halt. I could hear screams on the bus which had stopped opposite us in the far lane. It was tilting from side to side on its suspension like something out of a science-fiction movie and we could hear the shocked gasps of the pensioners on board who braced themselves against the seats in front.

I'm told that the earthquake lasted up to five minutes, although in some ways it felt like mere seconds and in others it seemed to last an eternity. Eventually, I returned to the school on the sixth floor. I knew the earthquake was serious as I looked at the unbroken view to the east and saw twenty miles away in Tokyo bay a large column of black smoke spiralling into the afternoon sky, which I later found out was a damaged oil refinery. The trains had all stopped, and long lines of commuters made an odd sight tramping the several-hours-long journey home. Millions of office workers filled the street like a slow and oddly dressed sponsored walk.

Glynn was well known amongst the teachers of the company as being unable to speak in anything other than innuendo. It was difficult to get any common sense out of him. On this most surreal of days, true to form, he sat crowing in his Alan Partridge-esque manner.

"Ooh, that was a big one! Oh, I think a big crack has just developed! Whoa, at last I can tell people that my bed was shaking last night!"

All the nervous humour born out of relief was put aside when we returned to our homes and discovered that a huge tsunami had engulfed Honshu's north-eastern coast. Whole fishing villages and towns had simply disappeared, whole communities wiped off the map by the surging ocean which carried cars and boats and buildings and people with it, miles inland. The video footage was harrowing. The by now iconic images of the wave breaching the sea walls, recorded on shaky handy cams by terrified residents perched on roofs was unforgettable. Tens of thousands of people had become homeless overnight. The earthquake lasted mere minutes and the tsunami was brief enough, but once the shaking had stopped and the waters had receded revealing the true extent of the damage, the third disaster became apparent. The Fukushima Daichi nuclear reactors had been inundated by the tsunami and there was a meltdown in reactor number two. As brave workers battled to bring the reactor under control the whole world watched. Was this another Chernobyl unfolding before the eyes of the world's media?

Frantic phone calls from home urged me to return to the U.K. in the wake of alarming BBC news reports that the meltdown at the nuclear reactor was worse than had at first been thought.

"Just get on a plane and come home!" insisted various members of my extended family citing reports they had heard of radiation sweeping towards Tokyo.

Although I felt concerned, I and many others like me felt a strange urge to remain in Japan.

My apartment building was undamaged, but it would not be entirely true to say all of Tokyo's buildings escaped the ravages of this massive tectonic event. My American friend Jake (the one who'd had the wine chucked over him at the Christmas party by the drunken Sunderland fan) was not as fortunate. Returning home that evening, he noticed with no small amount of alarm that there was a crack going from the foundations of his three-storey apartment block to its roof. Mustering all the 'look on the bright side' chipper Brit within me I posited the idea to a panicked Jake over the phone that I'd no doubt it was just a superficial crack in the building's façade. When I visited his home a short while later, it did indeed look bad, but in the weeks to come I never heard that it had suddenly collapsed so I guess luckily my forced positivity was borne out by reality.

After three days we received a phone call from our company headquarters telling us that there'd be no school for a further seven days due to the triple disaster. I could have stayed in Tokyo but when Jake and Tim told me they were off to Kyoto to do the tourist thing I decided to join them. I'd been to Kyoto three years earlier with my mum. I'd already seen the sights, but I had nothing better to do and it couldn't harm being four hundred miles from the rapidly disintegrating Fukushima Daichi power plant rather than a mere two hundred back in Tokyo. So, I hopped on the bullet train with the intention of meeting the pair who were already there. I was tired and irritable from nights of snatched sleep, being woken by aftershocks and drifting back into a slumber of troubled thoughts, always on edge and on guard. After the surreal few days spent in Tokyo after the quake, the gravity of the situation was really brought home to me when I saw families hurriedly boarding the same bullet train heading west, except they had a lot more luggage than the flimsy holdall I carried. These people were getting the hell out of Dodge.

Initially, in the vein of childish bravado I'd thought I'd stay in Tokyo. I didn't want to be one of those 'flyjin', a derogatory adaption of the term 'gaijin' which was quickly coined for the ex- pats who got out of Japan in the immediate days and weeks after the quake. There was a certain pride amongst those who stayed and stuck it out and a barely concealed derision of those who didn't. Most returned when things had settled down, but some didn't. It was with a certain jingoistic pride that some of the British ex pats, me included, noted that while the American embassy in Tokyo advised their residents to leave Japan, and the French embassy actually laid on flights for their residents in Japan to return home, the British embassy website with all the Blitz 'we'll get through it' spirit suggested their citizens just do as they see fit.

Of course, if the proverbial had truly hit the fan, had the geiger counters[90] in Tokyo started reporting levels of radiation that they were getting up north, we might have been singing a different tune. The panicked phone calls from loved ones at home continued to implore us to return. While the BBC and other Western news outlets continued to tout the next Chernobyl or worse, we watched the platitudes on NHK and the downplaying of the incident by the Japanese government and weighed up our options. We might have felt more panic if we'd known that the Japanese government, as it later turned out, was drawing up contingencies to evacuate the whole of Greater Tokyo. Just the thirty-seven million of us then. But it didn't happen, and we mostly stayed.

I arrived late in Kyoto and had booked my own hotel room. I'd meet Tim and Jake the following day. I was tired and dazed, and I soon discovered that the aftershocks were hitting Kyoto almost as badly as Tokyo. I couldn't sleep. I staggered out into the hallway to get a drink from the vending machine and noticed a little machine selling movie cards. For 500

---

[90] A device used to detect and measure the amount of radiation.

yen you could purchase a card and select a movie to watch in your room. The selection was scant. I eventually settled on 'Inception'. It is a good film, but it will forever be marred for me by the conditions under which I first watched it.

I shall try not to ruin it too much for those of you who have not seen the film, but as the main characters drifted in and out of sleep uncontrollably for the next couple of hours so did I. As I woke, startled every now and then, my hotel room shaking and juddering with powerful aftershocks, I'd see Leonardo Di Caprio and Ken Watanabe on my TV screen being tossed around by the same forces of nature. I drifted off again and once more awoke. They were in Kyoto. I was in Kyoto. They fell asleep once more and so did I. Then they woke as the ancient city rumbled beneath them, and then so did I as the exact same ancient city rumbled beneath me. And I wondered where reality stopped and where my dreams began. I dreamed of the film, the people in the film dreamed and I eventually awoke to a calmer dawn.

I moved out of the first hotel to share a room with Tim, the mad plum blossom viewing American in the mustard trench coat. He needn't have worried about the aftershocks or the nuclear radiation, the tar in his fags would surely kill him first. I would be woken by him every morning at seven am coughing so hard I marvelled at how his organs stayed inside his body. He'd light up his first Golden Bat of the day and pour himself the strongest coffee ever known, piling the grains two inches thick.

After three days in Kyoto, we returned to Tokyo. Rumours abounded after a week or two that Tokyo residents should stop drinking their tap water as it might be contaminated. I'd been drinking it since the meltdown and figured the damage was done, if any, so continued to drink it. Besides the only alternative was bottled water and with the panic buying at the convenience stores post-quake, that had all gone. Mixed messages began springing up about the danger of being caught out in the rain. Apparently, so people said, there was a high likelihood of the rainfall containing nuclear radiation. One or two friends were clearly and understandably feeling the strain, desperately showering if caught out in a downpour and praying to who knows what that so much of what we read and heard was over-exaggerated hyperbole.

The following weeks were tense if not scary. The aftershocks rattled on, waking you in the night or interrupting a lesson or bus ride. Some of them were nearly as powerful as the main quake itself. It might seem hard to draw any positives from such a disaster, and had we been the poor sods two hundred miles further north whose whole towns and villages had literally been washed off the map, I doubt we'd have found any. But somewhere I suppose, the universal truth that bonds are forged in adversity rang true. I felt more 'Japanese' than I ever had, having lived through it with them. After all, fear and anxiety do not discriminate.

The muted lights of Shibuya and Shinjuku, a usually dazzling neon glare, were haunting. They were a visceral reminder, if we needed one, that nothing was immune from the power of Mother Nature. Train lights were dimmed, and Tokyo grew dark in an effort to save power. The seemingly irrepressible sleepless city of bright lights had been subdued, providing a daily lived reminder, an ever-visible indication that all was not well. It was easy to forget that on a far more practical level, in addition to causing radioactive fallout, the melting of Fukushima Daichi[91] had reduced the nation's energy producing capacity.

It is common these days for people old enough to remember, to ask others where they were when JFK was shot. Where did they watch the moon landings? When the news of Princess Diana's death was broadcast, what were they doing? For me it was hard to forget the day the twin towers fell in New York. I had just turned 18 and watching the second plane slice through the building on a live TV news report, I looked on in awe and fear. I was in a café in Greenwood, Nova Scotia in Canada just outside of the CRAF base. On sofas all around me equally awed airmen were letting their takeaway coffees go cold as they sat watching in alarm in olive green flying suits festooned with sewn on badges. Minutes later their pagers bleeped, and they dashed back to base. That left a lasting impression on me, and no doubt anybody old enough to remember it will be able to recall vividly the circumstances in which they found themselves that day.

In the same vein, it became commonplace to discuss the events of March 11th. The locations and experiences were as varied as you'd expect. There

---

[91] A Nuclear Power Plant in Fukushima prefecture which suffered major damage from the March 11th, 2011 magnitude 9.0 earthquake and tsunami. Several of its reactors were permanently damaged. Radiation from the plant leaked into the air and sea.

were friends on buses, on underground trains (not ideal), there were friends in skyscrapers, asleep and even one sitting on the toilet. In the weeks that followed the quake we all had our 'emergency bags' packed and ready beside our beds. These were rucksacks containing a torch, spare batteries, water, chocolate and a helmet amongst other items. Of course, the hope was that you wouldn't ever need to use the emergency bag.

In late 2009, I had moved from my flat to the one above me. The floor plan was exactly the same as my old flat, except it had a balcony instead of an outdoor space, plus it had a sleeping platform accessed by a ladder from my living room. The design of my new flat was a double-edged sword. The advantage was that my new living room minus the bed had a little more space and, as well as my futon, the platform had a little space for storage. The downside was that I was constantly terrified of rolling off the platform in my sleep and crashing the ten feet down to the floor. There was nothing to stop me rolling off except for a wooden lip about an inch high at the platform's edge. This was bad enough in normal times, but during the huge aftershocks in the aftermath of the big quake my paranoia rose to new levels. When I moved into my new flat, I found a bucket on the balcony with a rope in it with little rung-like plastic discs along its length. For months I had wondered what on Earth it was for, but it eventually dawned on me that this was my escape mechanism should the front door buckle and become inaccessible after an earthquake.

If another 'big one' happened during the day, then at least you'd hear the alert over the public address systems in the street. If you had the TV on, then a little red light would appear in the corner of the screen accompanied by a bleeping. In either case, the warning you got was only seconds as it was impossible for the warning to be any longer. By the time the sensors in the ground detected movement, you had mere moments to do something. I almost wondered in those moments when the red light appeared whether I'd rather not know. It was like hitting the brakes and watching the car slide into the wall. I didn't want time to think. I didn't want a countdown like some kind of Tom and Jerry timer on a cartoon bomb. At least when it happened at night, by the time you'd woken from your slumber and realised what was going on it was more or less over. Given that many bars and restaurants in Tokyo were underground, it always made for a tense few seconds as the aftershocks rattled the glasses and the light fixtures in the ceiling wobbled above your head. I suppose if you are going to be buried alive underground a pub's not a bad place to have it happen.

Japan was wounded and, though we all knew what it had been through in its recent history and that the country and its people had the fortitude and resolve to survive against the odds, it hurt. Aside from the jokes and the stiff upper lips and the getting back to normal and the pretending that we in Tokyo had really suffered, we were all aware, but maybe not enough, that a few hundred miles north it would be a long, long time for things to get back to normal. Not for them the suspiciously exaggerated accounts of a near miss disaster that looks great on social media.

Not for them the 'Are you alright?' messages of concerned friends and family and the bathing in the afterglow of a pseudo victim mentality. Not for them the bragging rights, the Facebook 'Checking in as safe' status updates, and 'one year ago today' show off, attention seeking rubbish.

Their lives had been turned upside down. It would be a long time before the miles of debris was cleared. It would be a long time before the villages and towns were rebuilt from scratch, a long time before the reactors were demolished or entombed. It would be a long time before the millions of tonnes of contaminated soil was bagged and buried safely; before the seawater was safe and the sea-life which lived within it. The scars would live on, those on the land and those in people's minds. Over a hundred thousand houses were completely destroyed and many more were damaged. Nearly twenty thousand loved ones died in the tsunami alone.

The effects of the nuclear radiation from Fukushima Daiichi remain largely unknown. Radioactive particles spread across the Pacific and around the world. Scientists and medical professionals alike have feared a greatly increased risk of certain cancer types particularly among children, although data on the subject is far from conclusive. The effect on people's mental health, particularly in the worst affected areas, is incalculable.

I'm not well-informed enough to criticise the Japanese government or TEPCO[92] or any other

---

[92] Tokyo Electric Power Company, responsible for the operation and maintenance of the Fukushima Daiichi Nuclear Power Plant. During and

agency involved. It's not my country and it's not my place. What is undoubtedly true however is that questions remain. They remain as to how avoidable it was; as to whether the right actions were taken, at the right time, in the right order and by the right people. Many of these questions have yet to be answered. Some may never be answered. The aftermath, the weeks and months and years to come saw vociferous anti-nuclear power demonstrations. They saw charities set up to help the beleaguered people of Tohoku. As much as aid, money, clothes, food, housing, medical supplies and manpower for the rebuilding is needed, in the long term there's something else that is and will continue to be in demand. Transparency.

---

since the disaster, TEPCO was and continues to be the subject of huge scrutiny and has been criticised for its response and lack of transparency.

Chapter 20

Twenty Asylum Seekers a Year

A changing Japan

The bamboo that bends is stronger than the oak that resists.
Japanese proverb

Perhaps it is all too easy to attribute cliched behaviours and attitudes to a whole nation and its people. Surely the larger something is the harder it is to grasp or to define in any neatly- packaged way, and Japan, which is home to 125 million souls, is not small. If I ever read the ramblings of a Japanese bloke who'd spent half of his twenties living in London and had travelled around Britain a bit, would I agree with his ideas of 'the British' and the way they think and act or would I think, 'What the hell does this guy know?' On the other hand, perhaps viewing society from years spent on the inside but with an outsider's objectivity and sense of perspective, the notional Japanese man would be well-equipped to cast a spotlight upon Britain and all its little quirks and eccentricities. Of course, you would hope he didn't feel like an outsider at all, and at the very least that he wasn't treated like one. And as embarrassing as it is to admit, it goes without saying, unless he was a complete nitwit, he almost certainly would have picked up the lingo in my country far faster than I did in his.

It is now ten years since I left Japan. The nation's population hit its peak between 2008 and 2010 while

I was there at over 128 million. It has declined dramatically every year since and continues to diminish unabated at an alarming rate. Depending on which sources you read, between the years 2010 and 2020 alone the population of Japan decreased by between one and a half and two million people. Greater Tokyo was by far the most populous urban area on Earth when I moved there in 2007 with most estimates putting the figure at around thirty-seven million. Despite continuing to grow for several years after I left, it decreased in 2019 for the first time. Figures for 2020 show that Tokyo's population decreased once more, and the populations of both Tokyo and Japan itself are projected to decline year on year to the turn of the next century. Experts believe the population of Japan will level out at around eighty million, well over a third smaller than the country I knew.

On the surface this may seem of little significance. However, you don't have to be an expert in demographics or socioeconomics to understand that Japan's rapid population decline will have huge ramifications. Japan was Asia's original success story of the late twentieth century, the trailblazing predecessor of the burgeoning 'Asian Tiger[93]' economies to follow, which I somehow learned about in Year 9 Geography between flicking rubbers across the classroom and using a compass to scratch penises onto friends' metal pencil cases. As well as being the

---

[93] The Asian Tigers are the East Asian economies that rapidly industrialised between the 1960s and 1990s. While Japan was the original East Asian economic success story of the late 20th century, the term Asian Tiger may be used to describe Hong Kong, Singapore, Taiwan and South Korea ('The Four Asian Tigers') amongst others.

first to rise, it was certainly the one with the most dramatic ascent.

Post war, in the miracle of reconstruction and out of the ashes of World War Two, Japan had in the space of barely twenty-five years gone from zero to economic hero. In fact, in the mid to late 80's Japan seemed poised, according to some commentators, to overtake the U.S. to become the largest economy on Earth. Of course, it never materialised. The great economic crash of 1990 saw to that, the famed bursting of the 80's Japanese bubble. Land prices had become so hugely inflated that some experts believed the half square mile of land beneath Tokyo's Imperial Palace to be more valuable than all of California (America's richest state with a greater land area than the whole of Japan). Perhaps it was a sign of things to come that in 2010, a year before I left the country, Japan was knocked off its spot as the second largest economy on Earth behind the U.S. by China, a seemingly unstoppable economic force which has pulled away with an ever-increasing gap leaving Japan floundering in its wake.

With its awesome post-war economic resurgence and membership of the G7, Japan had gained a sort of Western status; 'of' the West but not 'in' the West. Yet Japan is in a different position to the partners with whom it sits around the G7 table with their ever-growing populations. The UK's population, which when I moved to Tokyo in 2007 was almost exactly half of Japan's, is surging, and unless a major shift in Japanese demographics takes place in the coming decades the U.K.s population could well overtake it before the century's end.

Though certain conservative elements of Japanese society and literature exceed the efforts of even the most ardent and blinkered anti-Japanese xenophobe at expressing just how group-minded the Japanese are and how the populace think as one, of course the truth is more complex. In common with elsewhere in the world, differences in attitudes and worldview are often clearly visible between those who are well-travelled and those who are not. An even starker gulf exists between those Japanese who have lived abroad and those who have not.

While to many people in Western Europe or North America it is a simple fact of life that we live in countries whose doors are open (or at least ajar) to foreign workers and their families and those seeking refuge, Japan has for decades only tentatively opened the door a crack with the security chain on. In 2017, while the UK was receiving criticism from campaign groups for accepting just 20,000 asylum seekers a year, by coincidence Japan received approximately that number of asylum applications, 20,000. How many were accepted? 20. I thought I'd misread it at first or that perhaps it was a misprint. Perhaps the true figure was 2000 or at least 200 but no, it was right, twenty.

Unlike its G7 table mates, until very recently a large increase in immigration to Japan seemed unthinkable, but as a response to the shrinking birth rate over recent decades, this has started to become a reality. Many foreign workers and their families are moving to Japan, seeking and gaining Japanese citizenship. This will undoubtedly do even more to challenge the, sometimes over-simplified, opinions people have of 'the Japanese' and, more importantly, the opinions 'the Japanese' have of their own increasingly 'diverse' society. I would be naïve to assume I am never guilty of possessing such cliched views myself, but I also believe that to indulge in large-scale censorship of one's own experiences and opinions for fear of ever happening to generalise is a mis-guided pursuit in faux virtue.

In many parts of the West, big cities have for several decades now been ubiquitous with multiculturalism, a heterogeneous mix of languages and skin colours, different religions and cultures. Needless to say, outside of Tokyo in the smaller towns and cities and especially in the countryside people would often stop and stare. A foreigner was an object of great curiosity and not by any means necessarily in a negative sense. Of course, Japan has for a long time been home to, amongst others, significant Chinese and Korean communities working in all sorts of industries, a fairly large community of Brazilians working in the car factories, Filipinos in nursing and care homes and Iranians in the export of cars, but they have always been subsumed as a very small proportion of a very large whole.

When I began to return to Japan on holiday from 2015 onwards, I noticed a sudden and increasing change in the face of the nation. The people that served me in restaurants, convenience stores and bars were now frequently of Bangladeshi, Pakistani or Indonesian origin. In the second decade of this century, it seems the realisation had dawned on the Japanese government that glaring gaps in the labour market don't magically fill themselves and Japan's unhealthily skewed age pyramid cannot be solved merely with tax breaks for families and ever-later retirement ages.

I am not blinkered enough to fail to recognise that I and the thousands of others working in Japan's English teaching industry did and do represent a large immigrant workforce, but the numbers for decades have remained fairly constant, and I am also not so arrogant as to suggest we were, are or will ever be anywhere near as vital to the country's economic survival or prosperity as the new wave of manufacturing, retail and service sector workers of predominantly Asian origin. How this conservative and largely ethnically homogenous country will adapt to an increasingly multicultural society only time will tell.

Japan is strangely liberal in many ways and yet fiercely conservative in others. The lack of structured religion and the traditions with which that entails, is perhaps a reason the Japanese are more open-minded than I had expected. Japanese society appeared on the surface far more accepting of various sexual orientations than I could ever have predicted, and Shinjuku had a district with a thriving gay scene. Indeed, a cult figure at the time I first arrived was called ' 'Hard Gay'. He was all over the TV screens in his tight black leather get up and muscular body like something from the YMCA video.

There are no ten commandments in Buddhism or Shinto so sleeping around while married was not such an enormous taboo, as long as there were no feelings involved. Sex and love seem quite separate things. Japanese marriages appear rather practical and, in many cases, loveless affairs. What really matters is working hard and bringing home the pay packet which, refreshingly perhaps, is traditionally handed straight over to the wives who handle the family's finances. She takes out what is needed to cover bills and food and the day to day running of the household, while the husband is given an allowance. I suppose it's sensible to ensure that the weekly groceries, the gas bill and the car tax are taken care of before 'Papa' manages to spend it all down at pachinko or on emptying the unwashed panties vending machine of its vital wares.

The Japanese have become, possibly by welcome happenstance, a pacifist nation. Most of the spleen of the right-leaning types is reserved for China and Korea. Aggro flares over war crimes and Korean 'comfort women[94]', and I've almost no doubt given what I've read that the Japanese were guilty for most of the allegations put to them. Of course, there is also, with arguably more justification, frustration and anger over the complex issue of the continued American military presence on the Japanese archipelago, a particular issue for the people of Okinawa, whose small islands at the country's far south western tip bear the brunt of the U.S. presence.

---

[94] Women forced into sexual slavery by the Imperial Japanese army in the countries and territories the Japanese army occupied in the period leading up to and during the Second World War. Some Japanese historians claim that all these women worked as prostitutes for the Japanese army voluntarily. While it is undoubtedly true that some did, most historians agree that many did not.

Perhaps fittingly for an island nation, it is islands located between Japan and its neighbours which form the basis of so much spleen. Japanese fishing boats clash with Chinese fishing boats and diplomatic ties became intermittently tense and then less so.

Sabre rattling on both sides of the Sea of Japan continues and with the growing might of China the future of Japanese security is far from certain.

The presence of U.S. military forces on and near Japanese soil, while an irritant, does understandably at least provide comfort. This is perhaps less a case of 'better the devil you know', than 'better the devil with whom you are friends and for whom you provide a useful and strategic location for military bases.' Standing up to a much bigger boy is quite easy when you have an even bigger boy on your side, even if he is at times quite annoying. It remains to be seen for how long and to what extent Japan will continue to be caught between its complicated relationships with its Asian neighbours and its American ally, and it will be interesting to see how the nature of these relationships change (or not) in the decades to come.

There is of course also North Korea, which has in recent years sent a series of missiles hurtling over the Japanese mainland to land in the Pacific. I was startled one morning on a recent visit to Japan when I heard a loud high-pitched beeping followed by a little red light that appeared on the TV screen in my Tokyo hotel room. It was my startling introduction to 'J' Alerts, a newly coined term for the short-notice warnings of a North Korean missile whose launch has been detected over or near to Japan. Oh great, I thought. Not only do I need to worry about earthquakes, volcanoes and tsunamis; I now need to reserve space in my nightmares for this new little excitement.

The missile launches, although we didn't know it at the time, mercifully turned out to be practice missiles which headed harmlessly over Japan to land in the Pacific. Nonetheless, lying in bed at night it was all too easy to ponder the potential results of an undershot, regardless of whether not it was armed with a less than friendly nuclear, chemical or biological warhead. The bleeping J Alerts on TVs, radios and smartphones, much like the earthquake alerts with which I'd become so familiar, are a mixed blessing. Do I really want to know? At least with earthquakes you face the beast head on and most of the time walk out unscathed, perhaps less anxious, almost able to offer up with swagger, 'Is that all you've got?' a luxury I doubt you'd have with even a remotely direct missile strike.

Dangerous transnational projectiles aside, the Japan-North Korea relationship is murky at best and is further complicated by the fact that many ethnic Koreans are long-term residents who are schooled in 'North Korean' schools inside of Japan. Every year a handful of Japanese people are abducted from the Japan coast in little fishing boats, in many cases never to be seen again.

Women's rights are slowly but steadily heading to the fore of political discussion. The pink-signed women-only carriages on the trains, the women's only sections in capsule hotels and campsites perhaps mask a sinister underlying truth. The idea that women-only train carriages would be laid on seems progressive and inclusionary, but anyone who stops to think about the issue for more than a moment should hopefully come to the conclusion that a truly egalitarian society is one that doesn't need them in the first place.

Fukushima left its mark no doubt but Japan, if nothing else, is resilient. The nation is no stranger to perseverance. Japan's relationship with nuclear power has forever changed but the case is by no means closed. Due to Covid-19 the 2020 Tokyo Olympic Games have been postponed until the summer of 2021 and will be a vastly different affair to those which have gone before it. It is a great shame. The games were supposed to be a visible symbol of the nation's recovery from its triple disaster for all the world to see. Once more the Japanese must rely on their ample reserves of patience and the strength of their resolve.

In August 2020 Japan's right-wing prime minister Shinzo Abe stepped down due to health reasons after a lengthy stint of eight years as the nation's leader (his second in office), quite remarkable by Japanese standards. His lengthy time in office is even more remarkable when I think back to my time in Japan in which I witnessed five (and nearly six) different prime ministers in just four years.

Japan's 125th emperor, Akihito, abdicated in early 2019 due to old age and failing health. Thus, the Heisei[95] era ended, a thirty-year period in which Japan underwent great change, from the huge economic crash at its start to the nation's chronically

---

[95] The period of Japanese history under the reign of Emperor Akihito which lasted from 1989 until 2019.

declining population, the triple disaster of 2011 and the awarding of the (now-postponed) Olympic Games.

It was an era of great change indeed but nowhere near as much as the monumental change seen under the reign of his father, the famed war-time leader Hirohito, emperor of the modern Showa era from 1926 to 1989. There are arguably only very few examples in modern history of a monarch or leader anywhere in the world whose country underwent such rapid and wide-reaching change during their reign - from the start of the war in China to Pearl Harbour, the atomic bombings of Hiroshima and Nagasaki, followed by the economic miracle of the nation rising from the ashes to become the second largest economy on Earth.

Akihito was succeeded by his son Naruhito in 2019, thus beginning the 'Reiwa' era of Japan's Chrysanthemum Throne[96], one which will undoubtedly, whether for better or worse, see huge changes.

---

[96] The throne of the Emperor of Japan.

Chapter 21

Sayonara

Saying Goodbye

Time flies like an arrow.
Japanese proverb

On 22nd June 2011, exactly four years and two months after I had arrived, I left Japan. Contrary to my friends' mick-taking jibes about me getting out because of the disaster in March, I had in fact by pure coincidence handed in my notice to resign the day before the earthquake struck. I was sad to leave my students behind and sad to say goodbye to Japan. Wanting different things from our futures, Yuka and I had split over a year before I finally left, and I was about to begin a new chapter in my life.

I returned to a lush green England at the height of summer with the intention of either joining the army or, failing that, the police. It turned out the army wouldn't have me due to the mild asthma and dicky back on my medical records and the police said I couldn't join as I'd been out of the UK for too long. The fabric of the nation had not been completely spared however because, after a couple more years teaching foreign learners in Bournemouth, I started teacher training and went on to become a schoolteacher. I may not have been deemed physically fit enough to defend Britain but, to my enormous relief, I was deemed mentally fit enough to be entrusted to educate its youth.

I spent the first few months bowing at each person I met involuntarily and receiving puzzled looks. I guess old habits die hard. The reverse culture shock was just as pronounced as the bemusement and discombobulated feeling I experienced when I first headed east, possibly more so. Home was familiar but simultaneously unfamiliar. It took several months, perhaps even over a year, to fully reintegrate.

In the four years between leaving Japan and going back for the first time my dreams, which usually consist of such delights as turning up for the wrong exam for which I haven't prepared, all my teeth inexplicably falling out, or finding myself out in public and suddenly realising I am totally and inexplicably naked, were interspersed with images of Tokyo and the people I'd met. The scenes in my mind were vivid but skewed. The memorable, the iconic and the bizarre were exaggerated and distorted, a disjointed mosaic of people, places and things.

The recollections linger in songs, and colours, in the smell of green tea and miso, but it is perhaps in odd sounds that I am transported back most viscerally. The noise of a harmonica conjures up for an instant the hot potato or tofu delivery man passing through Tokyo's narrow residential streets of an evening, while the sound of hollow wood on wood is the man coming round my Nogata neighbourhood at night to warn of the dangers of fire.

One day, several years after returning to the UK, I was sitting in a staff meeting at the school where I worked when someone downstairs slammed a door hard and the windows and structure of the building shook. Without thinking, I jumped to my feet and looked around, alert and on edge. Moments later I realised how ridiculous I must have looked to the other members of staff, none of whom knew I had lived in Japan.

"I thought it was an earthquake," I said limply before returning to my chair red-faced to bemused stares and shakes of the head.

It is testament to the ever-evolving city that when I return so much has changed. The Junior High School near my house has gone. The house opposite Whity Spot where the nice old woman had a rat in her kitchen has gone, replaced by a gleaming and presumably rat-less newbuild. Whity Spot was still there when I last visited but I'll feel sad on the occasion I return to find it too gone. I know it won't be long, it was built in 1985 and is in Japanese terms therefore nearing the end of its life. Okuma's shop is still thriving. If the wonderful old Mrs Okuma still lives, I hope her final years are painless and peaceful ones and that when she goes, she is reunited with her husband who'd been to Glasgow and London and Portsmouth in his immaculate navy whites.

Nogata's high street remains mainly unchanged. In a strange way I keep my fingers crossed that it retains its jumbled, chaotic appeal. Then again Japanese urban planners give far greater consideration to the needs of residents and the economy than the sentimental longings of a nostalgic foreigner. Last year when I saw huge construction barriers surrounding the Seibu-Shinjuku train line I was sad to be told by Jordan Chivers that they are planning to bury much of it underground. Yet again I'm sure it's a good thing in the long run, but I liked the line and its little crossings, shaded as they are by the low hanging cherry blossom trees in Spring, but things must change. It's silly really to wish for stasis because Tokyo was never the same for a single moment while I lived there. Everything was always temporary and meant to be, except for the temples and shrines, and I should never have expected Tokyo to remain fixed.

A British friend of mine who has travelled the whole world once said to me that he'd never been anywhere as different as Japan. He said that Tokyo was the kind of place where you could wake up one morning and not be surprised if the sky had turned neon pink overnight. I think this neatly sums it up.

When I visit Japan, I still get flashes of excitement. I still feel the flutter of the butterflies after all these years. Familiarity has not dulled the intrigue and I hope it never does. Just as old buildings have been torn down and new ones put up, old faces have grown older and had children and even older faces have aged and passed away. I have fond memories of the people and places of that other life in that other world and just occasionally I feel the excitement of stepping into that new world for the first time again.

Boxes of photos and diaries fill my cupboards besides trinkets and gifts and souvenirs. I am older now than the youthful man sitting on his bed forking corned beef vainly from a broken tin, but I've gained none of the certainties you assume time and age will bring. I am just as naive and nervous and bumbling. I'm just as foolish and make just as many mistakes, I'm just as opinionated and impulsive and hot-headed and just as highly strung. I arrived in Japan three months before I turned twenty-four. It changed me forever and I guarantee it would change anyone who visits the country, let alone someone who lives there.

***

Not long before I left Japan, I stayed at the Shinagawa Prince hotel. I hadn't asked for my towel and bottle of mineral water to be delivered by robot to my room but the moment it chirped outside my door and stared at me with its adorable little electronic eyes I was smitten. As I took my water and my towel and was about to shut the door it hovered awkwardly and batted its metal eyelashes and smiled sheepishly. "Thank you," I said, and it chirped, "yippee!" and whizzed off down the corridor with its blue light flashing.

It's not natural I'm sure to feel such an affinity for an inanimate machine. I stood there at my hotel room doorway watching the robot maid disappear around the corner and then summon the lift by itself. It then got in the lift and closed the doors and zoomed off, no doubt to perform another hugely helpful task. As I stood there a thought struck me. For all that the robot was just a jumble of wires and metal and circuits, its taped greeting and chrome smile felt more welcoming than the real greetings and forced smiles of the actual hotel workers. Maybe it was then, maybe it was at that moment that I was transported with a sudden visceral pang to the conversation I'd had years before when I was still fresh-faced and new and nervous.

"You reach your limit with Japan," my co-worker had said, "when you get to three or four or five years."

Standing there with my towel and my water, slightly too impressed by the robot, I began to wonder if I'd reached mine.

But I hadn't. For all its faults, this bizarre, eccentric, over the top, contradictory, schizophrenic, insecure, wonderful, beautiful land and its graceful, weird, lovely people is a second home to me. I know I love it even if I don't want to because when I see Japanese athletes competing in the Olympics or Japan mentioned on TV, I feel a frisson of excitement and butterflies in my stomach. It's not my home. My home is England and that is where I belong, but in those four years I learned more about myself than I thought I could in a lifetime. And for that I will always be grateful to Japan and its people.

Arigato.[97]

---

[97] Thank you.

Epilogue

Several years after returning to England, at a house party in the West Country, I was introduced to a Japanese lady by a mutual acquaintance. We chatted about Japan for a while, and she finally asked me a question that had been niggling her.

"I feel like I recognise you from somewhere," she said. "Have I met you before?"

Neither of us could identify a likely source. We continued to fetch food from the buffet, and I went on to make small talk with a few of the other guests. At some point later in the evening she rushed up to me, her eyes wide open.

"Hey, you're the guy from the poster on the train in Tokyo!"

The website

For photos, videos and more information about the book and its author please visit:

www.cannedcoffeeandkimonos.com

Glossary

A

aikido A Japanese martial art.

Ainu Also historically referred to as the 'Ezo', the Ainu are an ethnic group indigenous to Japan.

alien registration card Colloquially known as a 'gaijin card'. Foreigners staying in Japan for more than 90 days are required to register for such a card. Its purpose is to record information about Japan's foreign residents.

ANA All Nippon Airways, an international airline and the largest airline in Japan.

anime A style of animation originating in Japan.

Astro Boy, known in Japan as 'Mighty Atom' ('Tetsuwan Atomu'), is one of the most successful Japanese manga series. It began in the 1950s.

Awa Odori The largest dance festival in Japan. The dance originates from the ancient Awa region of modern-day Tokushima prefecture in the island of Shikoku. The origins of the dance can be traced back hundreds of years to a combination of Obon festivals of the dead and harvest festivals.

"a-ya-ka-sa!" The lead chant of the performers at Awa Odori festivals.

B

The Back of Japan See 'Ura Nihon'.

Banzai A spoof Japanese game show first aired in 2001 mocking the over the top and bizarre nature of Japanese game shows.

bonsai A Japanese art form of miniature trees in containers. The small trees are cultivated to replicate the shape and proportions of regular trees.

The 'bubble' The 'Bubble' was an economic bubble in Japan in the late 1980's which saw a huge inflation in the prices of property and in the stock market. When the bubble finally 'burst' in 1992 the Japanese economy immediately plunged into a deep recession from which many argue it has never recovered.

C

Charisma Man A comic strip about the exploits of an ex-pat in Japan. The main character is a blonde, blue-eyed foreigner. The various story plots revolve around the central idea that Charisma

Man comes across as suave, handsome, strong and virile while in Japan, when in fact he is just a plain, weedy loser back in his home country. His true self is laid bare whenever he encounters his arch nemesis 'Western Woman'.

Chiba A prefecture immediately east of Tokyo across Tokyo bay.

Cosplay deriving from 'costume play', is a hobby which first became popular in Japan, but is now a worldwide phenomenon, in which people dress up as specific characters.

D

decora A youth fashion characterised by clothes emblazoned with Hello Kitty and other childish cartoon characters.

E

Edo The former name of Tokyo. The name change occurred in 1868.

Edo era Also known as the Tokugawa period lasted from 1603-1868.

emoji Ideograms used in messaging on electronic devices. 'Emoji' is Japanese in origin originating from the Japanese characters 'e' meaning picture and 'moji' meaning character.

Engrish Sometimes known as 'Japanglish', a slang term for the misuse of English words and phrases by the Japanese.

F

First Certificate Exam An often abbreviated to 'FCE'. It is designed for students with an upper-intermediate English ability. It is a pass/fail test which, for those who pass, delivers a certificate which never expires. It is a common minimum requirement for non-native English speakers wishing to take a university course in an English-speaking country.

Fukushima Daiichi A Nuclear Power Plant in Fukushima prefecture which suffered major damage from the March 11th 2011 magnitude 9.0 earthquake and tsunami. Several of its reactors were permanently damaged. Radiation from the plant leaked into the air and sea.

futon A traditional Japanese style of bedding, a thin mattress that is laid out on a tatami floor and can be stored away each day.

G

gaijin A foreigner (literally 'outside person') sometimes considered offensive to foreigners but used widely by foreigners themselves in Japan. 'Gaijin' is a shortened form of the more socially acceptable 'gaikokujin' (both singular and plural).

gaijin card (colloquial) More formally known as an alien registration card. Foreigners staying in Japan for more than 90 days are required to register for such a card. Its purpose is to record information about Japan's foreign residents.

gaman a Japanese term with its origins in Zen Buddhism which means to endure extremely difficult things with patience, perseverance, tolerance and dignity.

gambatte translates approximately as 'Go on!'; 'Good luck!'; 'Do your best!'; 'Give it your all!'

geisha Female Japanese entertainers who perform traditional Japanese artforms such as dance, singing, playing traditional Japanese instruments such as the 'shamisen' (a three-stringed guitar-like instrument), tea ceremony, games and poetry.

Genpei War A five-year-long national civil war between the Taira (or Heike) and Minamoto clans in the twelfth century which resulted in a defeat for the Taira and their resulting demise. As a result of the Minamoto victory, the Kamakura Shogunate was established.

Golden Bats A Japanese brand of incredibly strong filterless cigarettes.

The Great Wave off Kanagawa A famous woodblock print by the artist Hokusai from the early 19th century. It is the first print in a series of work known as 'Thirty-six Views of Mount Fuji' by Hokusai. In the image an enormous wave threatens to engulf three fishing boats with Mount Fuji clearly visible and prominent on land in the distance.

Gunkanjima is what the island of Hashima, 9 miles offshore from the city of Nagasaki, is often known as. Gunkanjima means 'battleship island' due to its shape and silhouette. Coal mines were opened on Hashima in 1887 and in 1959 the tiny island's population peaked at over five thousand people. The mines closed in 1974 and soon after the island was abandoned. At the time of its use, it was the most densely populated piece of real estate on Earth.

gyaru A Japanese appropriation of the term 'gal' (girl). This style was particularly in vogue in the early 2000's and is characterised by tanned skin, dyed hair and garish and over the top clothing trends.

H

hanafuda The word translates as 'flower cards.' Hanafuda are a style of Japanese playing cards. Some games that are played with these cards are also known as 'hanafuda'.

Hanami Cherry blossom viewing party usually in public parks. These parties are characterised by people sitting in groups on blue tarpaulins under the cherry blossom trees, partying, eating, listening to music and getting drunk. Although it depends on the region of Japan, cherry blossom season by and large begins in April and lasts for around two weeks.

Hard Gay or 'Razor Ramon Hard Gay' is the stage name of the Japanese TV 'talent', comedian and retired professional wrestler Masaki Sumitani. Hard Gay is instantly recognisable for his tight black PVC fetish costume. In the mid to late noughties this character appeared frequently on national Japanese television.

Hashima, often known as 'Gunkanjima' (battleship island) due to its shape and silhouette, is an island 9 miles offshore from the city of Nagasaki. Coal mines were opened on Hashima in 1887 and in 1959 the tiny island's population peaked at over five thousand people. The mines closed in 1974 and soon after the island was abandoned. At the time of its use, it was the most densely populated piece of real estate on Earth.

The Heike clan The Taira clan are commonly referred to as the 'Heike' because of the alternative reading of the Chinese characters (see 'The Taira clan').

The Heisei era The period of Japanese history under the reign of Emperor Akihito which lasted from 1989 until 2019.

honne A person's true feelings. The 'private face' as opposed to the 'public face' (see 'tatemae').

I

IELTS stands for International English Language Testing System. It is used to test the English language proficiency of non-native English language speakers.

irasshaimase 'Welcome'. An honorific used when customers enter or patronise a company or business. Often shouted.

izakaya An informal Japanese bar that serves drinks and snacks.

J

JAL Japanese Airlines, an international airline and the second largest airline in Japan.

J Alert A nationwide warning system launched in early 2007. Its purpose is to quickly inform the public of various threats with the aim of speeding up evacuation times and coordinating emergency response.

Japanese Alps A series of mountain ranges in the centre of Japan's main island Honshu. The 'Japan Alps' or 'Japanese Alps' are sometimes divided into the Southern region (The Akaishi mountains), the Central region (The Kiso mountains) and the Northern region (The Hida mountains).

Japanglish Sometimes known as 'Engrish', 'Japanglish' is a slang term for the misuse of English words and phrases by the Japanese.

K

kamikaze A term which literally means 'divine wind'. The kamikaze pilots were a 'special attack unit'. The Japanese aviators flew suicide missions against allied ships in the Pacific in the final stages of the Second World War. Nearly 4,000 kamikaze pilots died during the war. The planes used in the suicide attacks were loaded with bombs, torpedoes and other explosives. Kamikaze attacks started in October 1944 but reached a peak in the late Spring of 1945 towards the war's end at the time of the battle of Okinawa.

Kanagawa A prefecture immediately south of Tokyo.

Kansai The 'Kansai' region is in the west of Honshu and is Japan's secondary centre of population and major conurbations.

Kanto The Kanto region is home to the Greater Tokyo urban area. It encompasses seven prefectures (counties) on the island of Honshu. Approximately one-third of the entire Japanese population live in the Kanto region.

karaoke Literally empty ('kara') orchestra ('oke'). Karaoke developed in Japan but is now a form of entertainment worldwide. People use microphones to sing along to songs whose lyrics are displayed with background videos on a television screen. Karaoke is a hugely popular pastime in Japan with karaoke parlours large and small (often open 24-hours) catering to the demand.

kimono A traditional Japanese garment worn by men, women and children. Kimonos are rarely worn as everyday dress except by geisha and maiko (trainee geisha) and sumo wrestlers, who are required to wear kimono in public at all times. Kimonos are most frequently worn by the older generation and in general are only worn for special occasions such as weddings.

koban A small neighbourhood police station or 'police box'

kohai A junior in a relationship to the superior 'Senpai'. The subordinate nature of the relationship may be due to hierarchy, age, status, level or experience. The Kohai should show respect, gratitude and a willingness to learn from their Senpai. The term is often used in a work or school context.

konbini Japanese for 'convenience store', a mispronounced abbreviation of the word 'convenience'.

ku A ward or subdivision of a city. The city of Tokyo proper has 23 special wards.

L

love hotel A discreet hotel with rooms rentable for as little as an hour.

M

mamachari Literally meaning 'mother's bicycle'. A standard cheap road bicycle with a basket at the front. This type of bicycle is by far the most commonly found across Japan and is useful for carrying groceries.

manga A style of comics and graphic novels which originated in Japan.

mansion In Japan a 'mansion' refers to an apartment in a large apartment building. Contrary to its use in the West, a mansion is far from a large house.

The Meiji era A period of huge change in Japanese politics, the economy and society at large. The Meiji era lasted from 1868 to 1912. During the Meiji era Japan transformed from an isolated feudal country to a modern, industrial nation state. Under the previous Tokugawa Shogunate Japan had been a closed country for over 200 years.

The Meiji Restoration The Meiji Restoration of 1868 consolidated powers under the emperor of Japan. The structures of Japanese politics and society changed significantly as a result. Japan quickly industrialised and took on western concepts and methods of production.

The Minamoto clan One of the four great samurai clans who fought and beat the 'Taira' (or 'Heike') clan in the Genpei War.

N

NHK Nippon Hoso Kyokai (Japan Broadcasting Corporation), Japan's national broadcaster, equivalent to the BBC of the U.K. Like the BBC, NHK is funded by viewers' licence fees.

ninja A ninja or shinobi was a covert warrior or saboteur in feudal Japan. Ninjas relied on stealth and their roles included surprise attacks, espionage and deception. Ninjas are often seen as the opposite of the samurai who fought openly and according to a code of martial honour 'Bushido'. Ninjas came to prominence in the 15th century and traditionally wore a black outfit with a hood and mask and used a wide array of weaponry from swords to throwing stars and nunchaku ('nunchucks').

O

Obon Japanese Buddhist custom to honour the spirits of one's ancestors. People traditionally return to their family and ancestral homes for a reunion. The festival lasts for three days and is a Japanese national holiday.

omotenashi The subjugation of the self in service to a guest or customer. Most readily seen in shops, restaurants and other customer service businesses.

onsen The term is used to encompass hot spring facilities and the traditional Japanese hotel resorts in which they can often be found. Onsen are distinct from 'sento' which are bathhouses for washing rather than places of relaxation.

origami The art of paper folding.

otsukarasamadeshiita A ubiquitous end of workday expression used between co-workers when leaving their workplace. The rough translation of this expression is 'Thank you for exhausting yourself today'.

P

pachinko An extremely popular pinball-type mechanical game originating in Japan that involves shooting little silver balls around the machine with the aim of landing them within the glowing plastic jaws at the bottom of the machine. The game is extremely repetitive, incredibly noisy and has incredibly bright, flashing lights. Although gambling in Japan is officially illegal, the silver balls that a player wins can be either exchanged for prize items or for a ticket which in turn can be exchanged for cash winnings in a separate nearby building.

Paris Syndrome A sense of disappointment experienced by tourists (often Japanese) visiting Paris for the first time when the city and the experience do not live up to their expectations. In extreme cases this can lead to psychiatric breakdown. The syndrome was coined in the 1980s by Dr. Hiroaki Oita, a Japanese psychiatrist working in France. The syndrome is characterised by a number of symptoms including anxiety, delusional states, hallucinations.

prefecture A geographical subdivision roughly equivalent to an English county. There are 47 prefectures in Japan.

R

rainy season In most of Japan the 'rainy season' lasts from the beginning of June to mid-July.

ramen Chinese noodles served in a broth, often served with pork and seaweed. Nearly every region of Japan has its own signature ramen style.

The Reiwa era The current era of Japanese history which began in 2019 under the new emperor Naruhito.

The Richter Scale The internationally recognised scale used to measure the strength of earthquakes.

The Ring of Fire A volatile tectonic region around the rim of the Pacific very prone to large earthquakes and volcanic eruptions. This area encompasses Japan, the west coast of the USA, the west coast of South America, the Philippines and New Zealand among other countries.

ryokan A traditional Japanese hotel with tatami-matted (straw-covered mats) rooms and usually containing public baths. In some ryokans, dinner is brought to your room and served to you by a maid at a table at which you sit cross-legged on the tatami floor.

S

Saitama A prefecture (county) immediately to the North of Tokyo.

sake Japanese alcoholic rice wine.

salaryman A Japanese salaried white-collar worker. Typified by businessmen in black suits who work in offices, commute to work by train and work incredibly long hours. Salarymen show great loyalty and dedication to their jobs and traditionally have spent long careers working for the same company.

samurai Japanese warriors, a military caste whose status eventually became hereditary in the 16th century. They existed from the 1100s to the abolition of Samurai in the 1870s and were roughly equivalent to knights of medieval Europe. Samurai lived by 'bushido' codes of martial values and honour. Samurai displayed great bravery and prowess in battle and showed unwavering loyalty to their retainers, the feudal landholders known as 'daimyo'.

The Sea of Japan The sea between the Russian mainland, Japan and the Korean peninsula. The 'Sea of Japan Coast' usually refers to the western Coast of Honshu, as opposed to the Pacific coast.

senpai A senior in a relationship to the subordinate 'Kohai'. The seniority of the relationship may be due to hierarchy, age, status, level or experience. Responsible for guiding and counselling their 'Kohai' junior. The term is often used in a work or school context.

sensei Teacher or instructor. Used as a title for figures of authority to show respect for their knowledge skills and teachings.

sento Public bathhouses found across Japan and distinct from 'onsen' which are hot springs and primarily used as resorts for retreat and relaxation.

shiatsu A form of Japanese bodywork or massage.

Shinto A religion originating in Japan, often regarded as Japan's indigenous religion, it is a religion of nature and pre-dates Buddhism's arrival in Japan from China and Korea.

The Showa era A period of Japanese history lasting from 1926 to 1989 under the reign of emperor Hirohito.

sumo The national sport of Japan. The sport is thought to be over 2,000 years old. The object is to force the opponent out of the ring or to the ground. The wrestlers lose if any part of their body except the soles of their feet touch the ground. Japan is the only nation in which sumo is practised professionally. The sport includes many traditional ritual elements and is intimately tied to the Japanese 'indigenous' religion of Shinto.

sumo stables Buildings where an organisation of sumo wrestlers live and train. Most sumo stables in Tokyo are located in or around the Ryogoku district in the east of Tokyo.

sushi Prepared rice with vinegar and topped with sliced raw fish, or another form of seafood or vegetable.

T

the Taira clan One of the four most important samurai clans that dominated Japanese politics, founded in 825 AD. Also referred to as 'The Heike clan' (see 'The Heike clan'). Orihime and Hikoboshi.

tatemae The opinions and behaviour displayed in public. The 'public face'. As opposed to the 'private face' (see honne)

TOEIC 'The Test of English for International Communication' is an English exam for non-native speakers.

Tohoku The North-East region of Honshu. It consists of six prefectures, Akita, Aomori, Fukushima, Iwate, Miyagi and Yamagata.

typhoon A tropical cyclone

U

Ura Nihon 'Ura Nihon' or 'The Back of Japan' is a term sometimes used for the Sea of Japan Coast in the west facing Russia and the Korean peninsula, as opposed to the more developed and highly populated Pacific coast of Japan. It is a somewhat derogatory term implying backwardness due to its out of the way remote location and how undeveloped it is.

W

wasabi Japanese horseradish used as a condiment for sushi and other food with a very strong English mustard-like 'hot' flavour.

'watashi wa' This is used as a pronoun at the beginning of a sentence about oneself.

Y

yaeba Teeth (canines in particular) altered to be like fangs. In Japan yaeba are associated with youth and with beauty.

yakuza A highly hierarchical traditional Japanese crime syndicates whose rough equivalents in the West are the mafia or other gangster organisations. The name derives from the worst possible hand in the card game 'Oicho-Kabu' which is '8-9-3' (ya-8, ku-9, sa-3). Yakuza are marked for life. Therefore, they are seen to be playing a losing hand in life. The number of yakuza, their activities and influence has dwindled in recent years.

Yamato race (or Yamato people) is a somewhat controversial term used to refer to the main ethnic group of Japan, often simply known as 'the Japanese'. The term distinguishes the settlers of mainland Japan (who arrived from mainland East Asia) from 'indigenous' minority ethnic groups which existed in parts of Japan and its empire for thousands of years previously.

Yasukuni shrine A Shinto shrine in Tokyo which commemorates and honours those who died in Japan's wars from 1868 to the middle of the twentieth century, including the Second World War. Controversially, this also includes convicted war criminals from World War 2. Visits to the shrine by Japanese prime ministers, the first of which occurred in 1975, have caused controversy at home but even more in neighbouring Asian countries which suffered greatly at the hands of Japan before and during World War 2.

yokozuna The highest rank in sumo. The word Yokozuna relates to the thick white rope belt they wear around the waist and symbolises their rank.

yubitsume A Japanese ritual to atone for offences and mistakes by amputating part of the little finger. In modern Japan it is mainly practised by the yakuza. The severed part of the finger is then submitted in a package to the yakuza 'boss'.

yukata A casual summer kimono worn by both men and women at special events such as fireworks displays and festivals.

Z

Zen A school of Buddhism which originated in China and came to Japan in the 12th century AD. A central tenet of Zen Buddhism is that anyone can achieve enlightenment, but they must follow the guidance of a 'master'.

List of Proverbs and Sayings in chapter headings

For some of the proverbs and sayings below no direct translation has been possible.

Opening One written word is worth a thousand pieces of gold. 書かれた一言は千個の金の価値があります。(Kaka reta hitokoto wa sen-ko no kin no kachi ga arimasu)

Chapter 1 Newly learned tactics are the origin of great blunders. なまびょうほうはおおけがのもと (namabyouhou wa ookega no moto)

Chapter 2 A man who never climbs Mt. Fuji is a fool. A man who climbs Mt. Fuji more than once is a fool. 富士山に登らぬ馬鹿、二度登る馬鹿 (Fujisan ni noboranu baka, ni-do noboru baka)

Chapter 3 To teach is to learn. 教えることは学ぶことです (Oshieru koto wa manabu kotodesu)

Chapter 4 Wherever you live, you come to love it. あなたがどこに住んでいても、あなたはそれを愛するようになります。(Anata ga doko ni sunde ite mo, anata wa sore o aisuru yō ni narimasu)

Chapter 5 We're fools whether we dance or not so we might as well dance. 私たちは踊るかどうかに関わらずばかですだから私たちも踊るかもしれない (Watashitachiha odoru ka dō ka ni kakawarazu bakadesu Dakara watashitachi mo odoru kamo shirenai)

Chapter 6 Better to be proficient in one art than to smatter in a thousand. の芸術に精通している方が、千を数えるよりもましです (Tsu no geijutsu ni seitsū shite iru kata ga, sen o kazoeru yori mo mashidesu)

Chapter 7 Gold coins to a cat. 猫に小判 (Nekonikoban)

Chapter 8 Like a barrel of potatoes. 芋を洗うよう いもをあらうよう (Imo o arau yō imo o arau yō)

Chapter 9 Unless an idiot dies, he won't be cured. 馬鹿が死なない限り、彼は治りません。(Baka ga shinanai kagiri, kare wa naorimasen.)

Chapter 10 If you understand everything you must be misinformed. あなたがすべてを理解しているなら、あなたは誤って知らされなければなりません (Anata ga subete o rikai shite irunara, anata wa ayamatte shirasa renakereba narimasen)

Chapter 11 Time spent laughing is time with gods. 笑って過ごす時間は神との時間 (Emi tte sugosu jikan wa kami to no jikan)

Chapter 12 A frog in a well does not know the great sea. 一舞の神にもりょんがあります(Ichi-mai no kami ni mo ryōmen ga arimasu)

Chapter 13 When you enter the village, obey the village. 郷ごうに入いっては郷ごうに従したがえ(Gō go uni nyū itte wa gō go uni jūsha ga e)

Chapter 14 The nail that sticks out gets hammered down. 出る釘は打たれる(Deru kugi wa utareru.)

Chapter 15 Better than a thousand days of diligent study is one day with a great teacher. 千日の勤学より一時の名匠 (Sen-nichi no kingaku yori ichiji no meishō)

Chapter 16 A frog in a well does not know the great ocean. 井戸の中のカエルは大海を知らない (Ido no naka no kaeru wa taikai o shiranai)

Chapter 17 Autumn is a second spring when every leaf is a flower. 秋は、すべての葉が花になる (Aki wa, subete no ha ga hana ni naru)

Chapter 18 We must never forget the explorer's spirit. 探検家の精神を決して忘れてはなりません (Tanken-ka no seishin o kesshite wasurete wa narimasen)

Chapter 19 After the rain, earth hardens. 雨降って地固まる (Ame no ato, chikyu was kataku naru)

Chapter 20 The bamboo that bends is stronger than the oak that resists. 曲がる竹は抵抗する樫よりも強い (Magaru take wa teikō suru kashi yori mo tsuyoi)

Chapter 21 Time flies like an arrow. 時間は矢のように飛ぶ (Jikan wa ya no yō ni tobu)

References

Wyatt, Caroline. "'Paris Syndrome' strikes Japanese" BBC News, 20th December, 2006. Web.
accessed 7th September, 2020
<http://news.bbc.co.uk/1/hi/6197921.stm>.

"Michael Fish revisits 1987's Great Storm", BBC News, 15th October, 2017. Web. accessed 16 October 2020 <https://www.bbc.co.uk/news/av/uk-19938165>.

Bibliography

Chapter 2. Climbing Mt Fuji and Looking for Love

Obon "Obon" japan-guide.com last updated 23 August, 2020. Web. accessed 13/3/21 <https://www.japanguide.com/e/e2286.html>.

Hokusai Katsushika Hokusai The Complete Works <https://www.katsushikahokusai.org/>.

The Edo era Edo Period (1603- 1868) Japan-guide.com. Web. Last updated 18 November, 2002 accessed 12/12/20 <https://www.japan-guide.com/e/e2128.html>.

Torii gates Britannica, The Editors of Encyclopaedia. "Torii". *Encyclopedia Britannica*, 10 Sep. 2019. Web. accessed 29 March 2021 <https://www.britannica.com/topic/torii.>.

Shinto Hirai, Naofusa. "Shintō". *Encyclopedia Britannica*, 10 Nov. 2020, Web. accessed 29 March 2021 <https://www.britannica.com/topic/Shinto.web>.

Hottest day in Japan Takahashi, Shunji (Climate Prediction Division). "Summary of Japan's Climate in 2007" Tokyo Climate Center, Japan Meteorological Agency TCC News No.11 January 2008. Web. accessed 17 September 2020 <https://ds.data.jma.go.jp/tcc/tcc/news/tccnews11.pdf>.

Chapter 4. The Biggest City on Earth

Busiest train stations in the world Blaster, Master. "The 51 busiest train stations in the world-All but 6 located in Japan." Japan Today, 6 February 2013. Web. accessed 8 June 2020. <https://japantoday.com/category/features/travel/the-51-busiest-train-stations-in-the-world-all-but-6-located-in-japan>.

"The world's busiest train stations" RailwayTechnology, 8 August 2012 (last updated 28 January 2020). Web. accessed 9 June 2020. <https://www.railway-technology.com/features/featureworlds-busiest-train-stations/#:~:text=Shinjuku%20Station%2C%20Japan&text=With%20an%20average%20of%203.5,in%20terms%20of%20passenger%20throughput.>.

Shinjuku station "Shinjuku station is Enormous! Daily Passengers Equivalent to Population of Yokohama" nippon.com, 31 August 2018.Web. accessed 9 June 2020. <https://www.nippon.com/en/features/h00273/>. "Shinjuku Station, Tokyo" RailwayTechnology, Web. accessed 10 June

2020<https://www.railway-technology.com/projects/shinjuku-railway/>.

Shinjuku Station Shinjuku Transportation Guide. Web. accessed 11 June 2020 <https://www.shinjukustation.com/shinjuku-station-map-finding-your-way/>.

Edo Seidensticker, Edward G. "Tokyo-Yokohama Metropolitan Area". *Encyclopedia Britannica*, 7 Nov. 2016, Web. accessed 1 April 2021. <https://www.britannica.com/place/Tokyo-Yokohama-Metropolitan-Area.>.

The Meiji restoration (footnotes) Britannica, The Editors of Encyclopaedia. "Meiji Restoration". *Encyclopedia Britannica*, 19 Mar. 2020, Web. accessed 29 March 2021 <https://www.britannica.com/event/Meiji-Restoration.>.

City economies Florida, Richard. "The Economic Power of Cities Compared to Nations" Bloomberg CityLab, 16 March 2017. Web. accessed 12 June 2020 <https://www.bloomberg.com/news/articles/2017-03-16/top-metros-have-more-economic-power-than-most-nations#:~:text=Tokyo%2C%20the%20world's%20largest%20metro,largest%20economy%20in%20the%20world.>.

Chapter 5. Sensory Overload

Tanabata festivals "Tanabata" Star Festival) nippon.com, 4 July, 2015. Web. accessed 17/8/20 <https://www.nippon.com/en/features/jg00097/>

Koenji Awa Odori "Tokyo Koenji Awa-Odori" Tokyo Koenji Awa-Odori. Web. accessed 13 June 2020 <http://www.koenji-awaodori.com/language/eng.html>.

Astro Boy

Brianna Albert"AstroBoy: "10 Things You Didn't Know About The Iconic Manga" CBR.com. Web. 23 November 2020 accessed 23 March 2021

<https://www.cbr.com/astro-boy-manga-facts/>.

Yasukuni shrine

"Yasukuni Shrine" japan-guide.com. Web. page last updated 20 May 2020

accessed 2 April 2021

<https://www.japan-guide.com/e/e2321.html>.

Britannica, The Editors of Encyclopaedia. "Tōjō Hideki". *Encyclopedia Britannica*, 15 Jan. 2021, Web. accessed 5 April 2021.

<https://www.britannica.com/biography/Tojo-Hideki.>.

Chapter 6. White Gloves
Samurai Britannica, The Editors of Encyclopaedia.
"Samurai". *Encyclopedia Britannica*, 5 Mar. 2020, Web. accessed 3
April 2021. <https://www.britannica.com/topic/samurai.>.
"Samurai" Japan-guide.com. Web. accessed 15 March 2021
<https://www.japan-guide.com/e/e2127.html>.
emoji Cydney Grannan "What's the Difference Between emoji
and emoticons?" Britannica. Web. accessed 1 April 2021
<https://www.britannica.com/story/whats-the-difference-
between-emoji-and-emoticons>.
rui-katsu "Participants ease stress levels at crying events" the
japan times 22 June 2013. Web. accessed 12 November 2020
<https://www.japantimes.co.jp/news/2013/06/22/national/p
articipants-ease-stress-levels-at-crying-events/>.
The yakuza Britannica, The Editors of Encyclopaedia.
"Yakuza". *Encyclopedia Britannica*, 11 Feb. 2021, Web. accessed 30
March 2021. <https://www.britannica.com/topic/yakuza.>.

Chapter 8. Trains, Planes and Automobiles
The Ring of Fire Britannica, The Editors of Encyclopaedia. "Ring
of Fire". *Encyclopedia Britannica*, 22 May. 2020, Web. accessed 3
April 2021. <https://www.britannica.com/place/Ring-of-Fire.>.
Chapter 9. Gaijin
Yubitsume Bosmia AN, Griessenauer CJ, Tubbs RS. Yubitsume:
ritualistic self-amputation of proximal digits among the Yakuza.
J Inj Violence Res. 2014 Jul;6(2):54-6. doi: 10.5249/jivr.v6i2.489.
Epub 2013 Nov 27. PMID: 24284812; PMCID: PMC4009169. Web.
accessed 5 April 2021
<https://pubmed.ncbi.nlm.nih.gov/24284812/>.
Chapter 10. Lost in Translation
Dejima island "Historical Dejima Island" japanistry.com, Web.
accessed 17 October 2020
<https://www.japanistry.com/dejima/>.
Bosozoku Grinnell College Subcultures and Sociology
"Bosozoku". Web. accessed 30th March 2021
<https://haenfler.sites.grinnell.edu/subcultures-and-
scenes/bosozoku/>.

Wangan "Tokyo Shutoku Expressway" Japanistry.com. Web. accessed 21 March 2021 <https://www.japanistry.com/shuto-expressway-explained/>.

Chapter 11. The Robot Restaurant and a Skewered Penis

Ninja Cartwright, Mark. "Ninja." World History Encyclopedia. Last modified June 03, 2019. Web. <https://www.ancient.eu/Ninja/>. accessed 11 November 2020

Chicano style Keith Estiler "The Influence of Chicano Culture in Fashion as Told by Leading Latino Pioneers in the Industry" Hypebeast 20 February 2017. Web. accessed 13 January 2021 <https://hypebeast.com/2017/2/chicano-influence-in-fashion>.

yaeba Steven Simonitch "Why Japanese Women go for fake crooked teeth" 31 January 2013Japan Today. Web. accessed 25 March 2021 <https://japantoday.com/category/features/lifestyle/why-japanese-women-go-for-fake-crooked-teeth>.

Chapter 12 Banzai, Biscuits and Bearskins

Firebombing of Tokyo History.com Editors "Firebombing of Tokyo" HISTORY Originally published 16 November 2009. Web. accessed 28 March 2021 <https://www.history.com/this-day-in-history/firebombing-of-tokyo>.

Grant, R.G.. "Bombing of Tokyo". *Encyclopedia Britannica*, 2 Mar. 2021,
accessed 28 March 2021
<https://www.britannica.com/event/Bombing-of-Tokyo>.

NHK Britannica, The Editors of Encyclopaedia. "Nippon Hōsō Kyōkai". *Encyclopedia Britannica*, 14 Aug. 2008, Web. accessed 2 April 2021 <https://www.britannica.com/topic/Nippon-Hoso-Kyokai.>.

Paris Syndrome Chelsea Fagan "Paris Syndrome: A First-Class Problem for a First-Class Vacation" The Atlantic 18 October 2011. Web. accessed 3 September 2020 <https://www.theatlantic.com/health/archive/2011/10/paris-syndrome-a-first-class-problem-for-a-first-class-vacation/246743/>.

Chapter 13 'Get out of the Pool'
Hashima island Goldfarb, Kara."Japan's Abandoned Hashima Island is Full of Decay and Dark Secrets" ati, 30 May 2018. Updated 8 October 2018. Web. accessed 2 July 2020
<https://allthatsinteresting.com/hashima-island>.

Chapter 14 'You Can't Sit There, That's Takako's Seat'
Kohai and senpai "Japan's Senpai and Kohai System" lingualift. Web. accessed 1 April 2021
<https://www.lingualift.com/blog/senpai-kohai/>.
Sumo Britannica, The Editors of Encyclopaedia. "Sumo". *Encyclopedia Britannica*, 20 Apr. 2017, Web. accessed 3 April 2021. <https://www.britannica.com/sports/sumo-sport.>.
Kimono Britannica, The Editors of Encyclopaedia. "Geisha". *Encyclopedia Britannica*, 22 Dec. 2008, Web. accessed 5 April 2021. <https://www.britannica.com/art/geisha.>. "Sumo: The History and Rules" japanistry.com. Web. accessed 5 April 2021 <https://www.japanistry.com/sumo/>.
Atomic bombing of Nagasaki Wellerstein, Alex "Nagasaki: The Last Bomb" The New Yorker. 7th August. 2015 Web. accessed 3 June 2020
<https://www.newyorker.com/tech/annals-of-technology/nagasaki-the-last-bomb>.
Atomic bombs dropped on Hiroshima and Nagasaki "Little Boy and Fat Man" Atomic Heritage Foundation 23 July. 2014. Web. accessed 15 July 2020
<https://www.atomicheritage.org/history/little-boy-and-fat-man>.
"The Atomic Bombings of Hiroshima and Nagasaki" atomicarchive.com, Web. accessed 6 April 2021
<https://www.atomicarchive.com/resources/documents/med/med_chp10.html>.
"American bomber drops atomic bomb on Hiroshima" History, A & E Television Networks, originally published 1 September 2010, last updated 6 August 2020, Web. accessed 6 April 2021
<https://www.history.com/this-day-in-history/american-bomber-drops-atomic-bomb-on-hiroshima>.
Britannica, The Editors of Encyclopaedia. "Nagasaki". *Encyclopedia Britannica*, 27 Oct. 2020, Web. accessed 6 April 2021.

<https://www.britannica.com/place/Nagasaki-Japan.>
Britannica, The Editors of Encyclopaedia. "Hiroshima". *Encyclopedia Britannica*, 5 Oct. 2020, Web. accessed 6 April 2021.
<https://www.britannica.com/place/Hiroshima-Japan.>.

Chapter 15. The Good, the Bald and the Ugly

Narita"Leading airports in Japan in 2019, by number of passengers handled on international flights" statista. Web. accessed 5 April 2021 <https://www.statista.com/statistics/1187899/japan-leading-airports-by-international-passengers/>.

Chapter 16. Japan has Four Seasons

The Taira/Heike clan Hogetsu, Keigo. "Taira Family". *Encyclopedia Britannica*, 23 May. 2016, Web. accessed 3 April 2021. <https://www.britannica.com/topic/Taira-family.>.
The Minamoto clan Cartwright, M. (2017, June 16). Minamoto Clan. World History Encyclopedia. accessed 3 April 2021. Web. <https://www.ancient.eu/Minamoto_Clan/>.
Nihonjinron Manabe Kazufumi & Harumi Befu (1993) Japanese Cultural Identity, Japanstudien, 4:1, 89-102, DOI: 10.1080/09386491.1993.11827036 Web. accessed 29 March 2021 <https://www.tandfonline.com/doi/pdf/10.1080/09386491.1993.11827036>.
'Yamato race' Satoshi Horai,' Kumiko Murayama,' Kenji Hayasaka,' Satoe Matsubayashi,' Yuko Hattori,' Goonnapa Fucharoen, Shinji Harihara, Kyung Sook Park, Keiichi Omotof and I-Hung Pan "mtDNA Polymorphism in East Asian Populations, with Special Reference to the Peopling of Japan" 'Department of Human Genetics, National Institute of Genetics, Mishima, Shizuoka, Japan; Khon Kaen University, Khon Kaen, Thailand; 'Department of Anthropology, Graduate School of Science, University of Tokyo, Tokyo; Department of Biology, Sung-Shin Women's University, Seoul; 'International Center for Japanese Studies, Kyoto; and National Taiwan University, Taipei Am. J. Hum. Genet. 59:579-590, 1996. Web. accessed 2 April 2021 <https://europepmc.org/backend/ptpmcrender.fcgi?accid=PMC1914908&blobtype=pdf>.
The Ainu Britannica, The Editors of Encyclopaedia. "Ainu". *Encyclopedia Britannica*, 3 May. 2017, Web.

<https://www.britannica.com/topic/Ainu.>. accessed 1 April 2021

Chapter 18. "Read the Sign, Damn it!"

Henry Stimson and Kyoto Oi, Mariko. "The man who saved Kyoto from the atomic bomb." BBC, 9 August 2015. Web. accessed 13 August 2020. <https://www.bbc.co.uk/news/world-asia-33755182>.

Sato, Hiroaki. "Stimson's love of Kyoto saved it from A-bomb." The JapanTimes, 4 December 2015. Web. accessed 13 August 2020.<https://www.japantimes.co.jp/opinion/2015/12/04/commentary/japan-commentary/stimsons-love-kyoto-saved-bomb/>.

Satsuma fruit Marks, Michael. "Best Mandarin Orange" Ever East Bay Times, 21 December 2016. Web. accessed 2 August 2020 <https://www.eastbaytimes.com/2016/12/21/best-mandarin-orange-ever/>.

Training for Pearl Harbour attack Fuchida, Mitsuo. Edited by Roger Pineau. "I Led the Attack on Pearl Harbour" U.S. Naval Institute, Proceedings, Vol. 78/9/595 September 1952. Web. accessed 14 August 2020 <https://www.usni.org/magazines/proceedings/1952/september/i-led-air-attack-pearl-harbor>.

Ibusuki kamikaze museum Schonherr, Johannes. "Ibusuki Naval Air Base Memorial, Ibusuki, Kagoshima Prefecture" Japan Visitor, Web. accessed 14 August 2020 <https://www.japanvisitor.com/japan-museums/ibusuki-naval-airbase-memorial>.

The Meiji era Britannica, The Editors of Encyclopaedia. "Meiji Restoration". *Encyclopedia Britannica*, 19 Mar. 2020, Web. accessed 31 March 2021 <https://www.britannica.com/event/Meiji-Restoration.>.

Spirited Away "film by Miyazaki [2001]" Britannica. Web. <https://www.britannica.com/topic/Spirited-Away>.

Kamikaze Britannica, The Editors of Encyclopaedia. "Kamikaze". *Encyclopedia Britannica*, 7 Jan. 2020, Web. accessed 9 December 2020 <https://www.britannica.com/topic/kamikaze.>.

Chapter 19. Bad Things Come in Threes

The Great Tohoku earthquake of 2011 Oskin, Becky. "Japan Earthquake & Tsunami of 2011: Facts and Information" LIVESCIENCE, 13 September 2017. Web. accessed 3 May 2020 <https://www.livescience.com/39110-japan-2011-earthquake-tsunami-facts.html>.

"20 Largest Earthquakes in the World" USGS, Earthquake Hazards. Web.

accessed 4 May 2020<https://www.usgs.gov/natural-hazards/earthquake-hazards/science/20-largest-earthquakes-world?qt-science_center_objects=0#qt-science_center_objects>.

Great Tohoku earthquake (Honshu, Japan) Mag 9.0 11 March 2011 British Geological Survey, Earthquake Seismology. Last update 23 March 2011. Web.<http://www.earthquakes.bgs.ac.uk/research/events/tohoku/honshuMarch2011.html>.

2011 Christchurch earthquake"Christchurch earthquake EEFIT mission" British Geological Survey, Earthquake Seismology. Web..accessed 6 May 2020 <https://earthquakes.bgs.ac.uk/research/events/newZealandEEFIT.html>.

The Richter scale "Earthquake Glossary Richter Scale" USGS, Earthquake Hazards program. Web. accessed 8 May 2020 <https://earthquake.usgs.gov/learn/glossary/?term=Richter%20scale>.

tsunami Britannica, The Editors of Encyclopaedia. "Tsunami". *Encyclopedia Britannica*, 29 Oct. 2020, Web. accessed 5 April 2021. <https://www.britannica.com/science/tsunami.>.

Fukushima Daiichi nuclear accident Laforge, John. "Move Over Chernobyl, Fukushima is Now Officially the Worst Nuclear Power Disaster in History" COUNTERPUNCH 27 April 2018. Web. accessed 26 August 2020 <https://www.counterpunch.org/2018/04/27/move-over-chernobyl-fukushima-is-now-officially-the-worst-nuclear-power-disaster-in-history/>.

Fukushima Daiichi radiation Imster, Eleanor. "Tracking Fukushima radiation" EarthSky, 6 January 2015. Web. accessed 13 August 2020 <https://earthsky.org/earth/tracking-fukushima-radiation-across-the-pacific>.

"Fukushima: Radiation Exposure" World Nuclear Association Updated February 2016. Web. accessed 14 August

2020<https://www.world-nuclear.org/information-library/safety-and-security/safety-of-plants/appendices/fukushima-radiation-exposure.aspx>.

Chapter 20. Twenty Asylum Seekers a Year

Japan's declining population Kato, Hisakazu. "We need a sense of crisis over depopulation" the Japan Times, 5 September 2018. Web. accessed 26 August 2020 <https://www.japantimes.co.jp/opinion/2018/09/05/commentary/japan-commentary/need-sense-crisis-depopulation/>.

Kopf, Dan. "The world is running out of Japanese People" Quartz. 4 June 2018. Web. accessed 18 August 2020 <https://qz.com/1295721/the-japanese-population-is-shrinking-faster-than-every-other-big-country/>.

Harding, Robin. "Japan's population decline accelerates despite record immigration" Financial Times, 12 April 2019. Web. accessed 19 July 2020<https://www.ft.com/content/29d594fa-5cf2-11e9-9dde-7aedca0a081a>.

"Population total- Japan" The World Bank Data, Web. accessed 2 September 2020 <https://data.worldbank.org/indicator/SP.POP.TOTL?locations=JP.>

"Japan Population Growth Rate 1950-2020" macrotrends, Web. accessed 4 September 2020 <https://www.macrotrends.net/countries/JPN/japan/population-growth-rate>.

"Japan Population" Worldometer, Web. accessed 1 September 2020 <https://www.worldometers.info/world-population/japan-population/>.

Tokyo population trends "Tokyo, Japan Metro Area Population" 1950-2020 <https://www.macrotrends.net/cities/21671/tokyo/population>.

"Tokyo Population" World Population Review. Web. accessed 17 August 2020 <https://worldpopulationreview.com/world-cities/tokyo-population>.

Population Pyramids of the World from 1950 to 2100, Japan 2100 PopulationPyramid.net .Web. accessed 5 August 2020 <https://www.populationpyramid.net/japan/2100/>.

Asian Tiger economies Andrew Bloomenthal, Reviewed by Robert. C. Kelly, "Four Asian Tigers", Investopedia, updated 16 January 2021. Web. accessed 20 March 2021 <https://www.investopedia.com/terms/f/four-asian-tigers.asp>.

Japan's post war economic miracle and the bubble economy "Japan as number one Land of the setting sun" The Economist, Business 12 November 2009. Web. accessed 23 July 2020 <https://www.economist.com/business/2009/11/12/land-of-the-setting-sun>.

Ben-Ami, Daniel. "Briefing: Europe turns Japanese" IPE. April 2020. Web.

accessed 8 August 2020 <https://www.ipe.com/home/briefing-europe-turns-japanese/10044473.article>.

China's economy overtaking Japan's "China overtakes Japan as world's second-biggest economy" BBC News, Business, 14 February 2011. Web. accessed 9 August 2020 <https://www.bbc.co.uk/news/business-12427321>.

"China overtakes Japan as world's second-largest economy" The Guardian Global economy 16 August 2010. Web. accessed 6 July 2020

<https://www.theguardian.com/business/2010/aug/16/china-overtakes-japan-second-largest-economy>.

UK population trends "Population Pyramids of the World from 1950-2100 United Kingdom 2100" PopulationPyramid.net . Web. accessed 3 July 2020

<https://www.populationpyramid.net/united-kingdom/2100/>.

"Overview of the UK population: March 2017" Office for National Statistics Updated 3 March 2017. Web. accessed 5 August 2020

<https://www.ons.gov.uk/peoplepopulationandcommunity/populationandmigration/populationestimates/articles/overviewoftheukpopulation/mar2017/previous/v1>.

Immigration into Japan Ebuchi, Tomohiro and Yokota, Yusuke "Japan Immigration, Japan immigration hits record high as foreign talent fills gaps" Nikkei Asian Review. 13 April 2019. Web. accessed 23 August 2020 <https://asia.nikkei.com/Spotlight/Japan-immigration/Japan-immigration-hits-record-high-as-foreign-talent-fills-gaps>.

McCurry, Justin. "Japan had 20,000 applications for asylum in 2017. It accepted 20" The Guardian, 16 February 2018. Web. accessed 4 May 2020
<https://www.theguardian.com/world/2018/feb/16/japan-asylum-applications-2017-accepted-20>.

Comfort Women Lynch, Ami. "Comfort women". *Encyclopedia Britannica*, 6 Jun. 2019, Web. accessed 4 March 2021 <https://www.britannica.com/topic/comfort-women. Accessed 1 April 2021.>.

Zen Buddhism Bodiford, William+M.. "Zen". *Encyclopedia Britannica*, 25 Feb. 2021. Web. accessed 29 March 2021. <https://www.britannica.com/topic/Zen>.